INDIA'S MISSED OPPORTUNITY

Vande Mataram

India's Missed Opportunity

India's relationship with the Non Resident Indians

M.C. LALL PhD.
London School of Economics and Political Science

Routledge
Taylor & Francis Group
LONDON AND NEW YORK

First published 2001 by Ashgate Publishing

Reissued 2019 by Routledge
2 Park Square, Milton Park, Abingdon, Oxon, OXl 4 4RN
52 Vanderbilt Avenue, New York, NY 10017

Routledge is an imprint of the Taylor & Francis Group, an informa business

A Library of Congress record exists under LC control number:

ISBN 13: 978-1-138-63737-5 (hbk)
ISBN 13: 978-0-367-20922-3 (pbk)
ISBN 13: 978-1-315-20518-2 (ebk)

Contents

List of Tables

List of Figures

Preface

This is an important book that deserves to be read not merely by those with an interest in contemporary Indian politics, but by anyone who is concerned with the changing nature of international society and of the assumptions and preconceptions that underpin the foreign policies of its member states. As we enter the twenty first century it is clear that people everywhere are on the move, both legally and illegally. Already, the result is a world where the demographic and political maps diverge, often dramatically. Only a small minority of the worlds' states conform to the nationalist ideal of a nation state - one culture one state. Most are multi-cultural, home to diaspora communities, some of which have been long established, while others are much more recent.

How are governments to react to this phenomenon, which although not new in itself, has gained much greater visibility since the end of the cold war and in the context of globalisation? If we discount the pathological response of ethnic cleansing, the choice comes down to some variety of assimilation or accepting that communities can have dual loyalties and that therefore the presence of diasporas should be regarded as a foreign policy asset rather than a liability. Historically, the emphasis was on assimilation, although some countries that regularly exported people in significant numbers - China and Ireland for example - also benefited from continuing links with the enclave communities that their nationals established in foreign countries. With the development of the global economy, they have been able to look to these outreach communities as trading partners, sources of private foreign investment, and, more generally, as diplomatic 'friends at court'.

The interest of the Indian case lies in the fact that India was not one of these countries. At independence in 1947 the Indian diaspora was already large and widely spread over the face of the earth, and in many cases both affluent and deeply involved in international trade. Moreover, most Indian communities remained closely knit and were understandably reluctant to shed their cultural identities. Yet the Government of India did not initially regard overseas Indians as potential ambassadors, advising them instead to identify with the countries in which they were settled. In adopting this policy the Congress party leadership deliberately reversed the policy it had pursued prior to independence when it had been much concerned with the welfare of Indians throughout the British Empire. With independence, however, they believed that the national question had been resolved since theirs was a strictly secular and civic conception of the nation-state. The picture began to change in the early 1990s and today there is a more concerted Indian effort to court overseas Indians in the interests of overcoming some of the traditional constraints on India development.

Marie Lall's book takes an unsentimental and clear headed look at the legacies of the past and the problems that still need to be overcome if the country is to harness the energies not only of its own citizens but of overseas Indians as well. The world will not be fitted back into so many neat national containers so that this is a problem that many other countries will need to address. The Indian story may provide salutary lessons for them too.

James Mayall
January 2001

Acknowledgements

First of all I would like to thank Professor James Mayall for all the help and advice in completing this book which started out as a PhD thesis under his supervision. His moral support was especially appreciated during my four year long stay in India, where he continued guiding me, yet gave me the space needed to pursue the research in tune with local pace.

Thanks also goes to Professor Fred Halliday, who seven years ago decreed that I was not mad in wanting to start research on an area I had so little knowledge on, despite it requiring the learning of a new culture and a new language. It was due to his encouragement that I set out to do this work.

At JNU, New Delhi, I would like to thank Professor Aswini Ray, who allowed my two-year research affiliation at the Centre for Political Studies and was always available for friendly advice.

Benoi Thomas, Nihar R. Das and Rajesh Jha have to be mentioned for their help in getting hold of government, and especially parliamentary material, to which I had no access.

Furthermore I also want to thank Dr Arun Mehta and Prof. Aasha Kapur Mehta for their help and friendship during my stay in India. The coffee cum pop corn sessions during which I could bounce my ideas were a tremendous boost at all times during my research.

Thanks also goes to Tamara and David Delapraz who, for months on end, lent me their house in Delhi to use as an office when my flat became too small.

Turning the thesis into a book was not a simple task, but was greatly helped along by Dr Andrew Wyatt. Discussions with him and his proof-reading proved invaluable.

Finally and most importantly I want to thank my husband, Viren Lall for his patience whilst he watched the 'booklet' grow. His computer expertise, emotional, physical and moral support were essential to finishing first the thesis and then the book in this millennium. I am more indebted to him than I could possibly express.

1 Introduction

This book analyses the relationship of the Government of India with the Non Resident Indians since independence. In particular it is concerned with the dramatic shift in the Congress party's policy at the time of independence. Before August 1947 Congress was very concerned with the fate of the expatriate Indians. The policy adopted in 1947 by Nehru's government not only excluded the issue of expatriate Indians totally from Indian foreign and domestic policy formulation, but actively encouraged the Diaspora to integrate into their host societies. It then goes on to analyse the reason for the development of the relationship, or rather the lack of a relationship between the Diaspora and the Indian Government and how that in turn affected the economic development of the India to this day.

Despite there being diplomatic relations in pre-independence time, an official policy in the years after independence and a significant policy shift after liberalisation in 1991, India has to date never developed a meaningful relationship with its Diaspora. This is a problem in so far as the expatriate Asians represent a community of around 14 million people who are, generally speaking, economically successful and many of whom have maintained a certain degree of Indian traditions. It is also notable that many in the Diaspora have upheld private links with their region of origin through family ties, marriage and commerce.

The purpose of this work is to provide an in depth analysis of the failure of the Indian Government to make good use of its Diaspora and the reasons thereof.

An accurate definition or acronym for the Indian Diaspora is difficult to come by. Generally speaking the terms 'People of Indian Origin' and 'Non Resident Indians' have been used interchangeably by the government of India in parliamentary debates and other official literature as well as by the Indian press. There are different categories of expatriate Indians. They include:

- Emigrants under the British colonial system including indentured labourers and free passage migrants to South East Asia, Africa, the Caribbean and Polynesia;
- Free passage/Commercial emigrants who left India before and after independence for Africa, Australia, England, and the US/Canada;
- Brain drain[1] emigrants who left India after independence for higher education and better jobs in England, Australia and the US/Canada;
- Labour migration who left India on short term contracts for unskilled, semi-skilled and skilled work in the Middle East and the Gulf countries in the 1970s to this day;
- Migrants to other parts of the subcontinent such as Nepal or Sri Lanka pre and post independence.

Some of these expatriate Indians have maintained their Indian citizenship, some of them have acquired the nationality of their host society, but most have maintained links with the country of their origin. This was largely because as a group they did not integrate socially and culturally into their host society. Part of the problem the government of India faces by trying to regroup the Indian Diaspora under one definition or another is the fact that Pakistani and Bangladeshi citizens are as much of Indian origin as the migrants to South East Asia or Africa or the West Indies who left under the Colonial system. This is also the principal reason why the debate on dual nationality has stagnated miserably. The government of India argues that if any person of Indian origin received the inherent right to apply for Indian citizenship and was allowed to maintain his or her other nationality, it would by default allow Pakistanis and Bangladeshis to hold an Indian passport and this would pose a security threat to India. The term 'Non Resident Indians' (NRIs) appears for the first time in the 1984 parliamentary debates, but does not replace the other headings in the indexes of 'Indians abroad' and 'People of Indian Origin' or even 'expatriate Indians'. There is no clear delimitation on who is an NRI and who is not until after the 1991 reforms, when the definition is linked to citizenship.[2]

In this book the terms Non Resident Indians (NRIs), People of Indian Origin (PIOs), and expatriate Indians/Asians will be used interchangeably, as in a cultural sense they are all part of the Indian Diaspora. For the sake of economic investment after 1991 the Government of India accepts all these definitions. The NRI definition by the Indian Investment Centre given at the beginning of Chapter 7, is the official definition of the government for tax and residence purposes only. It is directly linked to holding Indian citizenship and by definition excludes all People of Indian Origin who do not hold an Indian passport. For the sake of social science analysis in this book these groups cannot be excluded and a multi-layered, broad, all encompassing definition is required.[3]

The book analyses the relationship between the government of India and the Diaspora from 1947 onwards, giving a brief historical background as to how the Diaspora came into being and as to what the nature of the relationship was before independence. The principal analysis ends in 1996, five years after the opening up of the Indian economy and before the elections bringing the BJP government into power, but relevant economic figures are provided until 1999. It covers the policies of the various Congress governments and then, of the United Front governments in the recent years. There is no mention of the Desai's government, which governed for two years after the period of emergency under Indira Gandhi, as there was no implemented policy shift towards the Diaspora.

With respect to the parts of the Diaspora mentioned and analysed in detail, the book limits itself to the communities in Uganda, South Africa and Fiji as case studies, as they best illustrate the Government of India's policy of non-involvement and non-commitment towards the expatriate Indians in difficult situations. The crises of Uganda and Fiji also show a significant development within India's public perception of the expatriate Indians and their lot abroad. This shift in perception though is not reflected in the government's policy making. Further mention of Gulf migrants and Brain drain migrants is made in chapter 6 to illustrate the changing profile of the Diaspora, but their particular relationship with India is not looked at in any depth. The communities in the West Indies and South East Asia, as well as the ones in Sri Lanka or Nepal are not mentioned as with very few exceptions (Burma and Sri Lanka) they were utterly ignored by the Government and no notable event brought them into the Indian news or consciousness.

Continuity vs. change

The Indian government's position is one of continuity of the Nehruvian attitude in the context of two changes in the post independence era: first the changing foreign policy priorities from a global, ideological framework to a regional, more realistic framework (Nehru to Gandhi) and subsequently a change in economic foreign policy from a relatively closed economy to a relatively open one (Gandhi vs. Rao). In this context it should be remembered that except with respect to China till 1962, India's regional policy was always based on realistic assumptions. Yet these shifts did take place with respect to international foreign policy formulation.

The factor of NRIs being a 'hidden asset' in terms of economic potential did not strike the Indian government until the 1990s. Even after liberalisation and the public realisation that the Diaspora could lift India out of the development problems she was facing, there was little the government was prepared to do to establish a relationship in order to cash in on that asset.

There are three switches in Indian foreign policy which have a bearing on the relationship with the Diaspora: the first at independence where India's priorities changed from being an anti-colonial nationalist movement which included all Indians around the world, to a nation state project with internal integration as a central priority. This move excluded the involvement of the Diaspora. The Nehruvian policy of encouraging the Indian Diaspora's integration into their host society remained valid from the 1950s through to the 1980s. The second change from a global ideological foreign policy in the Nehru years to a more realistic regionally oriented policy under Indira Gandhi could have affected government-NRI relations, but did not.

A new approach appeared in the second half of the 1980 under Rajiv Gandhi who handled the 1986 Fiji crisis. There was a public if not governmental attitude change compared to the 1972 Ugandan crisis. This was also the time at which potential NRI investments were discussed and the banking system for expatriate nationals, especially the Gulf workers was facilitated.

1991 brought about the third axis of change with the opening up of India's economy. In theory the barriers for investment were removed, but in practice many of the obstacles remained and the special incentives set up for NRIs did not prove to be particularly interesting to them. The NRI demands related to equal rights with Indian nationals and dual citizenship whilst the people and the government of India remained highly suspicious of NRI and other foreign involvement on the economic front. As a result the process of liberalisation stalled and foreign direct investment (FDI) stagnation set in.

This work falls within the wider study of International Relations because of the increasing importance of non-state actors and their power and role in influencing states and government policies. Diasporas are such non-state actors. They have to be viewed not only as minorities in their particular host society, but also as important entities vis-à-vis their country of origin. The case of India is a peculiar one as the Diaspora was ignored and held at arms length for the best part of India's independent history. Diasporas can through their economic power influence the development of their home country, and to a certain degree policy making, especially in the third world. In their host country they can influence policy making towards their home country. In the case of India both these influences have been minimal or non-existent.[4]

Diasporas fall into the country of origin's foreign policy concerns and this was the framework which was adopted for the analysis. India's foreign policy priorities at the time of independence were those of anti-imperialism and support for the new developing nations which were getting rid of their colonial masters. The Indian Diaspora was seen in this context as a legacy left by the British imperial system and thus viewed very negatively.

The other framework needed to understand the role and importance of the Diaspora was the way in which the territorial state of India came into being at independence and what view the Indian government had of that state. The creation of postcolonial states often involves a high degree of nationalism and in some cases a high degree of national consciousness. In the case of India the particular sense of an all embracing 'nation' was a modern creation of the political class over and above a wide range and number of divergent civil societies. A national consciousness, if there was one, was directly created by the independence movement and its leaders, the Nehrus, Gandhi and Patel at the beginning of the century. But the sense of Indian consciousness at the eve of independence included the Diaspora which had expatriated themselves under the British colonial system. It started to exclude the Diaspora only after independence. It is also notable that the sense of national consciousness varies from region to region and that it is the regions to which the individual expatriate Indians remain attached. Unlike for example Israel, which is a state born out of the nationalism of a Diaspora, India created a territorial nation-state and within this process cut off the Diaspora. The political identity which was being created, was linked closely to India's economic and social transformation for which a nationalist framework had been adopted. The system developed for India after independence was separate linguistic and cultural units combined to form a centralised republic where power and authority were centralised.[5] Unlike the old Soviet Union, defined as a multinational community of republics, each one representing its own nation, the Republic of India is defined culturally as one nation, composed of a constellation of sub-nationalities, each forming a state making up this nation.[6] Therefore after the establishment of the Indian State, the concerns were of national integration and of nation state building. With the switch from a nationalist movement to a nation state project there was no place for ethnonationalistic concerns within the new state's foreign policy. The new political identity could not include the 'satellites' of expatriate Indians living all around the world. The book contends that this is because India is a weak nation, made up of innumerable civil societies, which have been bound together to form a strong state with new priorities with regard to foreign policy formulation.

Certain assumptions have been made with regard to the Indian Diaspora. They include the fact that the Diaspora, wherever dispersed, remained culturally Indian and attached to an Indian consciousness which bound them to the motherland by way of religion and tradition. This is what prevented their integration with the host society and their loose ends position vis-à-vis India.

The following questions have been addressed and discussed:

- Why did India not cultivate a relationship with the Diaspora after independence?
- Why did the basic relationship not change despite India's opening up and in light of its economic liberalisation?
- What are the consequences for India?

The structure of the book is based on six main chapters, besides introduction and conclusion.

Chapter two deals with the historical development of the Diaspora, establishing how Indians came to emigrate and live overseas and how they maintained links with the country of their origin. This chapter is divided into a historical, social, political and economic section, describing the Diaspora's role within the host societies and the ways Indians established a distinct cultural and social identity. The main focus is on Indians in Africa and Fiji, as these are developed further in the case studies, but Indian communities in other parts of the world are also mentioned.

Chapter three describes India's foreign policy formulation and explains why post-independence India did not maintain a relationship with the expatriate Indian communities. It describes Indian foreign policy priorities based on the ideology of economic self-sufficiency, anti-imperialism and non-alignment. Economic ties played a relatively minor role. The overseas

Indians were totally excluded as India developed its relationship with the decolonising host-countries ignoring their economic potential. The chapter is divided into four parts dealing with non-alignment, the Commonwealth and relations with Britain, regional foreign policy and foreign economic policy. This last part analyses India's attitude towards foreign investment from independence until 1991.

Chapter four looks into the relationship of the Indian government with the Indian Diaspora and analyses the differing position pre-and post-independence and the advent of the Nehruvian attitude. Pre-independence India was a nation interested in the Indians overseas and they were included in India's fight for independence. The development of a nation state project the priorities of which included the integration of the different regions and an independent foreign policy towards the newly decolonising states, and excluded any relationship with the expatriates. Cultural ties were maintained, but India disconnected in all other ways from the Diaspora despite its huge economic potential. The expatriate Indians were encouraged to integrate with the host society and openly pushed to identify with the priorities of the native population.

Chapter five describes three case studies involving the Indian government with the Indian Diaspora. The above described policy remained in place in times of crisis, such as Uganda (1972) or Fiji (1986). The government's attitude is also illustrated with respect to the South African Indian Diaspora. Although India fought the apartheid system, it cut ties with South Africa at the expense of the Indians living there.

Chapter six explains how the Indian policy had to alter in the light of changes in the world. Its internal economic crisis forced the opening up of the Indian economy. Foreign investment started flowing into the country but at a relatively low level, and certain incentives for NRI investment were opened up. The expatriate Indian community's profile has changed substantially and for some the NRIs represented potential saviours. But in effect the policy and the relationship did not change as the majority of the Indian population and the government of India remained closed to the idea of foreign investment. This was largely due to the perception of the expatriate Indian by the population in general and by the government in particular: these Indians left for economic gain. Before independence there was a certain responsibility and solidarity towards them as the unity of the Indian people was important in light of the independence movement and colonial rule which had allowed them to go abroad. Post-independence there was to be little comprehension as to why they did not come home. If they have not and if some are still leaving, that means that they are a part of the population of their host country and not really Indians anymore. Besides they are seen as cowards who avoid India's difficult economic circumstances. And they are perceived as traitors who abandoned their parents. So we face a case of 'mutual abandonment'; they disown their mother country which in turn disowns them.

Chapter seven looks at the results of the 1991 reforms and analyses them, showing that in effect the liberalisation policies have not brought about a changed relationship between NRIs and the mother country. Their investments remained painfully low as the Indian government gave only token concessions. A brief comparison with China is offered in order to establish that there are other models of mother country – Diaspora relationships which are mutually beneficial.

The book concludes that the relationship between India and the Diaspora is a curious one governed by the old ideals despite it having moved forward at the economic policy level in general. India's conscious choice at independence to exclude the rather rich Diaspora for idealistic reasons has meant that India has lost out in her development and continues to loose out to this day.

Endnotes

1 See chapter 6 for a detailed explanation

2 See chapter 6

3 Based on a discussion with Lord Desai on the 3rd November 1998

4 Diasporas with a certain degree of influence which come to mind are the overseas Chinese, the Jewish lobby, especially in the US, and the German Diaspora in parts of Eastern Europe and the ex-Soviet Union

5 For an analysis of India's statehood and the role of nationalism and civil societies, see: Kumar, R. 'L'Inde: Etat-Nation ou Etat-Civilisation?', Herodote no. 71, 4eme trimestre October - December 1993, Paris

6 Ibid., p.46

2 Historical background

Introduction

> South Asians overseas represent only a small fraction of the ethnic population displaced by imperialism and more recently by modern capitalism; likewise the complex overseas societies in which they have settled are only a subset of a larger body of racially and culturally pluralistic societies- all products of migration which are scattered across the globe.[1]

Studying the South Asian Diaspora involves social considerations such as race, culture, class and religion; economic and political issues seen in the larger historical and contemporary context of ethnic incorporation and race differentiation. Generally speaking studies have been undertaken from an anthropological, sociological, economic or historical point of view, focusing on the problem in a regional context. These approaches ignore the international relations aspect of the Diaspora's relationship with its home country, and the home country's relationship with the host country.

The total number of Indians living outside South Asia is quite small compared to the population of India: Estimates vary between 10 million to 18 million; on average the Diaspora's numbers are estimated at around 14 million, which represents only about 1% out of the more than 1500 million inhabitants of the region including the population of Pakistan, Nepal, Bangladesh, Sri Lanka and of course India.

Mass migration from South Asia took place within two broad periods and under two sets of circumstances: first under imperialism in the late nineteenth and early twentieth century; then since Indian independence after the mid twentieth century. The former was a function of the colonial expansion taking indentured labour, traders and administrators to colonies, the latter was migration of all forms of skilled, unskilled, entrepreneurial, and professional labour. Within those two periods people from all sections of Indian society emigrated abroad. In their host countries they socially recreated parts of Indian society, yet with large gaps, depending on what elements were missing. In colonial times there were significant differences between the 'far' and the 'near' abroad, as migrants in the regions closer to India such as Malaysia or East Africa could keep in touch with India compared to those who had emigrated to far away places such as Fiji or the West Indies. In the further away places it is notable that there was greater integration within the Indian population, who lost touch with the deep ingrained caste consciousness of India. Yet in societies located nearer to the subcontinent, social structures and divisions were maintained. One thing though is consistent for all the Indian Diaspora no matter where it went or at what time it migrated: There remained for all a distinct sense of cultural Indianess, deeply rooted in the knowledge of their subcontinental origins, which let them stay aloof of their host societies and hindered their integration into the new worlds they had chosen to live in.

The evolution of the Indian Diaspora is briefly described in the following chapter first from a historical point of view and then more specifically from a social, political and economic angle. The chapter will concentrate on the East African region and on Fiji as its prime examples, although for comparative reasons reference to other areas of emigration will be made.

Many ethnic minorities look back to their country of cultural origin for sympathy, spiritual sustenance and for the survival of their traditions. The interesting factor with the South Asian community in East Africa was the third dimension which had evolved out of imperial history: the reattachment to the UK through a passport which made them look upon Britain for protection and also economic survival. They were a minority who in the wake of independence of their host countries found themselves pulled in three different directions and therefore had severe problems: their ties were to India, the UK and their host country in which they lived. Unlike small indigenous minorities they had little political power, but could command a certain support from the outside during the colonial period.[2] In Fiji the relationship with the UK was different, as the Indian Diaspora was at the forefront of the independence struggle from Britain. They did not see in the British their protectors, in fact it may be argued that in this particular case the Melanesians were more attached to British rule in order to cement their political advantages. In general, since immigrant minorities are assumed to have the option to emigrate back, their future was not seen as necessarily tied to the country they resided in. Being weak politically was therefore quite unfortunate, but reinforced by the fact that the indigenous population viewed the Diaspora as alien. This state of affairs throws open a number of questions on the state of what amounted to be a triangular relationship.

The issues concerning alien minorities pose a number of questions on their integration with the host society and their rights within it. The colonial system had brought about artificial plural societies in which different groups lived side by side yet only interacting under very specific circumstances. The society which emerged at independence had to struggle with this legacy and build a new workable social system. Protection of minority rights did not mean the perpetuation of historically derived minority privileges, but the situation which developed after the independence of the East African states, though due to the economic disparities cultivated during the colonial years, was untenable. The solution proposed was integration, but this implied several assumptions: That there was a well integrated East African society into which the Asians did not fit; that the responsibility for integration lay with the Asians; and that the failure to integrate would cause their ultimate demise. Integration, a problem further described in the section on race relations in this chapter, goes beyond 'cocktail-mixing'. The Africans generally accusing the Asians of non-integration were the ones who assumed pseudo- European values and had alienated themselves from their own origins.[3]

The basic themes which emerge are first the continuous relative weakness of the Asians, since society was first controlled by the colonial power and later by the indigenous Africans. In both cases there were racial tensions of different kinds, although the Asian community had played a large role in the development of the region, quite disproportionate to their absolute numbers or percentage of the population.[4] And second the triangular relationship of the Diaspora with their host country, their area of origin and the ex-colonial rulers:

> Never a dominant power in East or Central Africa their capacity to determine historical factors has been limited. They have had no strong support from the governments of their country of origin; they have had no ambitions of aggression or annexation. At the same time they have displayed a poor sense of history and limited vision. It is therefore not surprising if they are seen as merely responding to the forces around them rather than influencing them.[5]

In the case of Fiji there was no question of minority rights protection for the Indian population: they soon had out-populated the native Melanesians, and were politically very active. Integration here again was not an option, and although the Indian population had integrated amongst themselves (unlike in Africa) they were not willing to mix with the indigenous population. Racial tensions arose over land ownership, which had been settled by the British colonial power in favour of the native population. Despite its political involvement the Fiji-Indian population remained relatively weak, bogged down by a system which had been created to their disadvantage. Here again the dominant theme emerging is their relative weakness vis-à-vis the natives.

The following chapter is divided into four sections. The historical part touches on all the major themes concerning the South Asian Diaspora and has a separate section on plural societies and race relations. The following social, political and economic introductions hope to give a broad overview on who the Asian expatriates were and what they represented in their host countries. Only after having gained a general image on the Asian Community overseas is one able to understand the dynamics of the political problems this generated in their relations to their country of origin.

Colonial and Post Colonial Period

In the late nineteenth and early twentieth century there was large scale emigration of South Asians to East Africa and other parts of the world, mainly as indentured labourers, a significant feature of the vast British colonial expansion in that period. The South Asians themselves were drawn from a colonial territory and were 'exported' to another for work purposes.

As the act of emancipation of 1834 abolished slavery, tropical colonies with sugar and cocoa plantations had sought other forms of cheap labour. The British colonial authorities arranged a system of indentured Indian immigration established in Calcutta and Madras. Labour was recruited in the hinterlands and signed contracts of at least five years which guaranteed them basic pay, accommodation, food rations, medical facilities and a free or partly paid return passage to India. Under this system 1.5 million persons migrated to Mauritius, Fiji, and East Africa. Because of the emerging economic opportunities in the receiving countries, only about one third of these migrants chose to repatriate at the expiration of their indenture contracts. As a result communities of varying sizes developed some growing into 'majority blocks' as in Mauritius, Guyana and Fiji.

In 1895 the plan to build a railroad from the coast at Mombassa to Lake Victoria in order to protect the upper sources of the Nile was approved by the British government. The Africans in the area were tied to the land during the rainy season and insisted on going to their plots to plant crops that were essential for the food supply in the coming year. Besides, the native population had not yet been initiated into a labour and money economy. As a result Indian labour was imported, which according to the British authorities could not only supply the demand but also provide the necessary outlet for India's excess population.[6] In East Africa of an estimated 32,000 railway workers 16,312 returned to India, 2,439 died, 6,454 were repatriated home as invalids and only 6,724 decided to stay.[7]

The second type of recruitment of 'cheap labour' was for South East Asia and Sri Lanka under the maistry or kangani system.[8] The former brought Indian emigrants to the plantations in Burma, the latter to the rubber plantations in Malaysia. All in all there were over 5 million emigrants, who had an easy return because of the close distance from the Subcontinent.

A third purpose for migration was commerce. Historically there had been trade for centuries between the East African coast and India. This counters the general assumption that Indian settlements began as a result of the colonisation movement. For over a thousand years Indians were at the centre of economic activity which opened up the East Coast of Africa to the wider world. In fact there is a reference in the 'Periplus of the Erithrean Sea'[9] to Indian merchants and seamen trading on the coast of East Africa. India's early trade with East Africa seems to have been sorely crippled by Arab piracy and then the arrival of Europeans in the Indian Ocean.[10] These Indians were not only merchants but also sailors, financiers and administrators, who were not all temporary visitors: 'In the early nineteenth century Indian settlements were already established and by the middle of that century their population in Zanzibar alone was estimated at five to six thousand.'[11] Therefore the Asians had an independent economic base in East Africa before the arrival of the colonialists, from which they most probably had penetrated inland ahead of the European powers.

The Indians who were brought in through the colonial system to trade or for clerical and administrative duties increased transportation, urbanisation and administration and pushed trade further into the interior. 'The 'brown man' fitted neatly into the free enterprise system, since he was not unaccustomed to the European ways and had some skill, considerable drive and above all high respect for money.'[12] Therefore there emerged the 'dukas',[13] small shops selling English and Indian imports and increasingly bringing the Africans into the monetary system. The relative success of the traders also encouraged free immigration where ambitious young Asians came to East Africa on their own initiative.

There had also been a scheme in the 1890s encouraging Indian farmers to colonise the areas along the rivers from the coast in East Africa. It was argued that the climate and the soil would be ideal for Indian agricultural exploitation. But the British East Africa Company, which was arranging for the settlement and development of the region, was never able to attract sufficient Indian farmers.[14] The settlement of Indian farmers failed not because of the lack or shortage of suitable lands but because of the competition it would represent to the Europeans. Besides Asians displayed little interest in agriculture despite many being from a rural background in India.[15]

Before the British, French, German and Italian conquests of the late nineteenth century the indigenous East Africans were not ignorant of trade, but the trade they had engaged in dealt mainly with slaves and firearms. The trade brought forth by the Asians was new and supported the incoming European settlers. Such traders were prepared to operate on very low margins of profit and the folk myth about the South Asians pioneering trade in a region of 'slumbering green savagery' seems now totally ridiculous.[16]

The other myth which developed and depicted East Africa as an 'America of the Hindu' can not be substantiated historically either. Many early Asian immigrants were clerks brought to run either the Zanzibar Sultanate or the infant administration of the British protectorates. There was never any large-scale immigration and never any aspiration to 'take over' the area in a colonial way.[17] The culture was not up for export, Indians overseas never representing more than 1-2% of the total population of the region. In fact out of the total estimated emigration of around 30 million between 1834 and 1937 almost 24 million returned to India, leaving a net migration of just over 6 million.[18]

> Ties with South Asia were at a minimum for indentured labourers since they were on average geographically furthest from South Asia, were highly restricted in their movements and activities while under indenture and were doubtless resolved to the severance of their ties to their homeland once they had decided to remain abroad following termination of their indentureship.[19]

Maistry and kangani contracted labourers remained much more linked since they were short-term migrants only and relatively close to home. On the other hand commercial migrants on the other hand remained well connected to their areas of origin through economic links, marriage networks, and frequent visits on social, religious or business grounds and through property ownership.

The economic activities undertaken later were often a function of the original migration purpose and as a result each migration 'type' in every geographical context occupied a kind of 'economic niche'.[20] For example: in Mauritius, Fiji and South Africa indentured labour became rural farmers; in East and Central Africa, they became the commercial middle classes. In both cases the settlements were a function of the relationship with the host society and its infrastructure which often imposed restrictions.

Under the colonial management there was to be a protector of immigrants who was supposed to look after the welfare of the South Asians: whether concerning the contract labourers, merchants, or clerical personnel, the colonial attitude towards South Asian migrants was generally one of favouritism towards what was perceived as a useful segment of the population. The colonial authorities supplied different and separate facilities for the different races and did so on a discriminatory basis. And yet the facilities for Asians were not only inferior to those provided for the Europeans, but also completely inadequate. Inter-racial contacts were discouraged and there were few incentives to go beyond the master-servant, or shopkeeper-customer level of interaction.[21] The Indians had in India already practised 'social exclusiveness' because of the caste and religious system, so keeping this within a framework of commercial administrative relations was natural to them.

Overall however there was an 'assimilationist philosophy' among the imperial powers and they usually paid little heed to overseas South Asians' grievances or aspirations.

Indian authorities, though did display much interest in the plight of their overseas children: Indian nationalists played a large part in the abolition of the indenture system recommended specially commissioned reports, and after India's independence in 1947, Indian commissioners were sent to Trinidad, Mauritius and Fiji.[22] After the First World War Indian nationalism in India fused with the resentment amongst the Indians living in British East Africa to articulate public demands for reforms which would entail equality between the brown and the white citizens of the British empire, that they should enjoy the same privileges regarding political representation, rural landownership and urban residence.[23] It counters the general belief that there was a lack of involvement on the part of the Asians concerning political advancement.[24] The political activities soon involved both the British and the Indian governments and became a matter of political concern. During the Imperial Conference in 1921 a resolution was passed that it was 'incompatible with India's status as an equal member of the empire that disabilities should exist upon the British Indians lawfully domiciled in some other parts of the empire.'[25] The British though declared in 1923[26] that 'in future disputes, the interests of the natives should remain paramount.'[27]

It is surprising that the Asians in East Africa achieved such political support in India during the 1920s since their numbers were very small. Perhaps the support was due to the fact that the community had a sizeable urban middle class element, well able to articulate their grievances and aspirations, compared to any rural or manual labour force.[28]

> Paradoxically the one reason why India was to behave so coolly towards Asians in Kenya during the 1960s was the absence of a substantive stratum of poor Asians among them- an absence that predisposed India now to agree that this particular category of overseas Indians was indeed an economically exploitative one.[29]

During the 1930s the British colonial office focused its attention on the increasing agitation in India. The struggle for independence and representation had already begun and 'every effort was concentrated on stemming the tide or working out some solution. East Africa took a back seat. Nevertheless the movement of Indian Independence attracted the interest of Indians and Africans in East Africa. Militant leaders of the independence movement such as Isher Dass and Makhan Singh made contact with some of the leaders among the African movement. Still the local Indian population was most interested in safeguarding whatever privileged status they had acquired vis-à-vis the African population.

In the inter-war years a strong immigration limitation policy developed, so that after the Second World War South Asians could only settle if they were needed for jobs where there were insufficient local applicants. European settlers more and more opposed Asian immigration. They pressed the British Government to do something, threatening to secede. As a result legal enactments were pushed through:

> ...presented at first as a move to ensure the supremacy of the white settlers, it was later pressed as a necessary protection of the Africans. It was alleged that the Asians exploited the illiterate Africans and prevented their progress by occupying all the jobs to which the Africans aspired. It was also said that that the social and religious influence of Asians was undesirable, that their culture and religion were backward, obscurantist and unwholesome.[30]

From this point onwards the East African Asians became visibly an urban racial minority and politically vulnerable once the British would leave since the colonial tripartite racial system would leave with them. They did not fit into the new world the African was trying to create for himself.

The position of the Indian communities had in political and social terms worsened since after the First World War period, 'while the white settlers' viewpoint backed by the towering authority of Smuts was dominant and the voice of black Africa was still ignored for (Eden to Halifax in May 1943) their prospect of self-government was still many generations away.'[31]

The Colonial Office suspected that the new independent government of India would interfere in the colonies, by mobilising all the communities of Indian origin throughout the territories as a sort of 'fifth column'. British citizenship was offered as a kind of counter-attraction.

But Indian Independence did not help the Indians in East Africa. The independent Indian government spurred the African leadership to seek their own independence and tried to force the South Asians to support and ally with the African nationalist movement during the 1950s. By that time the Asians found themselves in a very difficult position with no clear-cut political record. They had vehemently challenged the formation of colour hierarchy and race segregation in schools, hospitals and other public places, and also discriminatory policies concerning land, immigration and other legislation, but it was more for their own welfare than that of the Africans. Since the 1930s and 40s they had been proven to have no independent power-base which had isolated them even more. They therefore resolved to compromise with the British colonial system, trying to demand constitutional safeguards such as a separate electoral representation in the new independent parliaments to protect their own interests.[32]

Despite official Indian policy the British suspicion remained. The Indian government applied for representative Commissions to be stationed in East Africa, Mauritius and Fiji. Apa B. Pant, known for his earlier mediations between Indians and the British was appointed the first commissioner in East Africa.[33]

The period before the East African states gained independence saw the Asian community being drawn into politics once more. Political parties were being formed, and agitation and negotiations were under way. At first the traditional Asian political parties like the Indian Congress in Kenya was ambivalent as they were concerned with the privileges for the Asian community, but the younger, more radical members who wanted to form a government based on one man one vote campaigned for complete support for the Africans. So during the 1960-63 negotiations the Asians sided with the Africans.[34] This political role has to be kept in perspective, since it is doubtful that the whole community as such was enthusiastic about the prospect of independence.

In general one can say that the British Empire had provided the framework which had shaped the Indian community and although the Empire was 'blown away' the Asians were beckoned in three directions, on contradictory courses:

They had first wanted equality with the white population which they were not granted; they had then sought support of the government of India which at the time of independence backfired; and they had lastly supported the African movement and tried to become equal citizens in the colonies.[35]

Triangle of race relations

'One of the key historical factors has been the triangle of race relations. Colonial society was organised on the basis of racial communities and de facto, if not always de jure, on the principles of segregation and discrimination.'[36] Schools and voting were separated by race and at certain times the rights of dwelling and owning land were restricted according to race as well. This obviously stimulated racial tensions and communal rivalries, since any kind of categorisation on racial lines strengthens prejudice and produces stereotypes. The Asians were seen as dukawallas[37] who cheated their customers, were mean and secretive; the African was dull, unintelligent, lazy and dishonest and the European was the tough and aggressive man, but had done much for the development of the country.

In 1942 J.S.Furnivall had argued that there were societies with 'a characteristic political and economic constitution in which separate sections mix but do not combine.'[38] In these societies the mode of behaviour marked and excluded the members of one group from those of another and was therefore 'plural'. In such a society there is no common social will and no commonly held set of wants and values which means that it can only be held together by the use of political force exercised by one dominant section.[39] East Africa was thought of as such a 'plural society'.

The conflict between the Europeans and the Asians was due to the fear of Asian competition, yet often represented as protective measures for the innocent Africans who otherwise would be exploited by the evil Asians. Often, too it would be contended that Asians were only temporary residents with no real stake in the country. They were there to make as much money as possible before returning to India. In the mean time they were drawing on the country's wealth by sending money to their relations back home. By cultivating this myth of return and other accusations, the Europeans wanted to safeguard their own aggrandisement. In fact only few of the commercial emigrants went back and since they regarded themselves as permanent residents they saved and invested.

The urban concentration of Asians aggravated matters: there was no integration, it pushed property prices up and since there were only few African enterprises they retained a privileged group image. Those Asians who did contribute to the agricultural development in East Africa (e.g. cotton) found themselves in conflict with the African farmers who resented the Asian monopoly of marketing and ginning.[40] As the new economic opportunities opened, rivalry between the Africans and Asian businessmen was bound to develop and increase. The attitudes of the Africans towards the Indians depended in some ways on the different social classes they belonged to. There were the politically aspiring educated middle class, the economically aspiring middle class and the lower class participating in the money economy. It was the new class of emerging African traders who cultivated the stereotypes for political purposes. The Asians came off worst in almost everything when compared to the colonial powers except perhaps in the political field.[41] The whites were culturally arrogant, politically dominating and patronising besides being exploitative. The Asians were economically weaker, equally arrogant and exploitative but politically powerless. It was the irritating reality that the Asian, although himself from a colonised people, was socially and economically superior to the African and quite keen on maintaining racial differentiation downwards. 'To bow before the Indian was not to bow before the master, feared, detested and respected, but to submit to the slave.'[42]- A humiliating position.

Indians came to be hated by the indigenous society because they were part of the colonising system, even though they were under British 'supervision'. Black attitudes towards this group arose out of the social, political and economic dynamics created by this context: These attitudes were in fact taken over from the Europeans, assimilated and internalised. Asians themselves, being a colonised people and in many ways weaker than the British were manipulated to serve the colonisers' economic interests: they became a class of middlemen- a buffer between the colonisers and the Africans. They were seen as exploiters only concerned with their own economic welfare. Besides all this, the Asian's special way of life and social customs helped consolidate black African attitudes.[43] Their culture was not to be an example to be followed or imitated (unlike the European values); there was no element of conquest. So for the African the Indian was the 'other absolute'.[44] Not all economic activities resented by the black African were the result of white manipulations: there was capital flight from East Africa although perhaps not to the extent it was advertised, and the bargaining process made some feel that they were being cheated.

Apart from the economic field there were few incentives for closer social contacts. The empire had tolerated the emergence of caste and sectarian communities. The disparities of cultural and religious backgrounds were too great. Asians had been used to living within exclusive communities in India already. So they felt it unnecessary to establish social contacts outside their own social circle. Added to this were a feeling of cultural superiority and a snobbish disregard of the African socially. Towards the white community the Indians had no such feelings, partly because white control was firmly established in India. It was only on the 'sun-down' or 'cocktail' level that there was real integration between the different groups in East Africa. There was also an unwritten bond between meat eaters and alcohol drinkers across the caste and language lines in the minority.[45]

So the whole situation was not a bilateral problem, but one with a colonial dimension. The British had organised a tripartite racial division. After shipping hundreds of Asians into East Africa for their own economic interests the British only took the Asian economic interest into account at the expense of the African interests. The situation did not just develop, but was specially created.[46] This way the Asians were always seen as a group and any rights they achieved they got as a function of being seen as a 'group', by virtue of being Indian.[47] But their internal differences weakened the community and undermined their ability to meet challenges and crises. Nevertheless it also enabled them to survive any change of system, since their future was not linked to any particular regime.[48] Integration into the African culture and society was seen by many as the only viable solution. Often intermarriage was suggested as a form of assimilation. This however would not have solved the problem for three reasons: The historical compartmentalisation of races and the Asian practice of endogamy made such marriages highly unlikely, race not being the only problem but economic and social positions would not have been remedied by such marriages and if successful, would have become a form of disintegration since the original community would have been replaced by a new minority.[49] The lack of integration was not viewed by the Asian community as disloyalty to the system or government. Yet this is the way the African community perceived it.

The case of Fiji

Emigration of Indians to Fiji as indentured labourers began in 1879, soon after it became a British colony when 13 Fijian chiefs signed a formal Deed of Cession with Britain on October 10, 1874. An agreement between the two British governments of India and Fiji was signed as a result of which about 60000 Indian labourers were sent to Fiji between the period 1879 and 1916 to serve in the sugar plantations. In 1916, when the last batch of indentured labourers arrived Fiji some 40000 Indians decided to remain there. A few Indians, mainly Punjabis and Gujaratis came after 1890 and became traders and other professionals. However restrictions were imposed by the colonial government in the late 30s on those wishing to come to Fiji from India. Today's Fiji Indians are the second and third generation descendants of those labourers.

In India the migrants were recruited under the supervision of the colonial government. Local officials in the Ports of Calcutta, Bombay and Madras managed the routine affairs concerning emigrants. The recruiters - Arkatis, were appointed by the emigration agent and licensed by the protector of Emigrants. They went into the field to draft potential labourers. The Policy was that for every 100 men, 30 women had to be recruited. To ensure the supply of labourers Arkatis generally portrayed a false but rosy picture of the distant land.[50]

Indian labourers were brought to Fiji for several reasons: After the abolition of slavery in 1833, American labourers were no longer available for plantation work. So indentured labour from India was seen as a reliable source of cheap labour. Secondly, Sir Arthur Hamilton Gordon (1875-

1880), the first governor of Fiji, ruled the country through the tribal chiefs. He wanted to guarantee Fijian interests and their exclusive right over the land of the country. Consequently law forbade the sale of Fijian land and leases were permitted only for up to 21 years. Fijians were required to work on their own plantations, and this shortened the supply of labour for European settlers. To facilitate the labour supply for European plantations, he proposed the introduction of Indian labour with which he had had experience in his previous governorship of Mauritius and Trinidad. Gordon also realised that the sugar industry would be the mainstay of the island's economy for which he needed a regular supply of cheap labour and indentured labour from India was a convenient option. It also suited his policy of protecting the natives from becoming slaves in the fields of white settlers. Moreover demand for Indian labourers also increased with the creation of the Colonial Sugar Refinery Company (CSRC) in 1882, which became the dominant manufacturer of sugar in the country. On the other hand the deplorable socio-economic conditions of Indians in their motherland forced them to try their luck in an unforeseen land.[51]

The indenture contract was called Girmit, under which these labourers were to work for five years on the sugar plantations. This term could be extended for another five years. After that they were entitled to return home to India at government expenses or were free to live in Fiji as independent citizens. As an alternative to repatriation many Indians were offered land on lease for cultivation so that the supply of labour could be maintained in the future. Those who remained in Fiji after the indenture period concentrated mainly on agriculture for their living. At the same time many Indians started experimenting in the field of trade and commerce. They opened shops became hawkers and bakers, while some took boat licences for trading purposes. A little later they also entered into the transport and construction industry. Within two decades these industrious Indians made remarkable progress and some of them even acquired a status similar to that of the European settlers.

Although the British had in Fiji again created a tripartite racial system, with communal representation and special reserved rights for different races, there was in the case of Fiji no real triangle of race relations. During the British colonial period the Indians did aspire to proportional representation but their physical distance from India did not give them the impression that they could rely on the mother country to protect their interests in the new world. The Indians were disliked by the local population, not because of their economic wealth, but because the natives felt threatened by their numbers. This was not a case of economic superiority, as the best of the land had been reserved for the native Fijians.

Social

'Asian' is the synonym in East Africa for all people of Indian or Pakistani origin; 'Indian' being generally reserved for temporary visitors, when not referring to the people in India.

It is impossible to deal with the Indian minority in East Africa or anywhere else 'en bloc': there is virtually nothing of sociological significance about the minority which would hold for all its constituent groups.[52] One has to take into consideration linguistic and communal divisions, trans-group relations, in-group coherence and a whole range of other elements when looking at the Asian community from a social angle. Sectional and communal divisions in Hindu society have been studied in the South Asian area, revealing strong horizontal and vertical divisions perpetuated through the caste system. The same holds true for the Indian Diaspora overseas. In fact caste corporate groups and divisions between corporate units are not only the base of Indian society, but are a crucial tool of analysis:

> The Asians appear to have been divided not primarily along the horizontal lines of proletariat and bourgeoisie but according to the vertical divisions of Muslim and non-Muslim, and more specifically of Ismaili, Bohra, Shah, Patel, Sikh, Goan, and other religious communities. Within each of these categories there were those who were rich and those were relatively poor with considerable gradation between (...) Within these separate communities there was no entrenched class cleavage.[53]

The cultural composition of the emigrants varied greatly from host country to host country. In East Africa about 85% were Hindus, there were some Sunni Muslims (mainly traders) and a few Sikhs.

In East Africa, as back in India, religion ranks supreme. A secular value system has never been the structure of Indian society, and the Asian emigrants brought their non-secular scale with them.[54/55] The code of behaviour was based on a combination of religious principles and self-interest, which resulted in their seeing little correlation between law and morality.[56]

The workers recruited for the Ugandan Railways came mainly from Hindi speaking North India (Bihar and UP) whilst the maistry and kangani labourers bound for South East Asia and Burma were chiefly South Indian and spoke Tamil or Telugu. In East and Central Africa the traders were mainly of Punjabi or Gujarati extraction, as were the emigrants to South Africa, Fiji and Mauritius. There were also some Goans who did not wish to be classified as Indians, since they spoke Portuguese and had adopted some forms of the Portuguese lifestyle. Hindustani was the lingua franca amongst the East African Asians, but there were strong groups of Gujarati or Punjabi speaking Asians. Amongst the Gujarati speaking Muslim groups there were the strongly emancipated Shi'a Khoja Ismailis, followers of the Aga Khan; the Shi'a Khoja Ithna-Asharis (followers of the 12th Imam): and the Bohras, of Gujarati Brahmin extraction. To contend that there was no caste consciousness among the Islamic Asians is a foolish claim, endogamy among the Islamic groups mentioned was as rigid as amongst the Hindus.[57] In fact divisions tended to be clearer than within the Hindu community.

It should be noted that the Hindu community in East Africa, like the Muslim community hardly ever acted as a united body. 'Among the Hindus as also among the Muslims, the most striking feature is their division into small units or communities; but unlike the Muslims, the Hindus do not form their communities around religious congregations, even though there do exist cults with temples and congregations.'[58] The caste arrangements of the different home districts in India had not been reduplicated since no complete cross-section of Indian society from any one district was re-established overseas (certain being more heavily represented than others), and then because each district having its own local hierarchy, no caste from outside that area would have accepted it.[59] On the other hand communal divisions were transplanted. Modernised Hindus might convince the casual observer that there are few divisions left or that they will vanish soon. Most agree that communal divisions must go, but they are unlikely to vanish over night. Social life in general remained ritualistic sometimes still performed by the women in public. Marriage rituals too were quite unchanged from the Indian base: with the basic rite of the circuambulation of the sacred fire, the seven steps, the ascending of the stone by the bride being identical for all Hindus. It also remained an expensive affair since the tradition of dowry was maintained. Death rituals were maintained, if simplified. 'And the feeling of ritualistic pollution is all but non-existent.'[60]

There are no secular social institutions of an indigenous kind in India: any kind of club is a western import. It was the parochial communal groups that had created educational, medical and other important facilities, where the Indian Association had not made an effort or failed.[61] These parochially founded and supported educational institutions became gradually interracial in their staff and student recruitment. The Aga Khan's support and further immigration brought about many of the recreational and educational institutions from the Subcontinent during the 1920s and 30s.

Generally speaking interpersonal relations between men and women were as 'obtuse' as they are in India. It is only the last generation that has been partially westernised. The elders who were in charge of the community as a whole and the households at large had little if any formal education. As a result occidental influence was seen as loose or immoral and quite undesirable: any form of open westernisation was frowned upon. Ismailis in particular were criticised because of their tendencies to westernise.

The African and European allegation that Asians 'don't mix', since they don't intermarry and don't really socialise with others can be explained by the fact that even amongst themselves Indians of different caste, linguistic or religious backgrounds rarely socialise and are certainly not expected to intermarry.

In Fiji however, while a basic 'Indian culture' was maintained, there emerged a new society of immigrants, which was different from their motherland. They had lost their caste by crossing the ocean.[62] Hence the caste system no longer remained the sole guide to social interactions and relationships. In Fiji they were all indentured labourers and coolies. They acquired a new identity: Fiji-Indians. It was in Fiji that there was the highest degree of intra-Indian integration.

In general one can say that the South Asian communities experienced some form of 'cultural homogenisation' since they found themselves clustered together despite their regional differences and their traditional religious isolationism. But a cultural divide remained between North and South Indians, especially where they arrived in comparable numbers (e.g. Fiji) The complex caste system could only be maintained if the Indians could remain in the privileged position of high economic status, retaining contact to India and if they could isolate their women. As a result only urban traders and administrators could perpetuate such a position.

South Asian emigrants found themselves in ethnically plural contexts. For example they represented only 2% of the population in Kenya, but 70% and 49% in Mauritius and Fiji respectively. The class composition of these societies fitted within the framework of ethnic pluralism. Contract bound manual workers found themselves at the bottom end of the scale but the Punjabi or Gujarati merchants became an established middle class. Regardless of the class they belonged to, Indians were often discriminated against institutionally: the apartheid system in South Africa, or the Africanisation projects of Kenya and Uganda, or policies favouring 'sons of the soil'-bhumiputras in Malaysia or the Melanesians in Fiji are just a few examples.

As a result of this, community development took on an interesting course: A collective sense of ethnic identity was imposed on the South Asian community: Competition for control over resources, geographical segregation, political organisation and efforts to maintain cultural traditions in an alien society contributed to that trend.[63] They were generally speaking treated like outsiders because of their different habits and beliefs. The Indians considered 'intimate relationships' outside their caste as polluting influences.[64] Therefore there was a certain distance which was maintained with those they did business with. There was also a tendency to favour their own kind when it came to giving business: an Asian would always go to another Asian for a service if faced with a choice, since he would feel more at ease when negotiating the purchase. Consequently ethnic interrelations were minimal, save for economic interaction and what is known as a 'plural society' emerged. Ex-indentured population experienced a rapid increase, which was of much concern to the non-Asians. The merchant class however remained few in numbers but was concentrated in urban settings.

Basically the Asians wanted to pursue their traditional ways without anyone interfering. Laws were enacted in East Africa for the application of personal or religious matters such as marriages, divorce and so on. This helped preserve the cultural identity of the Asians but also made inter-communal and inter-racial contacts very difficult. This and their persistent contacts back with the 'motherland' made the South Asian community a self-sufficient and ethnocentric one.[65]

Political

The historical background section has described some of the main social and economic features of the Asian expatriate communities in East Africa and Fiji in a historical perspective. In this part the political activities of the Asians will be looked at in greater detail.

'The tumultuous struggle of the Asians against the white settlers in Kenya has sometimes been misinterpreted as a desire on their part to make Kenya an outpost of Indian settlement.' The evidence for that lay in A.M.Jeevanjee, the first Indian to sit on the Kenya legislative council appealing in 1912 to the Indian National Congress in India to exert pressure on the British in order to annex Kenya to the Indian empire. Earlier already, in 1904 Lyttleton who was secretary of state in the Colonial Office had described East Africa as the natural outlet for Indian emigration.[66]

The struggle though between the Asians and the Europeans in the 1920s and 30s was not motivated on the Asian side to 'own' Kenya but to secure equality and better treatment in a colonial context. The whites had often rested their claims of superiority on the fact that they had colonised and were the first settlers in East Africa, an allegation found untrue in the history section of this chapter. They also contended that non-Europeans could not measure up to the European standards because they were at a lower evolutionary stage. As a result the Asians and Africans were denied equal rights, such as the right to own land and the right to representation on the Legislative and Executive Councils of the countries. In Uganda both the Europeans and the Indians were denied privileges in the possession of land. Therefore there was never any real threat of the settler community taking over the country and there were no sharp rivalries as in Kenya.[67] Post Second World War the Africans took over the political battle against the imperial power, and Asian political movement declined visibly.

When looking at the political organisation of the Asians before independence one realises that a great majority never actively participated in politics. Both community and individuals reacted to political events as they came along in an 'instinctive search' for survival and security. There were three organs through which they could articulate their interests:

First, the Asian political organisations were usually associations or congresses rather than political parties, for example in Uganda there was the Central Council of Indian Associations and in Kenya the Kenyan Indian Congress.[68] Their function was to serve as a two-way channel of communication between the Asian Community and the governments. The colonial governments found them useful for selecting representatives for the legislative or executive councils. The contacts between the various associations and their constitutions were ad hoc. The two other organs were the press and the individual who had contact with government officials.

When African nationalism came up, it was not a new experience to the majority of the Asians, since they had watched and/or experienced the

Indian independence movement since the 1920s and 30s. They had a better understanding of and sympathy for the African demand for independence than the European settlers. Added to this was the fear for their own future and the question if the perpetuation of British rule might not be the safest option. The position of the newly independent Indian government was that the Asians had to identify with the Africans.

Most of the Asians had accepted the inevitable conclusion of self-government for the Africans but were worried about their own future since they were a rather privileged separate economic class and yet a vulnerable, easily identifiable immigrant minority.

At first Asians were kept away from the emerging African political parties, once these opened their memberships to the Asians in 1961 only few joined. Often they would enrol because of some short-term considerations based on personal relations with the leadership or local political issues. Having been locked out of the political party system had made many Asians look for a 'middle ground' that did not in fact exist.[69] European politicians like Michael Blundell had increasingly courted local Asian support, as the African majority became 'a serious possibility'.[70]

As independence drew nearer many Asians also sent their money abroad as security in an uncertain future. Politically though they tried to adapt: 'It was this passivity and ability to accept a fundamental redefinition of the political and social situation that was to ease the adjustment of the Indian to the changing demands of an independent Uganda.'[71] This was true for all East Africa.

Independence changed the character of Asian politics in East Africa since there was a vast ideological difference in the attitudes of the colonial government and the newly independent African governments towards racism. Whilst the imperial system had worked on the base of racial separation the Africans did not need this 'divide and rule' policy. In fact the new governments believed that their interests would be served best by forging national unity between their people. There was therefore no place for the Asian community as a distinct political entity in the new political system of East Africa, and there was to be no representation on racial lines. At independence most Africans ceased to be British citizens, and most Asians were offered the new citizenship of their respective country.[72]

Up to the dissolution of the British Empire the Asians did not have to choose between East Africa, India and the UK. They could stay connected to all three in different ways. Independence though demanded a conscious commitment and found the Asians carefully calculating possible loss and gains in the light of coming Africanisation.[73]

In Fiji, as the economic conditions of Indians improved they started desiring political rights. But their initial demands for political representation were denied. Indians formed the British Indian Association and their demand for equal political rights became more intense when D.M.Manilal, a lawyer from Vadodra (Gujerat), arrived in Fiji in 1912. In 1916 the British rulers nominated Badri Maharoj, a pro-government Indian to the Legislative Council. But it did not satisfy the Fiji-Indians.

To redress their economic and political grievances Indians went on strike in 1920 and 1921. In the first phase strike was confined to the Suva-Rewa regions. Popular Indian demands were to repeal the masters and servant's ordinance, a minimum wages fixed by law, abolition of the hut tax and various other forms of assistance for Indian farmers. The government suppressed it and it ended abruptly. In 1921, the strike lasted much longer but was peaceful. In both these strikes the British used natives as constables to maintain law and order which further strained the relations between the two sthnic communities. Fijians also feared an Indian dominance in future in the absence of Europeans.

In 1929 Indians were enfranchised on a communal basis. According to this provision the people were divided on the basis of their ethnic group into separate electorates and the different ethnic communities were represented by their own kind.[74] The Indians were given 3 representatives to the legislative council while Europeans and Fijians were given 6 and 5 seats respectively. Thus though the Fiji Indians got the franchise, they were not given equal political status with the Europeans and the Melanesians.

During the second world war Fiji Indians refused to join the army when their demand for equal wages with the European soldiers were denied. In 1943 they organised a strike to press the government in support of their economic and political demands. It was a blunder on the part of Indians and it damaged their future position in the country and they became an isolated group. Meanwhile the Indian population increased rapidly and 1944 established their numerical superiority. They became the largest ethnic group in the country and this frightened the native Fijians. Comparatively speaking Melanesians were very loyal with respect to the British colonial system. They found that being on the side of the colonial masters was of advantage to them since it was the British system, based again on race divisions, which could guarantee them their rights with respect to land and political representation. Independence would mean the demise of a system that suited the native Fijians more than their Indian counterparts.

In the 1950s Indians became more politically conscious. A federation party was formed by the Fiji-Indians to achieve their political objectives. In reply the natives formed the Fiji Association in 1956. Several other small parties, amongst others the Suva Rotuma association and the General Electors Association also came into existence during this period. In 1960 the Federation Party merged with the National Democratic Party and thus emerged the National Federation Party (NFP), a multi-social party but predominantly based on Indian support. In 1956 the Fiji Associations and other constituent organisations formed the Alliance Party under the leadership of Ratu Mara.[75]

In the 1960s the process of decolonisation started. In 1963, Fijians and Women were given the franchise. The first general elections were held in the same year but results came in favour of maintaining the status quo - the supremacy of Fijian chiefs and the Fijian establishments. It was shocking for the Indians community who expected their defeat. The Fijians were reluctant to accept any change in the political system because of a deep-rooted fear of Indian domination and because they had seen the British as their protectors. In 1965 a constitutional conference was held in London and a new constitution was introduced in the next year. The new constitution enlarged the council membership who were now to be elected by universal adult suffrage but the electoral system combined communal Fijian and Indian rolls which clearly divided the people along racial lines. The Legislative Council arrangements were modelled in such a manner, that it ensured the control in the hands of Fijians and Europeans. It gave 14 seats to the Fijians, 12 to the Indians and 10 to the Europeans in the 36 members' seat of the council. It thus gave parity to the Indians, who now constituted 51 percent of the population and the Europeans who were less than 10 percent. Indians were highly dissatisfied with this arrangement and soon it become clear that this constitution would not last for long. Demand for complete independence started. Indians were more vocal and championed the cause of freedom. The Fijians were initially hesitant but fearing Indian designs to dominate they also joined the campaign. Because of internal and external pressures another constitutional conference was convened in April-May 1970 where the decision was taken regarding independence, and on October 10, 1970 Fiji became an independent state.

The constitution of 1970 established a parliament consisting of two chambers - the House of Representatives whose members were to be directly elected and the Senate, which was a nominated house. In the 52 members House of Representatives Indians were given equal representation with the Fijians. Both the Indians and the Fijians were given 22 seats - 12 communal and 10 national each, while the General Electors, which included Europeans and Chinese were given 8 seats - 3 communal and 5 national. The senate had 22 members. 8 of them were nominated by the council of chiefs' nominees, 7 by the Prime Minister, 6 by the opposition leaders and 1 by the council of Rotuma. The electoral system was quite complex and voters were divided on the racial lines. Each voter had to cast 4 votes, one in a communal electorate and three in the national electorate. Thus in any election communal interests was bound to play an important role.

At the time of independence native Fijians were a minority (42 percent) and the constitution safeguarded their rights. The senate, which had significant delaying power, was controlled by the Fijians. Control of the natives over land was also preserved. On the other hand Fiji-Indians, the largest ethnic group of the country were not in a position to form any government of their own without the support of the Melanesians. They had less than 43 percent representation in the parliament. So when elections were held in 1972, the Alliance Party came into power by winning 33 seats while Indians supporting the NFP won only 19 seats, and Ratu Mara became the Prime Minister.[76]

In the April 1977 election the Alliance Party was reduced to being the minority party in the House of Representatives because of the poor performances of the Mara Government. They managed to get only 24 seats against the NFP's 26, one seat each went to the Fijian Nationalist Party and to an independent. But the NFP failed to form the government because of its internal quibbles and Ratu Mara was again sworn in as the head of a minority government. The NFP soon paid the price in the September 1977 election when it could secure only 15 seats while Alliance party bagged 36 seats. Ratu Mara and his colleges also returned to power after the 1982 general elections. In 1985 a new party - the Fiji Labour Party (FLP) was formed which had the support of various trade unions all over the country and across the racial lines. The FLP formed alliance with NFP and they fought the 1987 election under the leadership of Dr Timoci Bavadra. The coalition won the election by securing 28 seats while Alliance got 24 and with this ended the 17 years uninterrupted rule of Ratu Mara.[77]

Economic

The analysis of the economic role of the South Asian Community is crucial to understand problems and prospects in East Africa, since most of the Asian settlement was a response to the economic opportunities in the region. The Asian population increase was from 200 000 in 1948 to 372 000 in 1963, i.e. an increase of nearly 86% in 15 years. An estimated 43% of this was due to immigration.[78]

The East African settlement contrasted with the pattern established in other countries through their high urban concentration. This had far reaching economic and social consequences: it accounted for the 'Indian look' of urban areas, facilitated the organisation of close communal groups, increased isolation, and economically reduced the community's dependence on other races. This was further enforced by a high proportion of businessmen, lawyers and doctors in the Indian community.

There had been a lot of diversification of the Asian economic activity over the past decades. The early immigrants came from petty trade and agricultural backgrounds and had worked their way up into the wholesale and retail trade, into the private sector as clerks or then again joined the government as subordinate staff. Their business was limited to specific townships and confined by their not being allowed to own land. Professions and skilled employment were on the increase and in the post war years the economic activity diversified and balanced. The scarcities due to the war forced the East African countries to become increasingly self-reliant, and the Asian enterprises contributed to this forced industrialisation. Quite a number of Asian youths went abroad to the UK, India or Pakistan for education and came back with higher technical and professional qualifications. Around 45-50% of the total Asian working population came to be in wholesale, retail trade, banking or insurance; 10% in the manufacturing sector or in the public services.[79] During the colonial period there were high inequalities in income and wealth distribution. The Europeans were at the top, the Asians in the middle and the Africans at the bottom of the pyramid. Only a small group of Asians could justifiably be described as affluent; the majority belonged to the middle income group. No exact numbers and percentages are available because of the lack of data collected at the time, but surveys taken between 1965 and 1967 show that Asians constituted around 30% of the total high and middle manpower in East Africa. They provided 30% of the doctors and high-level business executives and 20% of the engineers.

The Asian economic role was an important one, since they extended the monetary economy into the subsistence areas and therefore provided the region with the necessary prerequisites for any economic development. They also acted as main outlets for produce from the indigenous rural economies and did this job at the lowest possible cost, working on very low profit margins. The Asian dukawallas slowly became an important factor in the functioning of the East African economies.

The Asians were also at the heart of trade with the rest of the world. In the early days this was especially the case with India. Close ties with the homeland remained as a result of marriage and family connections. As a consequence they also relied heavily on India as their source for imports and market for exports. Trade was at first connected through family members and with the expansion of business, import and export contracts with established wholesalers or industrialists based in the Indian ports developed. 'In the early twentieth century India happened to be the best source of supply for most of the commodities needed in East Africa, with the result that the Asians had a distinct commercial advantage.'[80] India was advancing in many new industries and therefore provided iron and steel hardware for much of the construction in East Africa. After the First World War India's importance decreased, partly because of new tariff policies and the emergence of other trading partners. India's comparably low economic growth and partition did not improve the situation either. Furthermore many of the Asians who had been at the base of the import-export trade were slowly but surely assuming a different economic role.

All in all the main Asian contributions to the East African economies took the form of capital, high level skills and entrepreneurship and small and large sector retail trade. There was also a high propensity to save and until the late 1950s most of it was invested locally.[81] They also extended credit to aid the African and European farmers in times of crop failure, or to subsidise transport and basic industry. 'The Asian's financial role was never understood by the colonial governments, which generally regarded the Asians not only as entrenched in their position, but also as exploitative, and dishonest in many of their business activities.'[82]

It was the importance of the Asians in the economic sector which fuelled a lot of the criticisms: their role as middlemen and their prominent positions in the purchase and marketing of cash crops, as well as their dominating the wholesale trade had given them the image of exploiters.

Since it is a common phenomenon all over the world to hate small-scale alien traders, it is understandable that the Asian community could not have escaped many of these accusations. It is true that their presence as a large economically sophisticated and isolated community retarded African participation in the national economies, but it is certain that without this same community, any kind of development would have been less advanced.

Asians were not as concerned with the process of Africanisation as with their own economic advancement. This turned out to be a short-sighted policy. In fact it was the principal cause of the deep-rooted hatred, which developed within the African community vis-à-vis the Asians. The petty 'crimes' of cheating and racial snobbery were not at the root of it. It is only in more recent years that the Africanisation programme forced them to consider African economic interests. But it has to be remembered that the Africans not being integrated into the economic development, was also a function of colonial discriminatory legislation, which impeded the acquisition of education and necessary training.

Independence brought with it profound changes in the racial divisions of economic functions. The ultimate objective of the newly independent governments was to increase national control and ownership of the economy and in some regions to eliminate capitalist elements in the commercial and industrial sector (especially Tanzania). The late 60s and early 70s brought the immigration and trade licensing acts, restricting the participation in the national economy to citizens only. This and other policies to accelerate Africanisation (such as training schemes) affected the Asian community and changed their position drastically. Everywhere there was to be a sharp decline in the number and importance of the Asian community, and all future development was dependent not only on their skills, but also on the attitude of the local governments towards them.

In Fiji the economic situation of the Indian Diaspora was different. Having been kept from owning land by the British Colonial system they very early on turned to other sectors of employment, which required higher education. They were to dominate universities and schools, the public service, and professions in the medical and legal field. In the field of commerce the Europeans and Australians retained control of the largest businesses, yet the Indians were quite successful in middle size enterprises. In all areas the local government tried to encourage the native population to become more active by giving them soft loans for businesses or keeping a quota system for certain professions as in the public services, yet with minor success.

Fiji-Indians had done a lot in the economic field to develop their host country, but the area where they achieved most success was not commerce, but in their strong political movement opposing British rule. After Independence they were not given equal status with the local population, but they continued never the less to be the backbone of Fijian development.

Conclusion

The chapter has tried to give an introduction on who the expatriate Asian communities were and how their situation developed. One can conclude that they were the 'victims' of a historical process in which they ultimately did not play a significant role.

Their economic contributions to their host countries development deserve more recognition than they have received. Their main problems were that as an immigrant minority they were small in numbers, marked out by race and wealth. At the time of independence they were suddenly confronted with a new style of government set on large-scale change. Not surprisingly the Asians did not attempt to help in the development of independent African enterprise, since many felt that making way for the native population would result in self-destruction.

With independence things changed: those who wanted to stay had to become citizens and needed to find a new role, something not quite so evident when one remembers the largely passive history of that community. The newly independent governments did not encourage Asian contributions, 'nothing like adequate use has been made of Asian skills and expertise' the governments preferring to engage expatriates at enormous salaries instead.[83] The main goal of the new administrations was to improve the lot of the native population and increase its control on private and public institutions. Much of the legislation designed to redress the economic balance in favour of the native population has been perceived as vindictive towards the Asian Community, especially since above the general lack of concern, the governments refused any kind of responsibility in this matter. Official policy was that of equal treatment of all citizens, no matter what their colour and races, as long as they were citizens. Despite this official policy sometimes race and non-citizenship issues were blurred. The process of 'Africanisation' in itself had racial connotations. So did the land reservation bill in Fiji. It tended to forget that the Asian population though a product of colonial society, also suffered from the colonial system and its legacy.

It was to be a real effort for the Asians to adapt to the new conditions since the set way of life of that community was encouraged, even enforced by the colonial regime. The compartmentalisation of society had resulted in separate schools and residential areas and sustained the isolation. This in turn had encouraged the stabilisation and maintenance of links 'back home' with India. This was only possible in Africa as Fiji was too far away Contacts and links with the 'outside' were maintained for security reasons: the average Asian felt that he would not be treated equally with the Africans. Besides, stemming basically from a commercial class with a strong belief in free enterprise the signs of 'creeping socialism' had been watched carefully in fear that they might challenge the established Asian commercial position.

It has been seen that the assimilative kind of integration with its radical ways ruling out diversity in order to create basic homogeneity did not work for the Asian community. Only the acceptance of the minority in a pluralistic context, encouraging diversity in religion and culture would give the Asian Communities a future in the host countries, especially since there was a lack of a defined, homogeneous society and culture into which they could blend.[84] Later there were many forces at work to break down isolation such as common schools and residential areas. Once the pressures on the community to change and integrate eased a better solution could be worked out.

The nature of the relationship between the host governments and the South Asian community varied a lot and depended on the kind of ethnic pluralism, which existed in each receiving country. Still in most countries of immigration, South Asians have suffered from discrimination or abuse of some kind or another. Therefore a certain kind of 'clustering' was maintained.

> Clustering serves not only a defensive function against racial harassment, but also provides a market for community services such as mosques or Gurudwaras, ethnic food stores and other specialist retailers. It also allows the re-creation of dense traditional social networks with all the implications this has for quality of life and transmission of culture.[85]

The total number of overseas South Asians is small by international comparison with other Diasporas, but they are found in diverse geographical, social, political and economic contexts. In each receiving country they have evolved differently depending on what percentage of the plural society they represented, what the reason for their migration was, how they consolidated and isolated and to what extent they fused (if at all) with the receiving society.

Endnotes

1 Clark, C., Peach, C. and Vertovec, S. (eds.), *South Asians Overseas - Migration and Ethnicity*, p.xix
2 Ghai, Y. and Ghai, D., 'The Asian Minorities of East and Central Africa up to 1971', p.2
3 Tandon, Y. and Raphael, A., 'The New Position of East African Asians: Problems of a Displaced Minority', p.7-8
4 Prunier, G., *L'Ouganda et la Question Indienne (1896-1972)*, p.7
5 Ghai, Y. and Ghai, D., 'The Asian Minorities of East and Central Africa up to 1971', p.2
6 Melady, T.A. and Melady, M.B., *Uganda: The Asian Exiles*, p.57
7 Ghai, Y. and Ghai, D. (eds.), *Portrait of a Minority - Asians in East Africa*, p.3
8 The kangani-maistry system of recruitment differed from the indentured system in two important respects: 1. Unlike the indentured labourers, the kangani-maistry recruits were legally free, having no contract or fixed period of service, and 2. More often than not the kangani-maistry recruitment was kinship and family based as opposed to the 'individual' recruitment of indentured labourers
Jain, P. (1990), *Racial Discrimination against Overseas Indians*
9 Written by a Greek sailor living in Egypt in the first Century AD
10 *Historical Relations Across the Indian Ocean*, Reports and Papers of the meeting of experts, UNESCO, Port Louis, Mauritius 1980
11 Ghai, Y. and Ghai, D. (eds.), *Portrait of a Minority - Asians in East Africa*, p.2
12 Tandon, Y., 'The Future of the Asians in East Africa', p.2
13 From the Hindi word dukan meaning shop
14 Melady, T.A. and Melady, M.B., *Uganda: The Asian Exiles*, p.53
15 Ghai, Y. and Ghai, D. (eds.), *Portrait of a Minority - Asians in East Africa*, p.3
16 Clark, C., Peach, C. and Vertovec, S. (eds.), *South Asians Overseas - Migration and Ethnicity*, p.151
17 Twaddle, M. (ed.), *Expulsion of a Minority - Essays on Ugandan Asians*, p. 2
18 Jain, P., *Racial Discrimination against Overseas Indians*, p.10
19 Clark, C., Peach, C. and Vertovec, S. (eds.), *South Asians Overseas - Migration and Ethnicity*, p.10
20 Ibid., p.10
21 Ghai, Y. and Ghai, D., 'The Asian Minorities of East and Central Africa up to 1971', p.5
22 Clark, C., Peach, C. and Vertovec, S. (eds.), *South Asians Overseas - Migration and Ethnicity*, p.11
Also see chapter 4 for detailed discussion

23 For details see: W. McGregor Ross in *Kenya from within* and W.K.Hancock in *Survey of British Commonwealth Affairs*
24 Ghai, Y. and Ghai, D. (eds.), *Portrait of a Minority - Asians in East Africa*, p.8-9
25 Ibid., p.12-13
26 Devonshire Commission; see chapter 4 for details
27 Clark, C., Peach, C. and Vertovec, S. (eds.), *South Asians Overseas - Migration and Ethnicity*, p.156
28 Twaddle, M. (ed.), *Expulsion of a Minority - Essays on Ugandan Asians*, p.2
29 Ibid., p.3
30 Ghai, Y. and Ghai, D., 'The Asian Minorities of East and Central Africa up to 1971', p.3
31 Twaddle, M. (ed.), *Expulsion of a Minority - Essays on Ugandan Asians*, p.22
32 Tandon, Y. 'The Future of the Indians in East Africa', p.3
33 Twaddle, M. (ed.), *Expulsion of a Minority - Essays on Ugandan Asians*, p.24-25
See chapter 4 for more details on Indian policy with respect to overseas Indians after independence, and the background of Apa Pant's mission in East Africa
34 Ghai, Y. and Ghai, D., 'The Asian Minorities of East and Central Africa up to 1971'
35 Twaddle, M. (ed.), *Expulsion of a Minority - Essays on Ugandan Asians*, p.17
36 Ghai, Y. and Ghai, D. (eds.), *Portrait of a Minority - Asians in East Africa*, p.4
37 From the Hindi word 'dukan' meaning shop, this means shop-owners
38 Morris, S. *The Indians in Uganda*, p.161
39 Morris, S. *The Indians in Uganda*, p.167
40 Ghai, Y. and Ghai, D. (eds.), *Portrait of a Minority - Asians in East Africa*, p.6
41 Twaddle, M. (ed.), *Expulsion of a Minority - Essays on Ugandan Asians*, p.81
42 Prunier, G., *L'Ouganda et la Question Indienne (1896-1972)*, p.200
43 Twaddle, M. (ed.), *Expulsion of a Minority - Essays on Ugandan Asians*, p.82
44 Prunier, G., *L'Ouganda et la Question Indienne (1896-1972)*, p.199
45 Ghai, Y. and Ghai, D. (eds.), *Portrait of a Minority - Asians in East Africa*, p.24 Ghai contends that since certain society divisions were maintained according to the cast and religious structure of India, there was nevertheless and unlike in India a common bond between those who had taken on a certain level of westernisation which included meat and alcohol.
46 Prunier, G., *L'Ouganda et la Question Indienne (1896-1972)*, p.92
47 Morris, S., *The Indians in Uganda*, p.196-7
48 Ghai, Y. and Ghai, D. (eds.), *Portrait of a Minority - Asians in East Africa*, p.12
49 Tandon, Y., 'The Future of the Indians in East Africa', p.5
50 Ahmed, A. 'Aspects of Fiji Indian History', p.1783
51 Ibid., p.1783
52 Ghai, Y. and Ghai, D. (eds.), *Portrait of a Minority - Asians in East Africa*, p.17
53 Gregory, G.R., *South Asians in East Africa*, p.356
54 Ghai, Y. and Ghai, D. (eds.), *Portrait of a Minority - Asians in East Africa*, p.27
55 The secular state which developed in India after independence was based on an intellectual construct developed by the elite of the time, who were trying to unify India, rather than create a society divided by caste and religion. Yet it has to be said from an Indian cultural point of view that at the time of its construction, the secular state was an artificial phenomenon.

56 Gregory, G.R., *South Asians in East Africa*, p.358-359
57 Ghai, Y. and Ghai, D. (eds.), *Portrait of a Minority - Asians in East Africa*, p.21-23
58 Morris, S., *The Indians in Uganda*, p.202
59 Ibid., p. 203
60 Ghai, Y. and Ghai, D. (eds.), *Portrait of a Minority - Asians in East Africa*, p.49
61 Ghai, Y. and Ghai, D. (eds.), *Portrait of a Minority - Asians in East Africa*, p.25
62 This was different from East Africa, as there the caste divisions remained, if in a cruder form. This is mainly due to the concept of 'far' and 'near' abroad, which was addressed in the introduction of this chapter. In the case of Fiji the links to India were greatly weakened and the social structure of the Indian Diaspora changed dramatically. In East Africa on the other hand frequent contact with the motherland made such a change of societal structure much more difficult
63 Clark, C., Peach, C. and Vertovec, S. (eds.), *South Asians Overseas - Migration and Ethnicity*, p.15
64 Melady, T.A. and Melady, M.B., *Uganda: The Asian Exiles*, p.70
65 Ibid., p.155
66 Ghai, Y. and Ghai, D. (eds.), *Portrait of a Minority - Asians in East Africa*, p.68-69
67 Ibid., p.68-69
68 These associations were modelled on the Indian National Congress back in India
69 Ghai, Y. and Ghai, D. (eds.), *Portrait of a Minority - Asians in East Africa*, p.89
70 Clark, C., Peach, C. and Vertovec, S. (eds.), *South Asians Overseas - Migration and Ethnicity*, p.157
71 Hopkins in Ghai, Y. and Ghai, D. (eds.), *Portrait of a Minority - Asians in East Africa*, p.93
72 The issue of citizenship will be discussed further in chapters 4 and 6
73 Ghai, Y. and Ghai, D. (eds.), *Portrait of a Minority - Asians in East Africa*, p.96
74 Ahmad, A., 'Indians in Fiji: An Interpretation' in Subramani (ed.), *Indo Fijian Experience*, p.12
75 Howard, M., 'State Power Political Change in Fiji'
76 Premdas, R., 'Military intervention in Fiji'
77 Howard, M., 'State Power and Political Change in Fiji'. The crisis, which was generated, is discussed in the Fiji case study, chapter 5
78 Ghai, Y. and Ghai, D. (eds.), *Portrait of a Minority - Asians in East Africa*, p.99
79 Ibid., p.103-4
80 Gregory, G.R., *South Asians in East Africa*, p.49-50
81 Ghai, Y. and Ghai, D. (eds.), *Portrait of a Minority - Asians in East Africa*, p.112
82 Gregory, G.R., *South Asians in East Africa*, p.353
83 Ghai, Y. and Ghai, D. (eds.), *Portrait of a Minority - Asians in East Africa*, p.177
84 Ghai, Y. and Ghai, D. (eds.), *Portrait of a Minority - Asians in East Africa*, p.212
85 Clark, C., Peach, C. and Vertovec, S. (eds.), *South Asians Overseas - Migration and Ethnicity*, p.23

3 Foreign policy

Introduction

The first chapter dealt with the historical background and established who the expatriate Asians were and why they were excluded from their host country's society. It also showed that they remained fundamentally Indian in their way of living and were attached to 'Mother India' in various social and economic ways.

Political elites in pre-independence India had shown great concern for its 'nationals' abroad. The British imperial system had made their immigration possible and the Indian government had supported that development. One can argue that at that time the definition of India (held by the Congress party and others) was largely based on a national movement, geared toward a nation oriented identity, which included the Diaspora. One could argue that India at the time saw itself not as a territorial but a de-territorial state. Yet political developments in pre-independence India also laid the foundations for a very anti-imperial, anti-racial course which would be followed by the ruling Congress party government after 1947. At this time a nation state project developed, which was to exclude the potential participation of the Indian Diaspora in the building of a new state that was India.[1] The Indian Diaspora was certainly never a domestic issue, and with the shift in political outlook within India they failed to become a foreign policy issue. As relatively strong economic communities, which remained largely uninterested in their host countries' politics, yet maintaining close family and commercial ties with the subcontinent, one might have expected the Indian Government to use them as a political and economic lobby in their host countries. Investment from their side could have been encouraged and would have constituted an additional source of economic assistance.

But the economic aspect of policy formulation remained largely in the domestic realm, and India's foreign policy ambitions were focused on the global problems of imperialism and racial inequalities. In Nehru's eyes the expatriate Indians had forfeited their Indian citizenship and identity by moving abroad and did not need the support of their mother country. In fact they were encouraged to integrate and fight for their host countries' independence. Their often having taken the colonisers' position due to their relative economic superiority to the indigenous populations did not encourage any support from their anti-imperialist motherland. So in the context of larger theoretical and moral problems of Indian foreign policy formulation the concerns of the expatriate Asians were largely forgotten.

In order to understand the highly theoretical and moralistic framework, which excluded the Asian Diaspora one has to look at the development of Indian foreign policy. This chapter sets out to describe this development and to explain why India's new view of the world excluded a potentially powerful economic asset until the late 1980s. The official stand of the Indian government and its policy towards the Diaspora in the 1960s-80s will be described and analysed in the following pages.

> Any country's foreign policy is the product of its past history, which it cannot change, its geography, which is normally very durable, its domestic circumstances, which evolve constantly and its environment, which is always in flux and largely out of the country's control. History and geography give continuity to foreign policy; domestic and international circumstances produce change.[2]

Both continuity and change are essential parts in analysing the foreign policy of a country, and India seems to have been less prone to change in the first 45 years of independence then in more recent times. It is generally agreed in the literature that India's foreign policy was very flexible and reactive in nature, yet on the other hand India held on to some principles and moral values, even at times when circumstances changed so radically that they had become obsolete. In order to understand why Indian foreign policy came to hold such a rigid moral course one has to look at the context in which it was formed.

India's foreign policy was formulated at the dawn of the Cold War in the shadow of superpower confrontation. Economic development was of paramount importance at that time, and India chose self-reliance over dependency. As a result external economic relations with the western capitalist economies played a minor part in India's foreign policy: 'For good and sound reasons India chose self reliance as an economic goal and the public sector as its tool and this became one of the first divides between India and the US and one of the first bridges with the Soviet Union.'[3]

Economic development remained largely a domestic issue. India's focus on politics rather than on economics within her foreign policy remained constant until the 1990s. Nehru's aims in foreign policy formulation were the following:

1. Balanced relations with the two superpowers;
2. Resistance to great power intrusion;
3. Non-alignment as a platform for projecting India's anti-colonial ideals;
4. Development of the Commonwealth as a global group;
5. Close and co-operative relations with China;
6. Help for India's economic development, suited to its goal of remaining self-reliant.

India generally perceived itself as a third world leader with a role to play. The Indian leadership has shown a far greater intellectual than practical interest in international affairs. This was partly due to the personality of Nehru, the architect of foreign policy. He had shown a particular interest in foreign affairs and was the one 'who put the issue of Indian independence in world perspective' by focusing on larger issues such as racial discrimination and imperialism.[4] This and India's position and size incited her to play a role in the international system.

There are two ways to play such a role: through the utilisation of force; and through the gaining of respect and moral authority. The two are generally mutually exclusive. At the time of independence India was economically and militarily weak, but the way she had gained her independence gave her some moral authority within the world community.[5] The Nehruvian model had three components: rhetorical, emulative and mediatory. Rhetorically anti-imperialism and anti-racism were the essential elements. At every possible occasion India raised its voice against apartheid, against the exclusion of communist China from the UN, against remaining colonialism in Asia and Africa. The emulative role was non-alignment: India refused to join the bloc system and believed that it should be able to judge and decide about each given situation as it came along, without owing allegiance to anyone. Nehru had not designed this system as a third bloc, but later it was often seen as such. As for India's mediatory efforts they were frequent in the early time after independence: Korea 1952, Indochina 1954, the release of American prisoners in China, the admission of new members to the UN (of which 5 were communist and 13 non-communist).[6]

Indian foreign policy was thus surely not reactive, but certainly in more than one way idealistic, and perhaps even unrealistic. Nehru said that:

> Individuals may become internationally minded and may even be prepared to sacrifice personal and immediate national interest for a larger cause, but not so nations. It is only when international interests one believes to be in line with national interests, that they arouse enthusiasm.[7]

But India believed for a long time that idealism and self interest were complementary to each other in its case: 'Idealism without self interest would be a hollow philosophy and self interest without idealism would just be the law of the jungle'[8] At this point one has to ask what India's national interest was and if it was in line with the idealistic aims it proclaimed. India wanted peace and peaceful coexistence in order to develop. India believed that any kind of conflict swallowed up the resources that could have been used for development. India wanted non-alignment, since the division of the world called for allegiance in one camp or another and as a result would cut out the possibilities of mutually beneficial co-operation with the other side. India wanted to preserve the integrity and sovereignty of her country, and was opposed to all forms of domination by others. India also shared the recent historical experience, hopes and fears of the newly independent countries of Asia and Africa. A rational course of foreign policy was to orient it towards this new group of states hoping to create a larger area of peace by fighting common dangers of imperialism and racism together.[9] In many ways ideals remained dominant, and although it looked to many that India's ideals coincided with her national interests, India had to learn that this was not always the case. Warren Ilchman had said about Nehru's India that the exclusion from involvement in foreign affairs during the colonial period produced an understanding of the world where the relating of domestic national interest to what the international system could provide and required was made difficult. This has certainly proven true.

Later, after Nehru's death, certain ideals pertaining to international politics in a larger sense had to be dropped, making place for a more regional, realistic and forceful policy. Yet India's foreign policy remained split between the real and the imaginary world for a long time, and politics and ideological concerns where more prominent than economic and realistic ones.

The following chapter divides itself into four parts: First India's involvement in the Non Aligned Movement (NAM) and her superpower relations will be analysed, then her role in the Commonwealth (CW), and her involvement in the third world as a protagonist of anti-imperialism. Her regional role will also be described briefly. The last part will look at India's foreign economic policy. It will be concluded that throughout India's 45 years of independence, till the early 1990s, her foreign policy was idealistically oriented, and that even changes towards realism under Indira Gandhi did nothing to strengthen the economic component in foreign policy. India's national interest was seen solely in political, ideological terms. As we shall see this led her to ignore some important and powerful opportunities.

Expatriate Asians have never been a part of India's foreign policy formulation. They were not considered an economic asset, a potential lobby, or anything else within the domestic or international affairs sphere. They were simply ignored.

Non-Alignment

Independent India's foreign policy was developed to a great extent in the aftermath of the Second World War where the most important feature was bi-polarity and superpower confrontation. South Asia in general adapted to that reality according to its own ideologies, political perceptions and geopolitical position within the area of superpower rivalry.[10] The choice for India was a limited one: either to join one of the two blocs or to remain separate. Although economically and militarily weak, independent India saw itself as the natural leader for all the countries wanting to rid themselves of colonial domination who wanted to follow a path of peaceful coexistence. Besides, emerging as the sixth largest state with the second largest population in the world, India felt it had an independent contribution to make to international politics and did not feel the need to be associated to any one bloc. As a result it became a founding member of the Non Aligned Movement (NAM).

Nehru's policy had a global orientation; his name has always been linked to NAM: 'His relatively idealistic view of internationalism is also proved by his frequent reference to the ideal of 'one world'.... He justified idealism in international relations by saying that realism as such 'leads to incessant conflict' and that the realist 'looks at the tip of his nose and sees little beyond, the result is that he is stumbling all the time.''[11] His worldview had developed during India's struggle for freedom and as a result his foreign policy always reflected the basic objectives of full independence and a respected international status in the world community. Full independence in this sense meant that India had the right to choose its interests and its policies, judging each situation as it came along. Nehru was also aware of the historic role the Indian national movement had played in the dismantling of colonialism and racism in general. Nehru wanted to uphold the moral image based on Indian values such as non-violence and tolerance, and propagated these ideas to the emerging third world nations.

Indira Gandhi maintained non-alignment as a central focus of Indian foreign policy, although from a much more realistic stand point: 'We will not allow ourselves to be led away either by the anti-Soviet or by the anti-American hysteria.'[12] Mrs. Gandhi's rejection of superpower dominance was accompanied by a rejection of power politics in general. She was against spheres of influence, or the concept of balance of power. But she also saw India's limitations in a regional sphere and retained a 'special relationship' with the Soviet Union.[13]

William Barnds gives three basic reasons for why India co-created and adhered to NAM: the major tasks were internal ones (political, social development and economic). Taking either side would divide a people in need of greater national unity. As the strongest power in the area India had no need for external support to bolster its regional position.[14]

Despite persistent attempts by the US and the Soviet Union India refused to be drawn into any kind of alliance or defence pact with either superpower, since it did not want its freedom of action influenced or restricted; in fact non-alignment allowed limited military dealings with all powers. Any kind of dependence on others was to be avoided. This concept also helped India avoiding direct involvement in any major conflict, which might not have been of direct concern to her, and allowed for greater economic assistance from abroad. The western political and economic system had been rejected since it was believed to be based on economic inequalities, and exploitation; historically it was it was this system which was accountable for the worst form of colonialism in Asia and Africa. The Soviet model was not favoured because it was based on violence and dictatorship. There was also a general belief that alliances for or against communism are largely a matter of convenience for the great powers, in view of that democracies had no qualms allying themselves to the Soviet

Union in the Second World War.[15] The Indian renaissance of political thought was essentially derived from the Indian cultural and intellectual traditions. Since the 1930s the Indian national movement stood firm on its own ideological ground, hoping to build a new system free of the evils of western democracy and communism.

NAM was non-bloc in character and created as an alternative world view to the Cold War, which was enfolding. NAM called for disarmament and the scrapping of nuclear weapons. As the movement grew, economic objectives rose to the foreground and the main aims can be summarised as follows:

- The non aligned nations should challenge the developed nations and compel them to share their wealth and resources with the non-aligned countries;
- The non-aligned nations should get a proper share in the management of various world issues, which are monopolised by the superpowers;
- There should be adequate economic co-operation among the countries of the third world to reduce their dependence upon the superpowers.[16]

Slowly non-alignment became synonymous with India's foreign policy. This did not mean creating equidistance from the Soviet Union and the US but establishing 'equi-proximity' with Moscow and Washington. India used the contemporary situation as it could, realising that it held certain advantages. 'This development (The US and Soviet Union being too close) can increase the possibility of a joint pressure on India to accept a particular view point, as may well happen if the US and the Soviet Union succeed in signing a treaty of non-proliferation of nuclear weapons.'[17]

The non aligned security strategy was based on disarmament and peaceful coexistence, but India soon enough realised that maintaining an adequate defence force was acutely necessary and that disarmament on all levels would only work if the superpowers themselves decided to reduce their military arsenals substantially. As for nuclear weapons, India did not see why they should remain reserved for certain nations and be off limits for others.

In general non-alignment could be seen as the international expression of domestic nationalism after independence. It enabled a country to judge each and every international problem in full freedom, but it did not mean neutrality or giving up the right of self-defence. India's policy was neither rigid nor infallible, but a dynamic concept which was able to adapt itself to changing conditions.[18]

As more and more states adopted this outlook it became clear that non-alignment was not so much an analytic concept as a term used to cover a wide range of approaches.[19] It differed from country to country depending on the history, the geography and the economic-political development. It was not so much a policy, as a policy formulation, not so much an objective as a framework, not an end in itself, but a means to an end. It assumed that the world would be a better place for everyone, if every country could and did pursue its destiny free from interference.[20]

Non-alignment also became increasingly institutionalised. The NAM members held meetings at different levels at regular intervals. Initially anti-colonialism and support for national liberation was a primary theme, due to the increasing membership of newly independent African countries. The concept of economic co-operation was of more recent origin, emerging from the realisation that the non-aligned countries shared some basic and simple problems such as a lack of health, clothing and shelter.[21] This in turn brought up the problem of the North-South dialogue. Its importance as a group also increased in the realms of the UN. The themes, which were developed and constantly reiterated, were concerns pertaining to colonialism, disarmament and economic matters.

NAM survived into the 1980s as a comprehensive political doctrine hoping to transform the international economic system, but its origins lay in the Cold War and its utility became questionable in the early 1990s. The question of NAM's utility and relevance to India have become particularly important. 'India (...) is no longer a new country. The Soviet Union is no longer a country at all. India need not fear American pressure to declare itself on the side of the capitalist West in a once and for all decision, for the ideological battle has been won by the west in no uncertain terms.'[22]

How did India come to chart a course that was without precedent? Isolation was a course India rejected. India gave priority to independence of judgement, world peace and non-involvement in blocs, in order to safeguard its own economic development and aid from the outside. Non-alignment was a 'common-sense approach' to India's foreign policy after independence combining 'pragmatism' with 'prudence'. It was the coherent guiding principle that countered the criticism that India's foreign policy was too often episodic and reactive.[23] Yet the question remains of how appropriate NAM was as a system for India: India's main foreign policy problems lay in the subcontinent itself; and by propagating a stand of higher morality than was in its own self interest, India found itself judged by standards established by Nehru and found itself wanting.

The question of how independent India really was is posed in the context of superpower relations. The following paragraphs will summarise India's relationship with the Soviet Union and the US, followed by an analysis on how far India compromised its non-aligned stand.

The Soviet Union

The cordiality and friendly co-operation, which characterised Indo-Soviet relations, were an outcome of domestic determinants as well as the international environment of the Cold War period. At first, after independence, 'Indo-Soviet relations were not even cordial, partly on account of the Soviet perception of India's independence, and partly due to India's adoption of the policy of non-alignment which was viewed by the Soviet Union as a strategy to justify collaboration with British imperialism.'[24] Stalin lived with the fear that South Asia might enter a hostile, western orientated alliance, but finally came to understand that accepting non-alignment was the necessary price to pay for friendship. For a while the Soviet Union tried to balance its relationship between Pakistan and India, yet in the 1960s Soviet assistance was badly needed. Despite the fight between communist China and non-communist India the Soviet Union stood by its promise it had made before 1962 to supply MIG 21s to India and even enabled her to manufacture them. As the major sources of foreign aid coming from the UK and the US dried up as the 1965 war began 'it must have occurred to Moscow that India could not pursue an independent foreign policy when she was dependent on the western powers not only to feed her teeming millions but also to defend herself.'[25] In 1965 the Tashkent conference which ended the war between Pakistan and India was held under the auspices of the Soviet Union. At that time India was suffering acute food shortages and in the wake of Indira Gandhi's move to power, India's internal stability was at stake. This was also the time of the Sino-Soviet split. From then on and more so during the 1970s the Soviet Union became an important partner for Indian trade in both the public and the private sector.[26]

The Sino-Pakistani axis had started to develop in the 1960s, more so after the Sino-Indian conflict of 1962. The growing rapprochement between the USA and China in the late 1960s made this power axis a global one and India felt seriously threatened.[27] China was very much against India's involvement in the liberation of Bangladesh (1971). At that time, India was not sure if Washington would oppose a Chinese attack on her, although she did not have enough troops to deploy along the Chinese border.[28] The Soviet Union had been courting India since the late sixties, and at this point in time India felt the need for a powerful friend. As a result the Indo-Soviet treaty of friendship was signed on the eve of India's involvement in the Bangladesh war. Although the treaty was by nature a security alliance, it was not a defence pact, which would have compromised India's freedom of action and political outlook. The operational part provided for 'immediate mutual consultation and the adoption of effective measures in the event of a military threat to either country'.[29] These military implications were clear enough for China and the US to understand that any further attack on India would certainly make the war uncontrollable.

As for the treaty, the benefits were mutual - there was structural support for the economy and the armed forces, besides India gaining a friend in an important position. Both economies were approximately at the same level of technology and both manufactured goods and primary products that could be exported to each other. From then onwards the relationship grew to the extent that India could be described as being the closest country to the Soviet Union outside the communist bloc.

When the Soviet invasion of Afghanistan occurred, India criticised but did not condemn the action. This is often held up to show that India was not really non-aligned as it always claimed. India's disapproval and calls for the pulling out of the invading troops were considered too little by the international community. At home Indira Gandhi pointed out that possibly Sino-American collaboration against the USSR had built up assistance given to the Afghan refugees and might have led to an escalation of western military presence in the area.[30] In the 1980s Mrs. Gandhi's government made it very clear to Moscow that despite the warm and friendly relations she was still disturbed by the presence of Soviet troops in Afghanistan. She was also very clear with the US by dissuading them from provoking possible Soviet retaliation by rearming Pakistan and verbally attacking the Soviet Union.

The United States of America

'India's relations with the US have been very complex. They have swung from one extreme to another ... Despite many common characteristics the two countries have different perceptions of certain key issues in international affairs.'[31] India and the US have no real clash of interests, their differences on international issues during the last quarter of a century have stemmed from divergent attitudes to other countries and other systems. The US' quest for bases in Asia resulted in a pro-Pakistani tilt, and the Indian concept of non-alignment was 'offensive' to American values. But to India the concept of equidistance implied the tacit acceptance of a power bloc structure. In fact at the base India was all but anti- American. 'The high prestige which the US had enjoyed in Asia until the second World War had been due to its detachment from European imperialism; when it began to form a ring of states in Asia this prestige was quickly dissipated.'[32] Nehru viewed the division of the world into two opposing camps as dangerous and clumsy. What annoyed him was that America was in the habit of thinking that its quarrels and controversies were the world's quarrels and controversies and that the world was supposed to submit to them.[33]

Yet as the world's largest democracy, with no interest in Marxism, and the potential of developing one of the world's largest markets, India might have been expected to become an area of American interest. The failure of Indo-American relations was in all likelihood due to conflicting perceptions: In America's eyes India was subscribing to a Marxist or socialist form of economic development through the planned system of industrialisation. Until the end of 1949 the US had no South Asia policy as such, and her interests in the region were not clearly defined. However the emergence of communist China increased the importance of India's strategic position, yet India remained non aligned. So between 1947 and 1949 the US stand towards India was mainly disinterested. As for the Indo-Pakistani dispute, the West took a rather unsympathetic stand towards India, especially concerning the Kashmir problem. To some, India remaining in the Commonwealth and Nehru's visit to Washington pointed towards a tendency to lean towards the West. But then India recognised China and remained outside the new bloc structure and this sealed her fate.

Later, between 1950 and 1959 there was a phase of open US hostility. The Korean crisis was a sore spot in Indo-American relations. Throughout the crisis India played a mediatory role which was disliked by the US.[34] Under the republican administration a Middle East Defence Organisation was suggested, which was to include Pakistan. It had been the debacle of Suez, which had led President Eisenhower to propose a new military assistance programme in the Middle East, since he abhorred the idea of a power vacuum. Although, unmaterialised, the MEDO pact threatened to come very close to India's borders, and was perceived as a threat by the Indian administration, bringing the Cold War to its back door.

As the 1962 war with China unfolded, the West and the US watched the events with 'sympathy towards India.'[35] In fact its decision to send India arms was by far the United States' most friendly act in the history of Indo-US relations. Yet as a result India was forced into negotiations with Pakistan over the Kashmir issue in 1963-4.

Indira Gandhi's first term started with the assumption that relations with the US could be dramatically improved.[36] Her concerns were to avoid food shortages by encouraging self-sufficiency, and regaining India's autonomy in international affairs. The two American ambassadors J.K.Galbraith and Chester Bowles, posted successively in Delhi at the time, both attempted to improve Indo-American relations by raising western aid for India. Part of the project was an American financed steel plant, which ended up being financed by the Soviet Union, as negotiations stalled.

As Indo-Soviet relations improved Indo-US relations began to deteriorate. The Nixon-Kissinger initiative towards China in 1971-72 worsened relations with India. The US hoped to create a new balance in Asia.[37] In fact it has been suggested that India's growing fear of China pushed her towards the alliance with the Soviet Union. (But then it might have been India's fear of an alliance between Pakistan and the Soviet Union, which led her to sign the treaty). Kissinger felt that the Indo-Soviet friendship treaty was a clear move away from India's non-aligned stance, and that India was out to break up Pakistan in order to dominate the subcontinent. This in turn would obviously mean an extension of Soviet influence. But at that time the US had to recognise that India was now a power in the region to be reckoned with.

At the same time India was opposed to the American involvement in Vietnam, which did nothing to enhance good relations. Furthermore India's explosion of a nuclear device in 1974 showed its ability to interfere with 'America's perceived global interest in nuclear non-proliferation.'[38] India had already refused to sign the nuclear non-proliferation treaty in 1968, believing that nuclear power should not be restricted to a small club of dominant 'haves' confronting the large mass of the 'have-nots'. Non-proliferation would only work if the superpowers agreed to dismantle their own arsenals. Indira Gandhi gave no assurances that such explosions could not be repeated in the future.[39] India firmly believed that the development of nuclear science and technology should not be impeded.[40]

The occupation of Afghanistan forced a radical review by the American administration of its South Asian strategic interests. Since the balance of power was thought to be Afghanistan-Soviet Union-India vs. Pakistan-US-China, the arms sales to Pakistan resumed.[41] Arms were also supplied to the western-backed alliance of Afghan Mujahidin. As a result the Indo-US relationship suffered, since India viewed this as gross interference in the region.

It was only in the mid 80s, following the election of Rajiv Gandhi that the US again expressed interest in improving relations and in June 1985 R.Gandhi made a successful visit to the US. 'The time has come for Washington to develop a policy that views New Delhi as more than a minor player in the global super power competition or simply one of dozens of third world or non aligned countries.'[42] Yet India remained fearful of US intervention in the South Asian region, not through direct intervention, but of the effects of its support for its regional allies such as Pakistan and parts of the Afghan Mujahidin.

It is interesting to note that Indo-US relations at no time affected the flow of Indian professionals to the US. No matter how bad relations were, India never interfered with the migration process, and the US did not apply special immigration sanctions to the inflow of Indian nationals. The Indian Diaspora in the US remained apolitical and did not have any effect on Indo-American relations.

Commonwealth, Britain, and Anti-Imperialism

Anti-imperialism became an aspect of Indian foreign policy due to India's own experience of British imperialism.

> The revival of memories of the greatness of ancient India, coupled with the study of British and French political thought during the Indian renaissance of the second half of the nineteenth century created a powerful resentment among the educated sections of Indians against British rule in India and the conversion of the Indian economy into a mere appendage of the British economy. The founding of the Indian National Congress was itself a manifestation of this anti-imperialist feeling among the Indian intelligentsia. Anti-imperialism gradually percolated down to the Indian masses in the course of the Indian freedom movement, especially through such struggles as the Swadeshi movement, the non-co-operation movement, the civil disobedience movement and the quit India movement.[43]

It was only after the First World War that the Indian leaders started opposing imperialism every where, rather then concentrating on the protest against British rule at home. By the time independence came, anti-imperialism and anti-racism had become a central focus in Indian policy formulation. Nehru, who was adamant on making India the moral example to the rest of the world, was ready to push these issues at an international level. He visualised a linkage between the Indian struggle for independence with the world-wide struggle against imperialism. The foreign affairs cell that was established in the office of the All India Congress Committee in May 1936 was to deal with such problems.

After independence one part of the British colonial legacy remained: India's continued membership in the Commonwealth (CW). In the 1920s and 30s Nehru considered the idea of India remaining within the CW, and consequently a Dominion of Great Britain to be ridiculous and humiliating. Britain in his eyes was the greatest enemy of national freedom and peace. But post war Britain aroused Nehru's admiration since she had fought for the cause of democracy and freedom.[44] As a result he became more amenable to maintaining relations with Britain and the CW after independence. However at this stage he still believed a republic could not be part of the CW. Britain was also keen on India's continued association with the CW. 'There was however one immediate factor which may well have been decisive. Pakistan was committed to CW membership. In view of pre-partition disputes over the division of assets, evacuee property, river water and above all Kashmir, did not that mean the likelihood of an anti-Indian CW if India seceded?'[45]

India had been a member of the CW since 1917 when it was admitted to the Imperial Conference, and the decision to remain was a sign that India could be magnanimous. Membership did not entail any diminution of Indian sovereignty or freedom in conducting relations with the rest of the world. Nehru also believed that the CW would outgrow its Anglo-Saxon image and become something of much greater importance. He justified India's stay in the CW with the benefits of co-operation in the field of economics, politics, education, diplomacy and defence. A majority of India's trade then was with the CW, and besides having her foreign exchange reserves tied up in the sterling area, there were a substantial number of communities of Indian settlers in various parts of the British Empire. Nehru also realised that fighting for India's ideals of peace and freedom for colonial people, against racism and for co-operation with Afro-Asian countries would be served better by remaining in the CW. It was to become a 'bridge' between the various races and cultures. This form of informal and non binding co-operation would suit India best, especially in the setting of the Cold War. Besides it gave India an international connection it needed as a new state.

The profile of the CW changed continuously after India decided to remain a member, and Nehru laid the foundations for the most fundamental changes. Since India had become a republic in 1949 it was relieved from the stipulation of owing allegiance to the British crown, thus paving the way that others would follow.[46] Through India's accession as a non-white state, the CW had de facto lost its image of a white man's club, and become a multiracial association. It had prospects for expansions in other areas of Asia and Africa, and it was India's objective to help other colonies achieve independence while still remaining in the CW. It had the potential of dealing with global political and economic issues, which were viewed as part of India's national interest and objective. India largely influenced the CW's concern for decolonisation and the second objective of racial equality followed suit.

> For India the struggle against racism was the continuation of the struggle Mahatma Gandhi had launched in Durban at the beginning of this century. India raised the issue as early as 1946 in the context of the discriminatory treatment accorded to the people of Indian origin in South Africa. Nehru early on saw the issue in the context of the even greater oppression of the African majority. At the UN, India contended that South Africa's policy of racial discrimination was a violation of the UN charter, particularly of those provisions on human rights.[47]

Although South Africa maintained that this problem lay within her domestic jurisdiction the CW took the issue up first informally then formally. In the 1960s the question of the acceptability of apartheid became more important. Nehru's 1961 attack, which later became known as the 'Nehru plan' or 'CW charter', argued that the CW could not be considered a free association of free peoples so long as a country practising racial discrimination was a member. He also emphasised that the concept of the CW as a multiracial society based on equality was rendered meaningless as long as this anomalous situation remained. In fact apartheid was an obstacle to the CW's growth, preventing other members from joining in. Nehru hoped that formal protest would force South Africa to change course, he still believed that one could fight racial discrimination more effectively within the Commonwealth than outside. Yet South Africa withdrew its application for continued membership and left the CW. Consequently the acceptance of the principle of racial equality as a condition of CW membership got 'de jure' recognition by the CW prime ministers. The question of racial equality had grown from the concerns about the Indian Diaspora to include all problems of discrimination and Nehru made sure that the Indian policy did not focus solely on the Indian expatriate communities anywhere in the CW.

At the beginning the CW had not only been an Anglo Saxon club (Britain, Canada, Australia and New Zealand), but actually Anglo-centric in character. The Indian membership helped that change, but the 'de jure' change came about with the establishment of a CW secretariat in 1965. Yet the relations between Britain and India remained unique: the similarities of their political structure, and the common history made for a strong link. Nehru maintained a personal relationship between the two powers despite their very different worldview. The subcontinent had been Britain's sphere of influence, but Britain slowly withdrew from a role concerning South Asian questions after 1947.

Britain also remained critical of India on certain issues such as Kashmir, or her attitude on the Suez crisis. On the Kashmir problem Britain was happy to throw the blame on Nehru's obstinacy, while the Indian government upheld their view that a plebiscite so long after partition would do more harm then good. As for Suez, India saw it as a fight between Europeans and non-Europeans, which greatly displeased the British.[48] Then there was the fierce criticism of British immigration policy in the late 1960s and 1970s. It induced the Indian government to 'keeping a close eye on the treatment of Indian immigrants'[49] under the guise of criticising racial discriminatory immigration policies. The Indian administration also felt that the British government had tolerated the sending of money and arms, as well as political support for Sikh extremism, which fuelled terrorism in the Punjab.[50] Despite the deterioration of political relations between the two countries the economic activity was not greatly affected: in the 1970s and 1980s over 47% of the foreign owned industrial assets in India were still British owned.[51]

The economic side of CW co-operation took shape in Singapore in 1971 when the CW heads of government declared the aim to remove wide disparities of wealth. Indira Gandhi wanted a wider perspective on economic relations to emerge from the CW. Britain ensured special treatment by the EEC when it joined, so that Indo-British trade relations could be maintained. Britain supported the establishment of a regular Indo-

EEC consultative machinery in concluding a separate Indo-EEC trade agreement, which embodied substantial concessions for Indian exports.[52] However, in general, the European powers were in retreat from Asia between 1966-1984. The interaction with India was largely on an economic base and the possibility of some common dialogue on both East-West and North-South questions were only explored during Indira Gandhi's second term.

India was anxious to play a big role in the freedom movements of Asia and Africa. In fact, as stated earlier, this had been one of her leading objectives in remaining in the CW. Pre-Second World War commercial contacts with other parts of Asia and Africa included exports (such as cotton textiles) and the settlement of Indians in small and big trading centres in the Arabian sea region.[53] India had an unusually long record of fighting colonial rule and the Indian National Congress evolved to become a model for other anti-colonial movements. India's involvement in anti-imperialism had started with the campaign against apartheid, which it pursued from 1946 onwards. But it did not end there. The mutual objectives of anti-colonialism and anti-racism created tangible collaboration between the two regions.

From the point of view of the Africans two developments in post independence India held special significance: the manner of merging the princely states into the Indian Union; (African nationalists wanted to unify the African continent) and the development of NAM, in which they saw that a weak nation could maintain autonomy in world affairs.[54] Yet Arab and African nationalists did not regard India as part of their natural grouping, since its culture was alien.

India's efforts were further hampered by the significant number of Indian immigrants who were implicit representatives of the British empire and its sphere of influence; and by the internal conflict between the National Congress and the Muslim League, which resulted in partition and the creation of an Islamic state on the subcontinent. This in turn undermined the basis for unity between India and parts of West Asia, while Pakistan used this for its own benefit.[55] Nehru's vocal policy of support to the newly emerging countries was particularly manifest at international conferences and at the UN. 'But the bases for India's relations with the newly independent countries between the Sahara and South Africa were tenuous and seldom warranted even the exchange of diplomatic relations.'[56] It was the CW which on the base of a common language, and similar governmental and educational systems, provided the means for a connection and an understanding between the African and Indian administration in the postcolonial era. The close connections that developed with East Africa led the Indian administration to ignore the interests of its own community in the region in order to back the nationalist leaders, such as J. Kenyatta. India only refused to support violent means, which would upset the British Kenyan government. As a result India disliked the emerging Mau-Mau movement and its violent methods. The decolonisation of Uganda and Tanganyika was less painful and dramatic and did not allow for a great scope of Indian involvement, yet New Delhi was adamant that the East African states should not be 'jeopardised by exerting any pressure upon them on behalf of the Indian settlers there.'[57]

Apart from pushing for decolonisation in Africa, India was keen to see stability and economic prosperity in that region. India had also made it a point of co-operating with other CW countries by becoming a centre for technology training and education, especially for Asia and Africa. 'Indeed these countries increasingly look to India for technical assistance, scientific, trade and commercial co-operation.'[58] While technical assistance is considered an important link in the co-operation programme, India also recognised the need for joint ventures, which were set up in countries such as Kenya, Tanzania, Uganda, Mauritius and Zambia.

The advantages of India's continued membership in the CW were various: the very character of co-operation in a family of nations enabled India to develop special relationships with countries she would otherwise not have had bilateral relations with. In practical terms India received support in 1962 during the Chinese aggression, from countries such as Britain, Australia and Canada, which had absolutely no obligation towards India.[59] The enthusiasm shown in the CW by successive Indian administrations however has fluctuated. Indira Gandhi in her first term was not particularly involved, due to an unmistakable shift in Indian foreign policy towards regional issues.[60]

The CW offered India multinational co-operation of a different nature than it had with the UN or NAM. The CW's advantage was that it linked countries with a common language and a common history. It had always been India's objective not to be isolated from the forces of nationalism in Asia and Africa. The CW proved an excellent forum within which to pursue these policies. India had played a key role in transforming the CW to what it is known as today, namely a forum that promotes co-operation and political stability. India believed that without this particular kind of communication and co-operation, stability in the third world could not be maintained.

Regional

Although India's international concerns remained steady, after Nehru's death the regional part of foreign policy formulation increased in importance. Unlike India's global role it was generally reactive in nature and not so much concerned with theoretical problems.

Regardless of the historical period, India has always been a dominant factor in South Asian politics. Her position became especially important after colonialism unified the subcontinent. Post-colonial, independent India dominates the entire area due to its geographic position: there is no other country equally big in size, and at the same time adjacent to all the other six states of the region only separated by either a land border or a coastal line. Landlocked countries such as Nepal or Bhutan could hardly survive economically without Indian co-operation; the Maldives and Sri Lanka might be less dependent due to their being islands, but their proximity to India's coast line still makes Indian influence inevitable.

This 'gigantism' (India holds 72% of the total land area, 77% of the total population, 85-90% of the total natural resources)[61] has also generated an atmosphere of regional mistrust. India is seen as the natural hegemon of the region. India also dominates for other reasons: despite the religio-cultural diversity the geographical unity is maintained by a relatively stable secular democracy, which contrasts with the other states, afflicted by inherently unstable political systems.

India's foreign policy evolved as a 'dual' pattern, encompassing a global as well as a regional role. 'It may not have been consciously designed or intellectually conceived, but dualism was the broad framework that was conceptually discernible in India's foreign policy behaviour during the Nehruvian era'.[62] Nevertheless the regional part of the policy formulation was at first rather ill defined and generally 'reactive' in nature. There the main emphasis was on establishing a security zone against possible threats from China in Tibet. Nehru believed that the broad concepts used in global policy formulation could also be used at the 'micro-level', subject to some minor adjustments. Yet after military impasses and defeats at the hands of the Pakistanis and the Chinese, India required a firming up of its regional stand.

After Nehru, India's global policy began to lose its effectiveness, yet slowly a framework for a regional policy began to emerge. From India's standpoint it was certainly more realistic, pragmatic, national interest orientated and consequently more forceful.

The main incident, which established India as a regional power, was the creation of Bangladesh. 1971 was crucial for India's position in the region: The flood of refugees that poured into India had severe effects on the economy and on India's social structure. Out of economic and strategic necessity India trained, armed and then gave combat support to the Bangladeshi refugees.[63] The intervention in East Pakistan was 'militarily conclusive and politically successful'. Bangladesh emerged as an independent state, India had defeated Pakistan for the first time since independence, and India had successfully defied Chinese and US pressure not to intervene militarily. As a result India was perceived as a regional power with possible hegemonic designs of her own. This in turn disqualified her from playing the kind of role Nehru had defined for her. It became necessary to assure the subcontinent that India did not have expansionist designs, though it had in effect become dominant in the region.[64] In fact subsequently it became one of India's main diplomatic aims to improve relations with its neighbours.

The Simla agreement, which resulted out of this conflict, remained controversial. It has been seen as an act of generosity, since Pakistan was not publicly humiliated. Pakistan had to accept the principle of bilateralism, which India expected would also apply for Kashmir. India did not demand any reparations, and returned 500 square miles of territory in the West. Bhutto had given priority to territorial issues over the liberation of prisoners of war, an issue which later became an embarrassment for India.[65] Yet the Kashmir issue was left open, and in effect with it the root of further regional problems.

Pakistan was not weakened: it became more compact and as a result a stronger military power, and with the forthcoming American aid it had made up more than its losses by 1975. Bangladesh for its part had always been poor, but was excruciatingly so after the war. The chaos that resulted after the war was largely blamed on India, which in itself did not improve regional relations.

Post 1971 India's regional strategy has four objectives:[66]

The upgrading of military power India continues to maintain and upgrade its military power since it feels surrounded by an uncertain, unstable regional set-up. Myanmar, Afghanistan and Tibet remain, even if not explicitly involved in a war, in a state of flux. Although these are relatively small and insignificant countries, the latter two are tied into greater balance of power equations. In addition there is the increasingly unstable and guerrilla like situation on some of India's borders. This is especially the case for the Northeast, where Naga and Assamese separatist movements have periodically created havoc.

Obviously the most significant reason in maintaining a solid military structure lies in the permanent confrontation with Pakistan. Although the communal question was at the root of Indo-Pakistani relations, it gradually developed into a Cold War issue as the great powers started taking sides.[67] The religious problem was diminished by the fact that India made it a point to maintain good relations with other Muslim states, notably in the Gulf. Yet the chance of it being handled and managed as a purely bilateral problem became impossible after the subcontinent divided itself into two opposing blocks: Pakistan-China-US vs. India-Soviet Union. The question of Kashmir evolved into a near civil war like situation, both parties claiming the state as their own. Furthermore India's May 1974 nuclear test at Pokharan, Rajasthan halted the process of normalisation in Indo-Pakistani relations which had been set in motion at the Simla summit in 1972. Because of these regional uncertainties, which were both internal and external in nature, a national consensus emerged on maintaining the armed forces.

Bilateralism A preference for bilateralism was one consequence of India's regional experience. India learnt that internationalising certain problems puts her at a disadvantage, as was observed with the UN dealings on Kashmir after the 1948 war. Keeping certain problems on a bilateral basis avoided the publicising of contentious issues. This in turn avoided the risk of a situation where India could find herself alone confronting a host of other countries opposing her. The belief in bilateralism also emanated from the tradition of 'non-interference' by other powers and the belief that India knew its region best.

Diminution of the Chinese influence The Chinese factor has been a sore point in India's foreign relations. Both China and India are the giants of Asia, both proud of their past civilisations and both sensitive about their economic backwardness in the 1940-50s.[68] Although China is a neighbour, it cannot be counted as part of the South Asian region, geographically set apart by the Himalayan mountain range. Therefore India and China are natural rivals, and the relationship was bound to be problematic. Nehru's political understanding involved advocating a policy of friendship, avoiding the isolation of newly communist China[69] and hoping to avoid the repetition of the errors committed with the Soviet Union.[70] In this way he hoped to establish a 'normal' world order where Indo-Chinese co-operation would lead the newly independent countries of the third world.[71] Throughout this time India upheld China's issues at the UN and recognised Taiwan as part of China.

When in 1950 China asserted its authority in Tibet, Nehru exercised restraint. In 1954 the two countries signed an agreement on Tibet which proclaimed the 'Panchsheel' doctrine; the five principles of peaceful coexistence:

- mutual respect for each other's territorial integrity and sovereignty,
- non aggression,
- non interference in each other's national affairs,
- equality and mutual benefit,
- peaceful coexistence.

Nehru had hoped to reduce China' potential threat by 'exposing it to the winds of international politics and blunting the edge of her isolation and military'[72] He emphasised that India had no territorial or ideological ambitions and that both nations had everything to gain from a co-operative relationship.

Yet in the 1960s the Indo-Chinese confrontation began on border issues, and evolved into a full-fledged war in 1962 in which India was defeated. 'It had become the function of the Chinese Foreign policy to make India the target of a virulent hate campaign and to discredit and debunk India's non-alignment and to destroy Nehru's prestige and all he had stood for.'[73] (India was an obstacle in China's militant line, which it wanted other third world countries to adopt. In order to discredit Delhi, Peking wanted to prove that the Indian foreign policy had become completely reactionary, that India's non-alignment was a myth and that its economic crisis was deepening. It also hoped to dissuade Moscow from assisting India further, and neutralise India's influence in the Afro-Asian community.[74] Later China shifted its position, moving closer to Pakistan, and gradually becoming a source of major military and economic aid to Islamabad.

The Indian humiliation of October/November 1962 made the nation realise that its relatively cooperative approach towards China had failed to provide the necessary security and that idealism was no substitute for realism.[75]

> After 1962 Indian leaders learned to lower their sights and to manage first the South Asian strategic environment. The 1962 military incident forced Indians to reassess the implications of Nehru and Menon's overemphasis on Pakistan as the principal geo-political problem. 1962 also forced Indians to recognise the importance of making India's north-east invulnerable to China's pressure.[76]

Still India felt it was threatened by both its immediate neighbours, Pakistan and China, neither of which subscribed to non-alignment, and therefore a modern defence force had become necessary.

A great deal of Indian diplomacy was focused on monitoring Chinese presence in the region, hoping to erode her influence wherever possible. On the other hand China found a willing ally in Pakistan to contain the expansion of Indian influence in the region. 'It is important to note that the understanding China has shown regarding Pakistan's membership of the western dominated military alliances preceded the deterioration of Sino-Soviet relations.'[77] But it is also interesting to note that the existence of this ongoing Sino-Pakistani military co-operation did not really influence Indian military behaviour either in 1965 or in 1971.

Chinese foreign policy regarding India has been reactive, defensive and offensive; it has been reactive since China could not remain indifferent to such a state as India on its borders, it has been defensive towards the movements in Tibet and offensive towards India as part of a programme to discredit India in front of the world, since its ideas could be threatening to the Chinese ideology. As a result the China factor remained a central influence in India's regional policy formulation.

Disallowing the destabilisation of any neighbouring states by any internal or external forces Finally India wanted to disallow the destabilisation of any neighbouring states by any internal or external forces. This includes the monitoring of ethnic conflicts in Assam, Bhutan or Sri Lanka, and the promotion of regional co-operation. There were of course many obstacles to regional co-operation, paramount India's size and position as a hegemon, but it was also integral for political and economic stability in the region.

India's foreign policy has shifted from the original Nehruvian diplomacy, founded essentially on global concerns, to a policy with more regional focus. This was partly due to the fact that India's internal and border problems have become more important, that the leaders themselves have taken a greater interest in internal affairs and that the surrounding countries have become increasingly unstable.

Policy towards Foreign Direct Investment

The basic problem with foreign capital and development

Like most underdeveloped countries, India suffered from a low level of income and a low level of capital accumulation. Consequently these countries have a stringent need for industrialisation and economic development. For instance, India launched an ambitious programme of industrialisation with the second five year plan of the mid 1950s: the Indian industrialisation strategy focused on the development of local capability in heavy industries including the machinery manufacturing sector.

In order to channel the country's scarce resources according to plan priorities, an industrial approval (licensing) system was put into place in the country, which would regulate all industrial investments beyond a certain minimum.[78] Since the domestic resources to carry out this programme were insufficient the country had to depend partly on foreign capital. To attain the broad objective of growth with social justice, India needed foreign capital resources, either in the form of foreign direct investment (FDI), foreign collaboration, aid grants from foreign countries or through imports.[79]

The foreign investment policy statement made by Nehru in April 1949 considered foreign investment necessary in supplementing Indian capital and for securing scientific, technical and industrial knowledge and capital equipment.[80]

At the time of Independence in 1947, India was host to a significant stock of foreign direct investment (FDI) largely owed to her erstwhile colonial masters, the British.[81] Immediately after independence the Government of India formulated its Industrial Policy Resolution of 1948 which was predisposed to strong governmental intervention.

First phase (1948-1960s)

In mid-1948, when the first survey of India's international assets and liabilities was under taken by the Reserve Bank of India (RBI), the stock of foreign investment in the country stood at Rs. 2,560 million, largely owned by British ventures.[82] During this period, the Government of India adopted a liberal attitude towards FDI inflows into the country and allowed a minority foreign ownership in its industries. The Industrial Policy Resolution of April 1948 recognised the positive role of foreign capital in the acceleration of a country's industrial growth and development. But it also realised that there was a need for the regulation of foreign capital in the interest of the nation. Thus, in April 1949, in his foreign investment policy statement Nehru was reported as having said that 'foreign investment is necessary in supplementing Indian capital and for securing scientific, technical and industrial knowledge and capital equipment. It was, therefore, encouraged on mutually advantageous terms, though the majority local ownership was preferred.'[83] Still the foreign investors were given all sorts of assurances with respect to no restrictions on the remittances of profits and dividends, and fair compensation in case of acquisition.

Keeping in mind the effects of the industrial policy resolution of 1948 with regard to the country's FDI flows, another Industrial Policy Resolution was drafted in 1956, wherein a list of industries were reserved for India's public sector. But the foreign exchange crises of 1957-58 compelled the Indian Government to adopt a more liberal attitude towards FDI flows into India. So, in order to attract more FDI, the Government announced various incentives and concessions like reduction in tax rates. In light of the launch of the third Five-year plan projects, 'the Government taking into account the gaps in capacity in relation to plan targets, came out with a list of Industries in the year 1961, where foreign investment was to be welcomed.'[84] Between 1948 and 1964 the FDI stock in the country more than doubled to Rs. 5.655 million from 2.560 million. The creation of local advantages led to a sharp jump in the manufacturing sector, where the FDI stock grew to over 40% from around 20% at the time of independence.[85]

Second phase (1960s-1979)

The first phase with a liberal attitude towards FDI flows lasted till the early-1960s. As a result there was a significant outflow of foreign exchange in the form of remittances of dividends, profits, royalties and technical fees.

These outflows of foreign exchange caught the Governments attention in the background of another foreign exchange crisis in the mid- 1960s. So, to check the future problem 'the Government of India streamlined the producer for inviting foreign collaboration and their approvals, and adopted a more restrictive attitude towards FDI.'[86] A new agency called the Foreign Investment Board (FIB) was created within the Government in 1968 to deal with all companies inviting foreign investment or collaborations with up to 40% foreign equity. Those with more than 40% foreign ownership were to be screened by a cabinet committee. Restrictions were imposed on the renewals of foreign collaboration agreements. 'From 1972 onwards the Foreign Exchange Regulation Act (FERA) come into force, which required all foreign companies incorporated abroad to register themselves as Indian companies with a maximum of 40% foreign equity.'[87]Due to the restriction during this period the FDI inflows decreased. The FDI stock increased between 1974 and 1980 by only Rs. 10 million.[88]

The main points of the FERA are as follows:

'Restrictions, regarding assets held by non residents, where the Reserve Bank of India (RBI) considers it necessary and expedient in the public interest to do so, with respect to any asset in India held by, or occurring to, or transferred to, or to be transferred to, either a person resident outside India or a person intending to become resident outside India, it may impose a condition that the said asset shall not be transferred, assigned, pledged, charged or dealt with in any manner whatsoever expect in accordance with any general or special permission, which may be granted conditionally or otherwise, by the RBI.'[89]

Special Accounts: 'Where in the opinion of the Central Government, it is necessary or expedient to regulate payments due to persons resident in any territory, the Central Government may, by notification in the official Gazette, direct that such payments or any class of such payments shall be made only into an account (hereafter in this section referred to as a special account) to be maintained for the purpose by RBI or an authorised dealer specially authorised by the RBI in this behalf.'[90]

FERA, it should be noted, put a general ceiling of 40% on the foreign equity participation and initiated a series of other complicated restrictions. Hence, the implementation of the provisions of the Act had left only a limited number of companies, engaged in specified activities to remain with more than 40% foreign equity.

Table 3.1: Trends in FDI flows into India (country wise) between 1948 and 1974

Country	Amount of FDI Flows (Rs. in Million) June 1948	March 1974
UK	2060	6891
USA	112	5309
West Germany	1	1808
Switzerland	53	449
Japan	--	416
Others	332	4557
Total	2558	19430

Source: RBI, March 1978. (Quarterly Economic Report 1994.)

According to Table 3.1, from India's first Industrial Policy Resolution of 1948 to the implementation of FERA in 1974, there had been a substantial increase in the FDI flows into India and the rise stood at 660% (or 7.6 times). Among the major investing countries, the United Kingdom had been the largest investing country followed by the USA.

Third phase (1980 - 1989)

Due to the restrictions of the 1970s India performed very badly on the international market. Its indigenous technology could not produce world class goods. As a result India's manufactured exports plummeted. Foreign investors did not invest in the Indian private sector due to the poor export quality. To overcome this situation the government of India developed an Industrial Policy Resolution in the 1980s emphasising:

(i) The modernisation of plants and equipment through the liberalisation of imports of capital goods and technology;
(ii) Exposing Indian industry to competition by gradually reducing the import restrictions and tariffs; and
(iii) Assigning a greater role to the MNES in the promotion of manufactured exports by encouraging them to set up export-oriented units.[91]

The Industrial Policy Statements issued in 1980 and 1982 announced the liberalisation of licensing rules and regulations. A host of incentives and exemptions from foreign equity restriction under FERA to 100% export oriented units were also announced. Accordingly, 25 industries were also de-licensed. The implementation of the policies during the early part of the 1980s gradually liberalised the imports of raw materials and capital goods leading to the expansion in the list of items on the Open General License (OGL). Nearly 150 items in 1984 and 200 capital goods in 1985 became part of the OGL. The import duties on imports of different types of capital goods were also slashed in 1985. Likewise, restrictions on imports of designed drawings were also removed.[92] Along with the policy of liberalisation of trade there was an increasingly receptive attitude towards FDI and collaboration. Investments and collaborations were also permitted on a selective basis, even in the non-manufacturing sector and in existing companies. In the tourism sector, 51% equity participation was permitted as a norm. It was also possible for foreign investors to make direct applications and obtain approvals, pending the establishment of a local company. 'The rules concerning the payments of royalties & lump sum technical fees were relaxed. Tax rates on royalties were reduced from 40% to 30% in 1986. A degree of flexibility was introduced in the policy concerning foreign participation and exceptions from the general ceiling of 40% on foreign equity were allowed on the merits on individual investment proposals.'[93]

Table 3.2: Trends in FDI flows to India between 1980 and 1989

Year	Amount in FDI Flows (in US $ Millions)	Growth Rate in percent
1980	87.0	--
1981	12.6	-85.1
1982	66.5	415.3
1983	61.3	-7.5
1984	99.5	61.3
1985	103.0	3.0
1986	85.0	-17.5
1987	83.0	-2.4
1988	173.0	108.0
1989	252.0	46.0

Source: Asian Development Review, Manila, No. 1, 1993.

According to Table 3.2 in 1980 India had received FDI inflows amounting to US $ 87 million. In 1989, this figure went up to US$ 252 million, recording an overall rise of nearly 190% (or nearly 3 times). However, trends of FDI inflows had been fluctuating. There was no clear-cut liberalisation policy. A large number of restrictions were still maintained. Another problem was that foreign investors were adopting a wait and watch policy before investing in India. They remembered that in the 1970s the Government of India had suddenly imposed restrictions on foreign investors and their investments.

Table 3.3: Trends of major investing countries FDI in India from 1981 to 1989

Year	USA	Germany	Japan	UK	Italy
1981	22.5	54.2	6.4	7.1	0.4
1982	50.3	35.4	251.12	16.5	39.9
1983	138.9	48.4	160.8	98.0	11.5
1984	89.5	28.5	61.5	18.1	7.7
1985	399.3	118.8	156.8	37.1	69.5
1986	293.6	201.6	56.2	77.2	23.3
1987	259.2	98.7	69.0	84.4	29.7
1988	971.4	309.9	174.3	139.1	278.7
1989	621.6	1203.3	87.8	334.6	69.1

Source: Indian Statistical Yearbook of different years.

According to Table 3.3, the adoption of a more liberal policy towards FDI in the 1980s, was marked by an increase in the FDI inflows, as compared to FDI flows taking place during the 70s. Between 1981 and 1989, the total FDI inflows into India increased 29 times whereas the major investing nations namely, USA, Germany, UK, Japan, and Italy had recorded on overall rise of FDI investment of 28%, 22%, 48%, 173% and 13% respectively.

In 1989, trends had changed considerably and as a result, the relative share of the two biggest investing nations namely; Germany and the USA had declined. In the case of the UK, the relative share had gone up to 4% and it remained as the third largest investing nation in India after Germany and the USA. This all shows that on the whole FDI flows in the 1980s improved compared to the FDI inflows to India in the 1970s.

Table 3.4: Number of collaborations in major sectors in 1980 and 1989

Sector	1980	1989
Chemicals	52	86
Electrical and Electronics	114	127
Industrial Machinery	121	108
Mechanical Engineering	29	63
Machine Tools	26	08
Total	526	639

Source: Indian Investment Centre, New Delhi.

As shown in Table 3.4 in 1980, the largest collaborations were in the industrial machinery sector constituting 23% of total collaboration. Next came electrical and electronics and their share stood at 22%. The third largest collaboration was confined to chemicals. In contrast in 1989 the largest collaborations were confined to electrical and electronics, their share stood at 20% followed by the Industrial Machinery with a share of 17%, chemicals with a figured at 13.4% and the mechanical sector at a share of 10%. During the decade of the 80s the total number of foreign collaborations was 7,128. During the period 1980 to 1989, only 1/4 collaborations had been of financial nature whereas 3/4 were of technical nature.

Fourth phase (1989-1991)

The decade from 1981 to 1991 witnessed an acceleration in the rate of economic growth to well above 5% per annum, as compared to 3% in the pervious two decades. However, this relatively higher growth rate was combined with an acute macro economic crisis that reflected itself in runaway inflation, Balance of Payments (BOP) deficit and mounting public debt. By 1991, India's economy was in a very poor condition. The foreign exchange reserves had fallen to such a low level that they were barely sufficient to buy two weeks worth of imports. The Inflation rate was running in double digits. Coupled with these danger signals, the basic macro indicators like the fiscal deficit was high and industrial production was depressed. The continuous high levels of deficits (both fiscal & BOP) compelled the government to resort to heavy borrowing to finance them, and consequently the public debt increased by alarming proportions.

In view of these developments of the economy, the government had to reformulate its economic strategy, which is better known as the New Economic Policy and the Economic Reforms Programme. Reforms resulted in the decontrolling of the private sector, reforms of the public sector, de-licensing of industries, liberalisation of the financial market, decontrol of the foreign trade and allowing the entry of foreign capital.[94]

India's economic foreign policy was for decades ruled by the ideals of Swadeshi or self-sufficiency and as it has been seen above FDI remained a controversial issue. It is also interesting to note that Non Resident Indians were never part of an active Indian economic foreign policy.

Conclusion

India's foreign policy was guided by a clear set of principles which have in different periods in time constituted a structure. Yet that structure changed to some extent depending on external and internal circumstances, retaining certain fundamental bases. A world in a state of permanent flux could not be confronted with a set of inflexible concepts, but India developed some objectives and interests she pursued consistently. In the early period India was more oriented towards the global scene, but priorities and needs changed later with time and India oriented herself towards a more relevant, regional foreign policy. Nevertheless India maintained certain highly theoretical principles.

Despite India not being a 'great power' it was too big a country to be a satellite of any other country or in fact to be ignored by the World community.

> When India had a traditional image, India used to play a notable role in world affairs. Today India is known as a sleeping economic giant, the fourth largest military power (in conventional weapons), and the largest and most stable democracy in the world. The odd thing, however, is that nowadays, India plays a much less active and important role in world affairs- for a variety of reasons, but especially because of the government's preoccupation with acute domestic problems and of the standing threat to India's security. [95]

Yet the basic parameters were constant: international involvement on a larger scale than the purely regional sphere was concentrated in international organisations such as the UN and NAM, or even the CW. These organisations gave expression to fundamental Indian beliefs, such as peaceful coexistence and cooperation between nations. The concept of balance of power which emated from nineteenth century European politics was alien to the South Asian region and India fought the creation of spheres of influences at all times.

It has been observed throughout this chapter that realism and idealism have both been part of Indian foreign policy, sometimes simultaneously. The Foreign policy focus developed from a highly theoretical, moralistic international role into a more regionally oriented policy. Realism in the South Asian region was necessary since the subcontinent has remained economically and politically divided. This in turn meant that India remained the leading power in South Asia. At home, economic failure and military humiliation had pushed India to rethink its role in the international community, especially since the aim of 'subcontinental harmony' and 'great power exclusion' was not attained.[96] India's objectives became definitely less altruistic in the 1970s and 1980s.

Although the external environment might have impinged strongly on foreign policy formulation there were certain important domestic factors which influenced its development. Leadership has been largely ignored in the earlier part of the chapter, and will briefly be considered here.

Nehru designed and conceived India's foreign policy and all the ideals and goals which went with it.

> He became a link, a bridge between warring ideologies, races and nations. He had fought against colonialism in Asia and Africa, but in later years as this imperialism was being liquidated, he tried to exercise some influence on the leaders of Afro-Asia, urging them not merely to flog the dead horse of imperialism, but to switch their minds from past to future, to tasks of reconstruction.[97]

He had seen through the inadequacies of the classical doctrines of balance of power and wanted to align national interest with world peace.[98] He himself led foreign affairs and his profound hatred of colonialism and war led to his idealistic view on how to conduct international relations in the post second World War world. He did not consult experts, and all foreign planning was under his supervision.

Although this direct supervision of foreign policy formulation was something his daughter did take from him, it was with her that the Nehruvian framework began to erode. Indira Gandhi had a more practical view of the world than her father did. The exalted vision the world had of India had vanished, and a lot of Indians at home believed that taking a more pronounced interest in the immediate region might benefit India's national interest.[99] Decolonisation had ended and the South African issue had been taken over by the other African states. The humiliating defeat at the hand of the Chinese and the aid India had received from the US, UK and France, contributed to the decline of her image. 'In the eyes of many this not only testified to India's inability to safeguard her interests, but also showed the alacrity with which she had sought external military assistance when for more than a decade India had been preaching self-reliance to everyone and had decried such initiatives by others.'[100] Under Indira Gandhi India abandoned the broader lines of her original international role. India was attempting to become militarily stronger. As for Indira Gandhi herself, she took great pains to control each and every foreign policy decision and to make all subordinate to her. The process of foreign policy making also became highly secretive.[101] She had inherited a strong and relatively autonomous Prime Ministry and asserted her authority early in her premiership.[102]

She ignored formal institutions and used the fact that public opinion manifested little interest in foreign policy. This allowed for the shift in Indian foreign policy to meet the regional challenges. Yet a consistent framework for those concerns was never developed and the regional policy's essential weakness was its reactive nature. Indira Gandhi still claimed that she had consciously continued her father's policy. She had inherited her father's resentment of the western domination of Asia, and she believed that in order to be self-reliant, India had to strengthen her independence, and to chose its own way. For this to be done India had to solve its own problems, which included backwardness.[103] The role in world affairs had diminished substantially, although ideologically and vocally she remained within the parameters Nehru had set for India on the international stage. She said: 'We are not tied to the traditional concept of a foreign policy designed to safeguard overseas possessions, investments, the carving out of spheres of influence and the erection of cordons sanitaires. We are not interested in exporting ideologies.'[104] Disarmament, resource diversification, international justice and the non-use of force were still things she called for. In contrast she understood the world's realistic power politics, but economic issues remained on the borderline of foreign policy making.

One can conclude that Indian foreign policy went from the Nehruvian global policy, rhetorically defined to fight imperialism and racism, to a far more realistic, regionally orientated framework. Post Nehru India learned to avoid idealistic and moralistic doctrines and rhetoric, yet, as we shall see later, not sufficiently to use its foreign policy assets in a more effective way for its own development.

Endnotes

1 See chapter 4 for details
2 Chopra, P., *The Crisis of Foreign Policy - Perspectives and Issues*, p.56
3 Ibid., p.57
4 Kapur, H., *India's Foreign Policy 1947-92, Shadows and Substance*, p.120
5 Ibid., p.122
6 Ibid., p.123-127
7 Kaul, T.N., *Ambassadors need not lie*, Vol. I, p.20-21
8 Ibid., p.21
9 Bandyopadyaya, J., *The Making of India's Foreign Policy*, p.108
10 Bradnock, R.W., *India's Foreign Policy since 1971*, p.84
11 Quoted in Nanda, B.R. (ed.), *Indian Foreign Policy - The Nehru Years*, p.182
12 Quoted in Tharoor, S., *Reasons of State - Political Development and India's Foreign Policy under Indira Gandhi*, p.94
13 Ibid., p.95-96
14 Quoted in Bradnock, R.W., *India's Foreign Policy since 1971*, p.87
15 Singh Joshi, M., *India's Foreign Policy*, p.2
16 Sisodia, S.S., *Foreign Policy of India, Indira Gandhi Era*, p.17-19
17 Khilnani Niranjan, M., *Realities of Indian Foreign Policy*, p.38
18 Quoted in Kaul, T.N., *Ambassadors need not lie*, Vol. II, p.1
19 Thakur, R., *The Politics and Economics of India's Foreign Policy*, p.15
20 Damodaran, A.K. and Bajpai, U.S. (eds.), *Indian Foreign policy - The Indira Gandhi Years*, p.198
21 Thakur, R., *The Politics and Economics of India's Foreign Policy*, p.19
22 Thakur, R., *The Politics and Economics of India's Foreign Policy*, p.31
23 Ibid., p.14
24 Chopra, S. (ed.), *Studies in India's Foreign Policy*, p.516
25 Ibid., p.27
26 Chopra, P., *The Crisis of Foreign Policy - Perspectives and Issues*, p.65
27 Bandyopadyaya, J., *The Making of India's Foreign Policy*, p.332
28 Ibid., p.332
29 Bandyopadyaya, J., *The Making of India's Foreign Policy*, p.332
30 Mansingh, S., *India's Search for Power - Indira Gandhi's Foreign Policy 1966-82*, p.4

31 Chopra, S. (ed.), *Studies in India's Foreign Policy*, p.523
32 Nanda, B.R. (ed.), *Indian Foreign Policy - The Nehru Years*, p.13
33 Dutt, V.P., *India and the World*, p.24
34 Pande, N.A., *India's Foreign Policy as an Exercise in Non-Alignment 1966-76*, p.185
35 Ibid., p.190
36 Dutt, V.P., *India and the World*, p.61
37 Ibid., p.67
38 Bradnock, R.W., *India's Foreign Policy since 1971*, p.101
39 Bandyopadyaya, J., *The Making of India's Foreign Policy*, p.336
40 Khilnani Niranjan, M., *Realities of Indian Foreign Policy*, p.41-2
41 Bradnock, R.W., *India's Foreign Policy since 1971*, p.102
42 Frankel, F., 'Play the India Card' FP, vol. 62, p.48-166
43 Bandyopadyaya, J., *The Mastering of India's Foreign Policy - Determinants, Institutions, Processes and Personalities*, p.69-70
44 Nanda, B.R. (ed.), *Indian Foreign Policy - The Nehru Years*, p.25-29
45 Prof. N. Mansergh quoted in Ibid., p.32
46 The formula agreed upon was that India would accept the King as the head of the Commonwealth, but not as the head of the Indian State
47 Damodaran, A.K. and Bajpai, U.S. (eds.), *Indian Foreign Policy - The Indira Gandhi Years*, p.211-212
48 Pande, N.A., *India's Foreign Policy as an Exercise in Non-Alignment 1966-76*, p.193
49 Bradnock, R.W., *India's Foreign Policy since 1971*, p.95
50 Ibid., p.95
51 Ibid., p.96
52 Damodaran, A.K. and Bajpai, U.S. (eds.), *Indian Foreign Policy - The Indira Gandhi Years*, p.226
53 Singh Joshi, M., *India's Foreign Policy*, p.79
54 Prasad, B. (ed.), *India's Foreign Policy - Studies in Continuity and Change*, p.261-2
55 Ibid., p.80
56 Singh Joshi, M., *India's Foreign Policy*, p.81
57 Ibid., p.82
58 Viviekanandan, B., 'India and the Changing Profile of the Commonwealth', p.37
59 Damodaran, A.K. and Bajpai, U.S. (eds.), *Indian Foreign Policy - The Indira Gandhi Years*, p.224-226
60 Bradnock, R.W., *India's Foreign Policy since 1971*, p.85
61 Kapur, H., *India's Foreign Policy 1947-92 - Shadows and Substance*, p.90
62 Ibid., p.92
63 Bandyopadyaya, J., *The Making of India's Foreign Policy*, p.334
64 Chopra, S. (ed.), *Studies in India's Foreign Policy*, p.30
65 Damodaran, A.K. and Bajpai, U.S. (eds.), *Indian Foreign Policy - The Indira Gandhi Years*, p.122-123
66 Kapur, H., *India's Foreign Policy 1947-92 - Shadows and Substance*, p.96-115
67 Grover (ed.), *India's Foreign Policy*, p.360
68 Khilnani Niranjan, M., *Realities of Indian Foreign Policy*, p.35
69 Dutt, V.P., *India's Foreign Policy*, p.278
70 Khilnani Niranjan, M., *Realities of Indian Foreign Policy*, p.35

71 Nanda, B.R. (ed.), *Indian Foreign Policy - The Nehru Years*, p.16
72 Nanda, B.R. (ed.), *Indian Foreign Policy - The Nehru Years*, p.17
73 Khilnani Niranjan, M., *Realities of Indian Foreign Policy*, p.36-37
74 Dutt, V.P., *India's Foreign Policy*, p.280
75 Chopra, S. (ed.), *Studies in India's Foreign Policy*, p.26
It is important to note that India concentrated its defence efforts solely towards Pakistan in the first decade after independence, Nehru believing that China was a friend and not a foe
76 Grover (ed.), *India's Foreign Policy*, p.361
77 Kapur, H., *India's Foreign Policy 1947-92 - Shadows and Substance*, p.111
78 Kumar, N., 'Industrialisation, Liberalisation & Two Way Flows of FDIs: Case of India', p.3229
79 Jenkins, R., *Transnational Corporations and Underdevelopment: The Internationalisation of Capital and Third World*, p.18
80 Kumar, N., 'Industrialisation, Liberalisation and Two Way Flows of FDIs: Case of India', p. 3229
81 Kumar, N., 'Industrialisation, Liberalisation and Two Way Flows of FDIs: Case of India', p.3228
82 Ibid., p. 3228
83 Ibid., p. 3229
84 Ibid., p. 3229
85 Ibid., p. 3229
86 Ibid., p. 3229
87 *The FERA Act, 1973* (Act No. 46 of 1973)
88 Kumar, N., 'Industrialisation, Liberalisation and Two Way Flows of FDIs: Case of India', p.3230
89 *The FERA Act, 1973* (Act No. 46 of 1973)
90 Ibid., p. 9
91 Kumar, N., 'Industrialisation, Liberalisation and Two Way Flows of FDIs: Case of India', p.3234
92 'FDI Flows to India: Pre & Post Scenario', p.147
93 Kumar, N., 'Industrialisation, Liberalisation and Two Way Flows of FDIs: Case of India', p. 3234
94 See chapter 7 for details
95 Bradnock, R.W., *India's Foreign Policy since 1971*, p. 84
96 Tharoor, S., *Reasons of State - Political Development and India's Foreign Policy under Indira Gandhi*, p.97
97 Nanda, B.R. (ed.), *Indian Foreign Policy - The Nehru Years*, p.22
98 Haksar, P.N., *India's Foreign Policy and its Problems*, p.98
99 Kapur, H., *India's Foreign Policy 1947-92 - Shadows and Substance*, p.130
100 Ibid., 132
101 Ibid., 186
102 Tharoor, S., *Reasons of State - Political Development and India's Foreign Policy under Indira Gandhi*, p. 362
103 Ibid., p. 88
104 Quoted in Grover (ed.), *India's Foreign Policy*, p.339

4 The Indian government's policy towards expatriate Asians

Introduction

The previous two chapters have demonstrated that in the post-independence era Indian foreign policy ignored the expatriate Asian community. Yet it is evident that the Indian government could not go on ignoring the 12-14 million overseas Indians around the world, and that their fate had figured strongly on the agenda of the pre-independence authorities.

India, it can be said was caught in a dilemma when it came to the expatriate Asians abroad: its foreign policy dictated independence from all foreign involvement, and its focus on non-alignment and good relations with the developing nations excluded a specific policy towards that community. Nehru had made the expatriate Asians aliens in a legal sense, and that status did not allow for any special relationship between them and the Indian state. This position had several drawbacks. One of them was that India could not get involved when part of the Diaspora was going through political, economic or social discrimination or even a severe crisis. The human rights issue could be addressed, yet strictly speaking it was none of India's business. The other drawback was that despite continuing informal ties, which remained between members of the Diaspora and their families in the place of their origin, they were not encouraged to part take in the economic development of India. It is questionable if the adoption of a rigorous statist policy in India was really of such long term benefit for the country and the population. It is also time to question Nehru's view of India in the post war world.

Therefore this chapter will in turn analyse the pre-independence policies concerning the Diaspora; then look at the development of the Nehruvian policy and its effect on India's foreign policy. It will also give an account of the legal aspects of the problem and towards the end explore the views held by the Diaspora.

It is divided into four parts: the first part stands in sharp contrast to modern India's attitude towards its overseas population, it gives an overview of the situation under colonial rule and the desperate efforts of the Government of India to protest in the name of the Diaspora for any ill treatment they had to suffer.

The policy which was developed under Nehru, adopted at independence and held fast until and well into the Rajiv Gandhi years is explained in the second part. This highly moralistic policy shifted India from its nationalist movement which had included the Diaspora to a nation state project which was to exclude them. The government of India pushed for the expatriate Asians to integrate with the society of their host country. This was partly to abolish remaining forms of imperialism, and partly out of concern for India's new stand in the world and the diplomatic relations that it was hoping to build with the decolonising world. The following section analyses the legal questions of nationality, and as the result of the overseas Indians' alien status with regard to India, their property and investment rights.

In the last part the point of view of the Diaspora is exposed. Their wishes and expectations stand in sharp contrast with what the Indian government was prepared to do between 1947 and the liberalisations of 1991.

The chapter concludes that India went through a major shift from viewing itself as a nationalist movement in the pre-independence era, to becoming a nation-state project with a mission to fulfil in the new world order and that this was at the base of excluding the Diaspora.

The Government's Policy Before 1947

As explained in chapter 2, the British Empire had favoured and even encouraged the expatriation of Asians for labour or commerce. The Indian Diaspora in Africa represented only a small fraction of the total local population (2.3% in Kenya; 1% in Tanzania and Uganda), yet 'the fortunes of the Indian Community in East Africa- along with those in South Africa- have loomed large in the politics of the Indian subcontinent, in a fashion that has quite overshadowed the troubles of Indians in Ceylon or South East Asia.'[1] Whilst the troubles of the expatriate Asians in South East Asia were directly related to their difficult working conditions; those of the community in East and South Africa were more of a political and social nature. Then again the expatriate Asians in East and South Africa were more an urban, middle class element, capable of complaining whilst the Indians in Asia remained manual, agricultural labour, and were not so vocal about their problems.

Before 1860 the Indian interest in Africa had been limited to the economic interests of the merchants in the coastal cities, who traded spice in Zanzibar, Dar-es-Salaam and Mombassa. In 1860 the first indentured labourers reached Natal, and with this started an extensive Indian settlement in South and East Africa.[2] This was also the start of an interest throughout India in political and social developments in Africa. The overseas Indians became a part of the imperialist system where white settlers had established their superiority over the indigenous population. From relatively small beginnings they developed a vast network of trade throughout the region. The protection of the British administration led to the recruitment of a large number of Indian immigrants and allowed them to expand into the interior of the country. The rapid growth of the white settler community in the first two decades of the twentieth century posed a fundamental challenge to the Asians residing there. Questions soon emerged about residential rights and other aspects of racial segregation. The two settler communities lived uneasily next to each other, but could not do without each other.

During the course of their expatriation the Indians went through three contradictory phases: first they aspired to become like the whites, claiming to be British citizens in Africa. Secondly they relied on mobilising the support of the Indian government through Indian nationalism. The Colonial office strictly opposed both moves. Thirdly they were pressured to become citizens of the places they had chosen to live in, something which was unacceptable to most of them. The Indian government paid attention to all the difficulties and grievances experienced by the Diaspora and most of the efforts to help them were undertaken at the beginning of the twentieth Century.[3] Domestic public opinion and Indian nationalists were particularly critical of the indenture system, which brought with it as many problems as it did economic benefits. It became a big issue both for the public and the politicians. It is noteworthy that between 1914 and 1948, Indian interest in Africa was purely nationalistic, concerned solely with the fate and problems of the Indian overseas community. No effort was made to include the African community in the fight for equality.

South Africa

The discrimination against Indians was particularly harsh in South Africa. There had been a split between the Union government and the British government when the authorities in Natal openly sided with the colonists and planters at the end of 1880. In 1894 the Natal government disenfranchised the Indians and in 1906 the Black Act made registration and carrying registration papers for Indians mandatory.[4] Gandhi started a protest movement (Satyagraha) to draw local and imperial attention towards the plight of the Indian population.

Gandhi was concerned not only with the problems of the South African Indians but with the lot of the Indians all over the world.[5] He made two trips back to India during which he wrote the 'green pamphlet' and addressed the Indian National Congress, the Chambers of Commerce and other organisations to rally support for their Indian countrymen, especially in South Africa. Gandhi's campaign in South Africa had the objective of bettering the fate of the Indian community there. During this time the Indian government maintained pressure on the Union Government as well as on the Colonial authorities in England to improve the treatment of the South African Indians.

In 1914 the Smuts-Gandhi agreement was signed, promising equal treatment in the future, but interpreted by the South African Government as a guarantee that most Indians residing in South Africa would return to their country of origin. In the eyes of the South Africans they were only temporary residents, despite the fact that earlier, Sir George Gray had clearly stated that the Indian families would remain as settlers after their term of indenture was over. In fact the Government of India would not have allowed Indian emigration to Africa had there been any suggestion that they might be transported back to India against their will.[6] The Indian position was that the immigrants had acquired rights in their new country and that on top of every thing else they were 'British nationals' in South Africa long before the Dutch and the Germans became nationals.[7] The Indian government responded to Smut's view by stopping indentured emigration to South Africa and subsequently abolishing the entire system. This was due to unrest in Bombay, which was becoming more and more intense, resulting in resolutions and memorandums to the Viceroy.[8] The last emigrants left India in January 1917.[9]/[10]

East Africa

In the East African region the problems resulted first from discrimination imposed by the Colonial authorities, then by the antagonism between Africans and Indians. They were denied proportional representation in the legislative, executive and municipal councils and were subjected to inferior transport, medical, prison and educational facilities.[11] The agitation for equality in East Africa started at the end of the First World War. An East African Indian National Congress was set up and a list of grievances was sent to the local and imperial governments. A deputation was sent to India to enlist the support of the Congress and the Viceroy. The expatriate Indians felt that they were backed by nationalists back home, some of whom, such as G.K. Gokhale or Mrs. S. Naidu, advocated an Indian protectorate in German East Africa, Tanganyika.

> It does not take a very learned student to realise that naturally and meritably East Africa is one of the earliest legitimate territories of the Indian nation going so far back as the first century of the Christian era. (...) East Africa is therefore the legitimate colony of the surplus of the great Indian nation, whether they went forth to colonise these unknown lands from an economic point of view or to satisfy their desire for venture...[12]

Several political parties, one of them being the Jana Sangh, claimed to establish a little India wherever there were people of Indian origin.[13] The fact that the Indian Diaspora in East Africa might suggest that India administer their region, greatly alarmed the European community in East Africa.[14]

British position

Before 1914 the British government was neither consistent nor united in its attitude towards India's problem in Africa. The Wragg Commission reported in 1887 that Indian traders had a right to go to any part of the British Empire, since by trading even in the most remote areas they were providing the white population with a useful service. The report also noted that the majority of white settlers wanted Indians to be indentured for as long as they stayed in the colony. They were afraid that the Indians would provide fierce competition in both agriculture and commerce.[15] In general the governors and other officials in the colonies had the interest of the white settlers at heart, but the colonial office in London had to juggle with pressures coming from the India Office and the Government of India as well. Some secretaries of state such as Chamberlain supported the European interests, whilst others such as Lord Granville pressed Indian claims.[16] During the passive resistance struggle in India the Viceroy, Lord Harding, criticised the South African racial policies, and was almost recalled to Britain. Yet in upholding Indian interests the Viceroy had the support and approval of the India office.

The British position was that the Indians were simply citizens of whatever colony they lived in. When India later applied to appoint agents in the West Indies and Fiji to help monitor the grievances of the Diaspora, the colonial office refused on the grounds that the Indians there were permanent residents 'enjoying harmonious relations with other sections of the local population.'[17]

But soon Britain found itself caught in an inter-imperial quarrel where white settlers were pitched against the expatriate Indian population; where the Indian government was arguing with other colonial governments; and where the Foreign and India office were at loggerheads with each other. In response the Foreign Office determined that in Kenya, as in the rest of East Africa 'the interests of the African natives must be paramount and that if, and when those interests of the immigrant races should conflict, the former should prevail.'[18] This was spelled out in the 1923 White Paper, also known as the Devonshire declaration. Yet the White Paper also denied the Indians equality of status with the Europeans in Kenya, causing outrage back in India.

By 1923 racial friction was out of control and the European settlers threatened to secede from the empire if no action was taken.[19] The white population demanded controls and restrictions on continuing Indian immigration. A bill to regulate immigration and employment was introduced into the Kenya legislative council in 1923. It gave wide powers to the immigration authorities and prohibited the entry of 'all persons who were unable to produce a certificate of employment before landing.'[20]

Government of India's position

The first Imperial Conference was held in 1907. However in the 1911 Imperial Conference India made sure that the overseas Indian problem figured prominently on the agenda.[21] India did not gain full representation until 1921, her membership having been debated at the Imperial War

Conferences of 1917 and 1918.[22] India also raised the issue of discrimination against overseas Indians at the Imperial Conference of 1917:

> What we particularly ask is that in the first place British Asiatics (sic.), that is Asiatics (sic.) of British nationality, should at least not be less favourably treated than other Asiatics (sic.). In the second place, we would ask that the freest facilities possible be given to educated Indians for travel, for study, or for visits, as apart from settlement, in the Dominions for any purposes. Lastly, we would ask that a kindly and sympathetic consideration should be given to those Indians who have already been permitted to settle in the Dominions.[23]

This was part of the reciprocity debate that would become an issue with India's membership at the Imperial Conferences. The reciprocity act (Resolution XXII of 1917) ensured that the governments of the British Commonwealth should enjoy complete control of the composition of their own population by means of restriction of immigration and that British citizens domiciled in any British country should be admitted into any other British country for visits and temporary residence.[24]

After the First World War India became an independent member of the League of Nations, and with it, several other League and para-League organisations (although until 1929 the Indian delegation was led by non-Indians).[25] The government of India used its voice at all international meetings to protest against the treatment of its overseas population.

In India in 1919 at the Amritsar Congress, it was declared that 'this Congress is of the opinion that the anti-Indian agitation now going on in East Africa is utterly unscrupulous and trusts that the government of India will safeguard the right of free and unrestricted emigration from India to East Africa and the full civic and political rights of the Indian settlers in East Africa including the East African territory conquered by Germany.'[26]

At the Imperial conference of 1921, the Indian government lobbied for the overseas Indian population living in the Dominions to be granted equal rights with the British. Whilst New Zealand, Canada and Australia were ready to accept Indian equality, especially in view of the enormous contribution to the war effort, the British did not support the proposal. In 1923 L.B.Shastri appealed against the colour bar in the colonies, but to no avail. The Indians were continuously denied the right of settlement in the Kenyan highlands which were reserved for the white population. At the 1923 Imperial Conference the issue of discrimination in South Africa was again taken up by Sir Tej Bahadur Sapru. In the case of South Africa the principle of reciprocity was not respected and the government of India wanted to send an agent to South Africa to protect Indian nationals there. The Prime Minister of the Union of South Africa explained that in South Africa it was not a question of colour, but that a different principle was involved, namely:

> That the attitude of thinking men in South Africa was not that the Indian was inferior because of his colour or on any other ground – he might be their superior – but the question had to be considered from the point of view of economic competition. In other words, the white community in South Africa felt that the whole question of the continuance of western civilisation in South Africa was involved.[27]

The British imperial authorities were not particularly interested in helping the Indian communities who were being discriminated against (although Indian ill-treatment had figured as one of the causes of the South African War against the Boers). This became evident in the case of the Canadian Sikh community in 1908 when the British government upheld Canadian legislation to limit Indian immigration into Canada.[28] It was therefore left to the Government of Indian to fight for the rights of overseas Indians. Since India was not a national government, it could maintain an interest in the welfare of the expatriate community, but could do no more than lobby with the Imperial powers or ban the export of labour to the Dominions. India's lobbying at the Imperial Conferences had some success as it overcame a reluctance to discuss the problem of expatriate Indians in general and made it one of the Conference's major issues. It seemed that the empire could no longer lightly dismiss the problem, even if that did not lead to any dramatic results.[29]

Despite the creation of the separate department of overseas Indians and its placing under an Indian member of the viceroy's executive council there was no substantial enlargement of the role of the Government of India. The separate department of overseas Indians had at its head Dr N.B. Khare.[30] He declared with reference to the Pegging Act and other anti-Indian measures that: 'Some means must be found for maintaining the dignity and prestige of Indians and the government of India even in wartime. (...) Had India been independent she would have considered this a *casus belli* against South Africa.'[31] The sanctions, which India could apply, were of marginal value.[32] This, it was felt encouraged the Dominions to maltreat the Diaspora.[33]

Only in 1943 a Reciprocity Act was passed which enabled the Government of India to 'institute counter measures'. This was to prove not very useful in practical terms. In fact India retaliated by issuing a notice that the rights of South Africans residing in India would be reduced in the same way as those of Indians in South Africa. When after the war in 1946 the Pegging Act in South Africa was reconfirmed and the Indian population was still represented by Europeans, the Indian government decided to terminate the Indo-South African trade agreement, and announced a trade boycott.[34] This was meant to harm South Africa economically, especially since during the war India had become South Africa's third most important source of imports. In fact India was exporting five times as much as she was importing, but a major item being imported was coal from Natal which was already in short supply.[35] Despite this the trade boycott came into force. Direct relations between the two countries came to a halt after nearly fifty years of negotiations on the Indian Diaspora, which numbered 282,407 in 1946.[36]

It is notable that India raised the issue of racial discrimination issue in South Africa at the UN before the advent of Indian independence. At that time the Diaspora was still very much in the picture of Indian politics. As the case study in the next chapter will show, India raised this issue with respect to the discrimination against Indians for a number of years before calling for the abolition of apartheid as a system, which then included the blacks and coloured in the anti- discrimination campaign. It is also notable that India did not raise the South Africa issue at the Commonwealth meetings in the early years of independence. Nehru was aware that if he challenged South Africa in the context of the Commonwealth he would give Pakistan an excuse to raise the Kashmir issue as this meant raising domestic matters, which might threaten the integrity of the association.[37] This was a major change in policy, as the South Africa issue had regularly featured on the agendas of the Imperial conferences, which were the predecessor of the Commonwealth meetings.[38]

As far as the nationalists claims in East Africa were concerned, they were not advocated by the Indian government, yet it still stood up for the rights of the overseas community when it came to the discriminatory land and franchise policies in that region. Indian agitation secured the end of certain policies of segregation in 1922, but restrictions on residence of non-Europeans on European owned plots remained in force till 1945.[39] The Indian government did not intend to use the Diaspora as a fifth column to support anti-Imperial movements in the British dominated African and Asian countries. Yet right from the start of India's own independence movement India felt it had to lead a new block of states and Nehru hoped that the Indian Diaspora would play a significant role in bringing about decolonisation.

Shastri became the spokesman for India at the League of Nations. He primarily presented the Indian case for equality, but soon found that the Indians were also dedicated to an emphasis of African interests. Shastri agreed to assert that Indian and European claims should yield to the interests of the African population. In this aspect he agreed with the Devonshire declaration. Yet the reiteration of the segregation policies this document also contained, made him and Indian public opinion furious. To him putting African interests first did not mean continuing discrimination against the Indians. The 38th Indian National Congress annual session in December 1923 declared that unless India became independent, the grievances of the Indian Diaspora could not be properly remedied.[40]

At this point, before the Second World War India maintained a nationalist policy. The government of India recognised that it bore responsibility for its overseas' population, and used its voice in all forums to propagate this claim. It also recognised the Diaspora as being part of the nationalist movement, which was to rid India of colonialism. To this end the Government of India sent deputations to various parts of the Empire.[41] This policy remained constant until independence in 1947. Other missions were sent to different parts of the Empire to report on particular problems concerning the Indian Diaspora.[42]

Table 4.1: Missions of Congress members to the colonies

Sno	Persons deputed	Country	Year	Purpose of mission
1.	G.K. Gokhale	South Africa	1910	To discuss the Indian question with South African Authorities
2.	C.F. Andrews & W.W. Pearson	South Africa & Fiji	1916	To investigate conditions of Indian labour
3.	C.F. Andrews & B.D. Chaturvedi	Malaya & Ceylon	1923	To examine Indian immigration in all its aspects
4.	M.A. Arulanandam, A.V. Dias, Periasundaram, L. Muthukrishna	Ceylon	1923	To investigate into the conditions of life to which the South Indian labourers in Ceylon were subjected

5.	Sarojini Naidu & George Joseph	Kenya	1923	To attend the Indian Congress in Kenya; to study the situation and to advise the Indian Community there on the steps they should take in carrying on their struggle against the insults and injustices heaped on them
6.	Shridhar Ganesh Vaze and B.D. Chaturvedi	Kenya	1924	To inquire into conditions of Indian settlers
7.	C.F. Andrews	Zanzibar	1934	To study conditions of Indian settlers
8.	Jawaharlal Nehru	Ceylon	1939	To confer with the authorities and representative associations and individuals on behalf on behalf of the Congress Working Committee and do all that may be possible to effect adjust and honourable settlement
9.	Jawaharlal Nehru, C. Rajagopalachari, A. Aryanayakam & G. Ramachandran	Ceylon	1946	To assure the Ceylon Indian Congress of the full sympathy of the Indian National Congress for the cause of Indians in Ceylon and to take necessary steps to secure redress for their grievances by investigating the matters in dispute

These missions, especially the ones in the 1920s and 1930s not only checked on specific problems of the Diaspora, but also rallied them to the cause of Indian independence.

With the advent of independence India had to review its position in several areas. This included its future relationship with the former colonial power Britain, its membership in the Commonwealth and the Diaspora, which was mainly located in the Commonwealth. At independence India debated whether or not to dissociate herself from the Commonwealth in her fight against racial discrimination. For decades there had been in India a widespread and standing grievance against racial discrimination, especially with regard to people of Indian origin in parts of the British Empire-Commonwealth. An association with an organisation where such racial discrimination prevailed could be considered an affront to the national dignity of newly independent India. Yet eventually in 1947 the Indian leaders came to feel that by joining the club of the five white nations, they were actually converting the Commonwealth into a new multi-racial association, thus enabling other non-white nations to follow suit later.[43] As a result of this move the relationship between India and Britain was also fixed, since by joining the Commonwealth, India implicitly accepted Britain as a friend and ally. As for the relations with the Diaspora, they are the main focus of the next section.

The Nehruvian Doctrine

> Imperialism simply means a relationship of subordination by a controlling power over another nation or society.[44]

India's imperial legacy had led to the creation of an Indian Diaspora. Now that the Empire was no more, the new Indian government found that it had to ask itself some very serious questions on imperialism and consequently on its relationship with the expatriate Asians. In the late 1940s and early 1950s the colonial era was on its way out but that did not mean that imperialism was over. Imperialism as a system would not even cease to exist once the traditional European powers had withdrawn from their colonies. Even then subordination by one group over another would still continue post independence. India recognised that economic dominance in one form or another meant a kind of imperialism and understood that in general the expatriate Asians were to be found in the controlling category. In fact in some cases they were seen as trying to step into the master's shoes to maintain a privileged position in the newly independent states via their position in that country's economy. Since the British imperial system had always kept the different racial groups separate, the expatriate Indians in general had had no inclination to align themselves with the African masses and help in the liberation struggle. In some cases they even felt that the British departure would take away the status quo they had enjoyed previously and the security which came with it.

As far as imperialism was concerned, India's new government was committed to the permanent withdrawal of colonial rule from Africa and all other colonised nations. Nehru believed that the people in Asia who had experienced decolonisation had a special responsibility towards the people in Africa and their struggle for freedom. He was vocal on the 'agony of the African continent throughout history.'[45] India was especially concerned about British Africa, hoping to exert some influence in London. It also decided to actively support the struggle against the British in East Africa despite the interests of some Indian entrepreneurs in the region.[46] India did not agree with the violent means employed in certain freedom struggles such as the Mau-Mau movement in Kenya, yet it would not distance itself from the ultimate goal which was that of self-determination and freedom for all nations.

Nehru soon spread the message that Indians who had left their country of origin to seek fortune abroad had to integrate with the local population, support their struggle and even put their cause first. According to him they had come to be economically successful as guests in these countries, now they owed their hosts support in their political path. His message at first was mainly intended for the Indians in the newly independent countries like Burma, Ceylon and Malaysia, but it was also aimed at the Indians in the other British colonies on the African continent where independence was still to come. In a Lok Sabha speech he stated:

> Now these Indians abroad, what are they? Indian citizens? Are they going to be citizens of India or not? If they are not, then our interest in them becomes cultural and humanitarian, not political. That interest of course remains. For instance, take the Indians of Fiji or Mauritius: are they going to retain their nationality or will they become Fiji nationals or Mauritians? The same question arises in regard to Burma and Ceylon. It is a difficult question. This house gets mixed up. It wants to treat them as Indians, and with the same breath it wants a complete franchise for them in the countries where they are living. Of course the two things do not go together. Either they get the franchise as nationals of the other country, or treat them as Indians minus the franchise and ask for the most favourable treatment given to an alien.[47]

Although this policy was rather new to the average Indian Nehru had held the same position throughout the 1920s, according to him the overseas Indian had to adapt to his host country and to become part of the indigenous population.[48]

The government of India soon followed Nehru's policy. Indians abroad were advised to accept local citizenship and cease to seek a separate and better destiny from their fellow countrymen. Nehru clarified that with respect to Indians permanently resident outside of India: 'The Indian Commissioners will not be entitled to discharge consular functions in respect of Indians who may not be considered to be nationals, that is permanent residents in these territories or to act as the spokesmen of such Indians.'[49]

In refuting imperialism Nehru believed they would guarantee their future in the emerging society.

> The Nehru policy was based on the unrealistic hope that within the broad pattern of African-Asian nationalism the separate identity of Indian immigrants would be forgotten. This did not happen. Instead of pan Afro-Asianism several nationalisms emerged. Thus the cry 'Burma for Burmese', 'Ceylon for Ceylonese' was followed in the 60s by the cry 'Kenya for Kenyans' (...) He treated the question of African freedom in the abstract. He himself was not clear about the magnitude of the specific nature of the problem of Indian settlement in Africa.[50]

Nehru ultimately hoped that the Indian Community would not be treated as an 'unwanted import' because India was treating Africans as brothers and comrades. All this was part of Nehru's commitment to eradicate all forms of imperialism from the post war world order.

To a certain extent this policy was also linked to the fact that all problems concerning the Diaspora were no longer inter-imperial matters to be solved under the auspices of one great regulatory power. Moreover they concerned sovereign or potential sovereign states with independent interests which had to be reconciled with India. India could not afford to be vociferous on the fate of Indians abroad and put potential good diplomatic relations at risk.[51] In the post war era the world was reorganising itself into power blocks, based on politico-economic systems and beliefs. Very soon Nehru realised that any form of alignment would be detrimental to India and a third way was devised. Nehru dreamt of combining economic mobilisation with political conciliation, a Soviet style economy with western policy.[52] Seeing India, as the model to all decolonising nations,

Nehru wanted a 'third world block' to follow certain moral principles based on anti-imperialism and non-dependency, and India had to go ahead with the good example. This also meant making friends with the countries fighting off the imperial system, and those who had already gained independence. A strong line on the fate of a small Indian minority in those countries, who had left India voluntarily to make a better life for themselves, would have been counterproductive for India.

Nehru concentrated on developing an 'Africa policy'. In the pre-independence era he had frequently pushed Congress to pass resolutions against racial inequalities which prevailed in places such as the Union of South Africa and Kenya. But it was Shastri's idea that Indian interests were subordinate to those of the African people.[53] The 1952 Foreign Policy Resolution called for the removal of all forms of colonialism from Asia and Africa and for the Indians resident in those countries to emphasise African interests. Both communities were urged to co-operate in non-violence. India frequently censured continuing imperialism such as the South African Union's application of apartheid, France's suppression of Algerian Nationalism and Portugal's mass reprisals in Angola. These basic tenets of foreign policy formulation were only reinforced by the emphasis on non-alignment and friendship with all nations. It culminated in the 'Panchsheel', a declaration of world peace and co-operation. This was to unite the Asian and African Nations under a common foreign policy, which was described by Nehru as the 'recognition of sovereignty and integrity of a country, non-aggression, non-interference in other countries either for political or ideological reasons, mutual respect and peaceful coexistence.'[54] In the long run this was to consolidate Nehru's aim of an Afro-Asian voice and voting block in the UN. In fact, had Nehru's government pressed on expatriate Asian rights and privileges, it would have disrupted possible future co-operation between India and the relevant host countries. Under no circumstances were the good relations between Delhi and the African States to be jeopardised by the problems of the Asian settlers there.[55] In fact India's involvement in African nationalist politics was quite damaging to Asian-European relations: the withdrawing European powers were worried that the Asians would take this situation as an opportunity to entrench their own position.[56]

South Africa was a special case, since even after independence from Britain the white ruling minority oppressed the African people. What started out as a protest against the treatment of Indians in the Union soon developed to include a wide protest against the discriminatory treatment against all non-whites. It was first brought up in the UN in 1946. Apartheid as such (not only referring to the Indians) was voted upon in 1952 under India's sponsorship. For a while other countries believed that India's interest in fighting Apartheid was based on the fact that there were a large number of people of Indian origin who were victims of the racial segregation. India though was very clear that if the Indian minority were given racial equality or privileges, it would not end the fight until racial segregation was totally abolished.[57] Nehru felt that the Indian community in South Africa should stand by the Africans. The African Congress did struggle against Apartheid, and the national struggle conducted after 1950 was organised jointly by members of the Congress alliance (both Indian organisations).[58]

The Government of India on its part cut all contacts with South Africa. In fact it should be noted that the resulting trade embargo and the absence of diplomatic representation caused inconvenience to the people of Indian origin, but that did not make the Indian government compromise. The case study following this chapter explains in detail the government of India's position with regard to visits to South Africa and other contacts between the Indian minority there and the mother country. Certain family ties were maintained, yet under great strain as the economic and political embargo from India was almost complete.

Africa had become one of India's foreign policy priorities.[59] Nehru wished for more than simply a diplomatic block based on morality and non-alignment; he believed that the third world developing nations had to co-operate and help each other in the way of technical and economic assistance.[60] In this light several industrial and educational projects were developed, including an India-Africa Development Association, constituted by Indian industrialists with the active support of the Indian government.[61]

The main objectives of this association were as follows: [62]

- a uniform policy of Indian businessmen dealing with African governments;
- to advise prospective entrepreneurs on investment laws governing collaboration in African countries;
- to investigate available opportunities of industrial collaboration;
- to create scholarships for African technicians;
- to focus on problems which hampered the free flow of trade between India and African countries.

In the long run Nehru saw the opportunity for trade and further technical collaboration which could prove a solution to many problems of the developing countries. Economic co-operation would bring prosperity but could also be underpinned by training programmes and other social services. In the 15 years of the Special Commonwealth assistance programme India provided over 1500 training places for nationals from Ghana, Kenya, Malawi, Mauritius, Nigeria, Sierra Leone, Tanzania, Uganda and Zambia. Hundreds of experts, such as doctors, engineers, teachers, accountants and architects were deputed to these countries under the same program.[63] It has to be clarified at this point that there is no evidence that India might have made use of the people of Indian origin for purposes of negotiations. These were simple government to government contracts with the sole objective to further Indo-African ties.

The 1962 Sino-Indian conflict provided further impetus for India's involvement in Africa. Africa's mixed reaction to the war showed India that it did not have such strong allies in Africa as it believed. It also understood that it had to work against Chinese penetration in Africa by increasing material support for the liberation movement in South Africa and by expanding economic co-operation with the rest of the continent.[64] The launching of the Indian technical and economic co-operation programme in the 1970s was a 'multi-pronged effort aimed at countering China's diplomacy' and driven chiefly by political expediency. Yet in those days South-South co-operation was not that popular in Africa and the programme fell short of Prime Minister Indira Gandhi's expectations.[65]

The one exception to the Nehruvian policy was the case of Ceylon where Nehru quite unsuccessfully tried to haggle out a deal for the Indians resident in this neighbour country. India strongly protested against the Ceylonese Citizenship Act which decreed that nationality could only be claimed by descent or registration (registration requiring continuous residency since at least 1946 or earlier) which excluded most of the Ceylonese Indians. Ceylon wanted India to take back a sizeable portion of their expatriate population. The fate of the Burmese Indians was quite similar, yet in this case India did not put any pressure on the Burmese Government and even signed a treaty of friendship in 1951. Needless to say both cases became quite messy over time and because of their geographical closeness to India could not be ignored and spilled into Indian politics quite frequently.[66]

Malaysia was another controversial case where the attitude of the government of India shortly after independence was not altogether consistent: the Nehruvian message of expatriate Indians identifying with the country of their adoption had not been clearly communicated to the Malaya Indians during Nehru's visit in 1946. When given the choice of Malaysian citizenship most Indians chose Indian citizenship although half of them were eligible for Malaysian citizenship.[67]

There are theories which proclaim that despite the clearness of Nehru's message and all official declarations on not wanting to use the expatriate population as a Trojan horse, post independent India still had 'use' for them. Srikant Dutt describes at length how India searched and found a controlling, imperialistic role for itself, using methods such as aid, foreign investment, contracts, insurance and banking to further its state capitalist system in need of expansion.[68] Since India through its size was a middle size power, hegemonic in its region, Dutt maintains that it had great power aspirations:[69] This included building a heavy industry, a modern arms industry (including the great power symbols of nuclear power, missile, and satellite development) and a well developed technical infrastructure. All this might have had its origins in a 'self perception' by India's ruling classes, or simply derived from the role it used to play during the colonial period when Indian army personnel were sent to fight and administrators and traders were to be found all round the world. Then Indians were the agents of a European colonial power.[70] Post independence however, Dutt states that in order to maintain its sub-imperialist power status, India used its Diaspora. For him they represented a pool of local contact men, ready at hand for India's political and economic aspirations, and a pool of capital in the form of remittances. They are to be found in all areas of the globe, from South East Asia, to the Middle East, from Africa to the Americas. Immediately after independence it was assumed that there would be increasing interest in the Diaspora because of Indian nationalism. Yet with the exception of the South African case no economic or political sanctions were taken to further the case of the expatriate community. According to Dutt a separate department concerned with the overseas Indian affairs located within the Ministry of External Affairs did exist until the mid seventies, and was revived later, but most of its work remained classified.[71] Although it seems to be impossible to get any exact information on this particular department, it was most probably linked to the movement to stop the brain drain, which was being noticed at the time.[72] Indira Gandhi was particularly interested in reclaiming Indian scientists from abroad for them to help in India's development. The first time any special department or agency was mentioned, was in 1986 when a special approval committee was constituted within the department of Industrial Development for the expeditious clearance of industrial proposals of NRIs. Then in 1987 an Indo-NRI Chamber of Commerce and Culture was set up to promote the overseas' Indian case. [73] In fact even the Department of Overseas Indians that had been set up in 1941 had been transformed into that of Commonwealth relations in 1944.[74] So one can argue that the Government of India had no central machinery to deal with overseas Indians until the mid 1980s.

It is true to say that India was caught in a dilemma when it came to the expatriate Asians straight after independence. The radical shift in policy and emphasis concerning the Diaspora took time. India was pushing the settlers to identify with their host country and acknowledged the legal jurisdiction of the foreign states and their settlers, yet there were diplomatic interventions to improve their legal status.[75] Nehru acknowledged the contradiction by emphasising that legally and constitutionally they were not India's problem, but that there was a certain interest in their welfare. Added to that was the emotional attachment of the Indians who had kinsmen abroad, who became a political force in the states where emigrants had departed from. This was reflected in the Indian Constitution where Part II Article 8 provided that any person living abroad, whose parents or grandparents were born in India could be granted Indian citizenship by registration.[76] The issue of Indian citizenship is dealt with in detail in chapter 6, but it is useful to note at this point that dual citizenship was not allowed at any point as India believed that you could not be loyal to two masters.[77] Yet Indians who had taken on a new nationality could, if they wished to return to India, revert to Indian citizenship, although this process was not without complications.

For some time diasporic Indians were also seen as representing India abroad. Nehru's 1960, 1961 and 1962 Republic Day addresses had references to the 'mother country' and their positions as ambassadors to their host countries. Although the affinities with the mother country could never become a political tie Dutt maintains that India was caught in a dilemma and that it led to a contradictory Indian policy towards decolonisation in the 1950s.[78]

Despite this dilemma Nehru realised that the interests of Africans and Asian settlers seldom coincided. There was the uninhibited pursuit of business gains and Nehru acknowledged that there was truth in the African allegations that Indian tradesmen and industrialists were exploiting the Africans as much as the British had done, a state of affairs he found unacceptable. Slowly, as migration had ended, public opinion as well started to become more indifferent.[79] India became supportive of Africanisation even to the detriment of Indian settlers. So as time went on the Indian Diaspora had to increasingly fend for itself.

Nehru's policy illustrated a change in the Indian perception of their country and its role in the world. There was a shift from a nationalist anti colonial movement to a nation state project and with it came entirely different priorities. Nationalism had been used to mobilise Indians in India and around the world to rid India of the British colonial power. At independence a new definition had to be sought for India, one which would also define the basis of an Indian identity. Nehru firmly believed that the only thing which could be the basis of a new Indian identity was its shared historical past. India's many civil societies differing on bases of language, religion and even race gave little other common ground for national integration. But national integration, consolidating the nationalist movement and creating out of it one state with a common way out of all these differing civil societies was one of Nehru's top priorities. India had inherited the structures of the Raj, which although national in form were imperial in content. As a result internal structures and policy formulations had to be changed, no longer to be based on the imperial legacy of divide and rule but unite and cooperate. With the new political elite (the Congress Party) and the new infrastructure services (the IAS) which transcended all civil societies, Nehru constructed the new Indian State, which would operate as a unified entity. Yet with the new Indian State being based on a shared past, religious tolerance and democracy the Indian Diaspora was excluded. This lay in sharp contrast to the policies promulgated before 1914, which have been described in the first part of this chapter. To an extent one can argue that it was an aspect of the time, of the 'new world order' after the end of the Second World War. Nehru believed that India had to be viewed as an irreproachable country by the rest of the world if it wanted to assume the leadership position for the newly decolonised and developing countries. To him this was the way of stabilising India's position in the world and giving it a kind of 'power'.

The exclusion of the Diaspora in post independence India can be looked at in one more way. One can also argue that it was a return to 'old traditions': India had a tradition of socio-religious restrictions on overseas travels. 'Anyone returning from 'overseas' (not overland) had to take the prayashita, perform purificationary yagna before he could rejoin his cast as a regular/participating member.'[80] The Arya Samaj today maintains that these purifications were installed by the priests themselves to enshrine their position in society, yet more traditional Hindus quote these traditions from Hinduism's most ancient and sacred texts: the Vedas. In those days it can be assumed that these restrictions applied to protect the stability and cohesion of society by keeping ideas of change far away from it. New ideas threatened the stability of the structure of Indian society which was largely based on intricate hierarchy and the acceptance of one's position within this society based on one's caste. The exclusion of the Diaspora after the advent of Independence can be seen in a similar light. Their not having shared in India's past and especially in India's struggle made the overseas Indians fundamentally different and to a certain degree could not be part of the new post colonial society. To a certain extent India came full circle, but this time for different reasons.

The Legal Aspects

Earlier in this chapter it has been shown that the Indian government's policy evolved vis-à-vis the expatriate Asians. From deep concern during the Imperial era, it developed into an ethical question of imperialism and moral responsibility under Nehru and remained so until the mid-late 1980s. This section proposes to look at the legal aspects of the problem, examining nationality, residency, property and investment rights of the Indian Diaspora.

> Nationality, in the widest sense of the term, is the notion of belonging to a distinctive national community; but in a narrower sense, it refers to the legal principle by which a society embodied in a state defines those who belong to it and those who are excluded from belonging.[81]

Pre-independence there was no question of nationality; Asians were till 1948 either British subjects or British protected persons. The British subjects had been born on British territory (British India or the Kenya Colony), the Asians born in India's princely states, or in any Protectorate or Mandated Territory were British protected persons. By law the difference between the two was that the British subjects were nationals of Britain and the British protected persons were aliens. But for all practical purposes such as employment, property, political or social rights, and diplomatic protection they were treated as equals.[82] In theory the British subjects were all equal; with the right to enter British territory, and the right not to be deported from it. Yet from early on, immigration restrictions were imposed, requiring permits to enter a British overseas territory. Permits were easier for British subjects of European stock to acquire than for others. In 1918 the Imperial Conference passed a resolution stating that the communities of the British Commonwealth could determine the composition of their own population, which in effect allowed the racially discriminatory immigration policies to be enacted in the self governing Dominions.[83]

It was when the British empire fell apart and decolonisation started first in Asia, then in Africa that the question of nationality became complicated. The Indians in India became Indians, which was simple enough; the same held for Africans in Uganda, Kenya or Tanzania, they became Ugandans, Kenyans and Tanzanians as soon as the British left. But what about the expatriate Indian population? On 1 January 1949, started an interim period whereby under the 1948 British nationality act the citizens of East Africa and the Indians residing there were 'introduced to the status of citizens of the UK and Colonies'.[84] This was part of the creation of the Commonwealth which was to provide a substitute for the empire and be a help in the decolonisation process. The Act was passed in order to guarantee the equality of status between the British subjects and the Commonwealth citizens in the future.[85] It provided that:

1. All British Subjects who had links with the UK would become 'citizens of the UK and Colonies';
2. British subjects who had links with other self governing countries of the Commonwealth would be regarded as potential citizens of their respective countries while some others would become 'British Subjects without citizenship';
3. Former British subjects and British protected persons who became citizens of any country of the Commonwealth would be called 'British subjects' or 'Commonwealth Citizens'; and
4. Categories 2 and 3 could become 'citizens of the UK and colonies' by registration after residing 1 year in a British territory.[86]

According to Twaddle the decision to accord this status to the people of the British colonies was pushed by the Colonial office, which was afraid that the new India, now completely national, would use its communities of Indian expatriates throughout the British Colonies as a 'sort of fifth column'.[87] Giving these Indians British citizenship was seen as a counter attraction. By this time the Nehruvian policy had already been clearly stated: the government of India was not going to infiltrate Africa through the Diaspora and was in fact encouraging them to take local citizenship (which first meant British, then after the British departed, East African citizenship).

In general the Indians did stick to their British passports once the British departed, feeling that they were neither East African citizens nor foreigners in the region. That technically made them aliens in their host country, a status they did not worry about at the time. It is also noteworthy that apart from the occasional visits to Britain and putting some of their savings into British banks they did not attach too much importance to their British citizenship. Until the 1962 Immigration Act, these British subjects could not be refused entry to the UK and could not be deported. Citizens of India and Pakistan also had similar rights, since under the British nationality act of 1948 they were considered British subjects.[88] Yet until the British departed from East Africa these same Asians were still subjected to racial discrimination such as separate schools, hospitals and hotels, restrictive residential rights in the highlands and diminished representation. For example Europeans had 11 members on the legislative council of Kenya and the Asians had 5, although their population was three times that of the Europeans. Despite the resentment, which that created, the Asians were not prepared to take up local citizenship and give up the citizenship of the UK and colonies.[89] The 1962 Immigration Act closed the doors to the 'British subjects' of the Commonwealth countries and to those Asians who were holding British passports issued in countries which had been dependencies of Britain in the past. The Asians simply exchanged their 'old' British passports for 'new' ones and felt safe. They opted for British citizenship because India was abolishing dual citizenship and they felt that the decolonisation in Africa would bring uncertainties with it, which might lead them to escape to Britain. Yet, the panic only started when the 1968 immigration bill announced entry quotas for Asian British subjects. Now the free entry into Britain was being questioned and the Asians felt caught in a trap. Until the new 1968 legislation was passed there had been no incentive for the Asians to choose local citizenship and the East African governments were not particularly interested in giving their citizenship to a large number of Asians.[90] On the advent of independence local citizenship had been offered with a deadline attached to it, but 'certain African governments were being embarrassed about the Asians who were or had become citizens since they would benefit as much from the policies of Africanisation to the detriment of the indigenous Africans.' The dilemma of the African governments was that the Indians might become 'paper citizens' to avoid the possible adverse effects of Africanisation.[91]

The Government of India at that time instructed its missions to persuade the Asians to exchange their British passports for local ones in order 'play a constructive role in African society' and 'showing that they were anti-imperialist'. In fact there would be no difficulty in their returning to India whenever they wished'.[92] The reason why these people were so adamant in retaining their British nationality was primarily economic. Their ties to India were that of language and culture, but they realised that they would never have the same opportunities in terms of earnings or for their children's education. They also felt that their freedom to move away would be more restricted with an East African passport.

It has to be noted that actually British public opinion favoured 'a common status for all', especially in the light of the Indian war efforts in both World Wars. Besides the British Government wanted to avoid 'statelessness' which could be brought about by decolonisation. Yet Australia, Canada, New Zealand and South Africa never treated all British subjects equally, denying in particular the Asians the right to settle. This idea of national exclusiveness soon took over from the notion of a common status.[93] Britain began to fear a wave of immigration, which would not be assimilated, and as a result immigration restrictions were introduced in the mid-late 60s.

The position of the Indian government is singular but not difficult to comprehend: Nehru, as explained in the previous section was adamant that all Asians living overseas accept local nationality in order to integrate better with the local population. He did not accept any 'special status' or any continuation of the old imperial system. But the Indian government was equally clear that those Indians, who at the time of independence wished to return to their country of origin, were welcome to apply for Indian citizenship. What the Government of India did not want was split loyalties among those living in one country, holding the passport of a second and investing in a third, all out of reasons of security or convenience. The Indian government also understood that the Asians who has been overseas for several generations were not prepared to come back to India and compromise their existing living standards, but then they would have to accept becoming 'local' and not expect to have a foot in the Indian camp as well. In fact with regard to Indian citizenship it is interesting to note that between 1947 and 1955 when the Citizenship act explicitly abolished dual nationality under the constitution, the matter of dual nationality was somewhat vague. India's constitution also states in Article 9 of Part II that 'no person shall be a citizen of India (...) if he has voluntarily acquired the citizenship of any foreign state.'[94] As a member of the Commonwealth India did not consider any Commonwealth country a 'foreign state'. Tinker contends that despite India not approving of dual nationality, some East African Indians who were intensely proud of India's newly independent status obtained an Indian passport without surrendering existing citizenship rights.[95] The ambiguous situation was only clarified when the Citizenship act was drafted and came into force in 1955 requiring anyone who had 'voluntarily acquired the citizenship of another country... (to) cease to be a citizen of India'.[96] In the latest definition no difference was identified between Commonwealth states and other states. India was greatly disappointed by the British attitude towards the British passport holding Asians. Indeed in February 1968 India announced that it would deny entry to the British passport holding Asians. By opting for British citizenship they had terminated Indian responsibility for them. In the summer 1968 the British and Indian government reached an agreement whereby any Asian leaving Kenya, could enter India if his passport had been endorsed by the British High Commission, granting him entry into Britain.[97] With this stand the Indian government hoped to force the British government to live up to its responsibilities which it had so lightly cast off through the various Immigration Acts and Bills.[98]

The expatriate Asians became aliens like any other foreigners and the government of India restricted their rights in buying/owning property and investing in their country of origin. It was only with the advent of the Janata government in 1977 that changes in government policy were being considered:

> There were to be changes in the entry laws, allowing overseas Indians to return to the 'motherland', even if they were foreign nationals. The government sponsored a seminar on overseas Indians and declared that henceforth the Indian Council for Cultural Relations would get involved. (...) The new policy seemed to be a seeking of balancing of interests of India while at the same time expressing legitimate concern about overseas Indians.[99]

Although the Janata government did not remain in power for very long, the debate on expatriate Asians had restarted within the Indian government.

With regard to the problems concerning the rights to own property in India, to be able to reside there and to invest, policies varied over time. Although by law they were aliens, some difference between them and non-

NRIs were made by the government with regard to the above areas. NRIs were already in the mid 1980s allowed to buy and own property, although only in specified areas. NRIs had to pay for the property in foreign exchange, could own no more than two at a time, which again were subject to a three year lock-in period before resale, and could use the property for personal residence or renting out only. If any of these properties were rented out the proceeds could not be repatriated, yet if the NRI wished to sell the property after the lock in period, he could repatriate the original investment from the sale proceed, 'but capital gains calculated at the rate of 20% of resale consideration shall not be allowed to be repatriated.'[100]

These guidelines had been set up during the 'liberalisations' of the early 1980s. The news was that NRIs with Indian passports did not need the approval of the Reserve Bank of India to buy property, which was still a requirement for other foreigners, foreign companies, or NRIs with foreign passports. Allowing NRIs to own properties it was hoped, would fuel investments flowing into the country, yet despite this, there were few investment proposals as the procedures for granting approval to the NRI project was intensely cumbersome.[101]

Other facilities which were developed or improved in the same period was the holding of stocks and shares, and the holding of bank accounts in India. Any NRI could invest in Government securities and units of Unit Trust of India and the National Savings/Plan Certificates of the Government of India through an authorised foreign exchange dealer. The acquisition of shares was subject to approval of the Reserve Bank of India, who allowed it only 'if the non resident investor furnishes an undertaking binding himself, his heirs, executors, successors, and assigns not to seek repatriation of capital invested or income earned thereon, irrespective of the manner of payment of the investment.'[102] Yet again for bank accounts the NRI did not have to be an Indian citizen and could choose between accounts, which allowed for repatriation and accounts, which did not.

The Diaspora's Point of View

The previous sections of chapter 4 have analysed the Indian Government's policy towards the expatriate Asian Community. In this section the point of view of the Diaspora will be taken into account.

As has been seen in chapter 2, emigration started in the 7th century AD and until the 14th century trade links all round Asia and Africa were established. Between the 15th and the nineteenth century Indians began entering and taking up residence in the colonies, mostly upon their own initiative. From the mid 19th century to the early twentieth century came the bulk emigration as indentured labourers and later, again as part of the colonial system, as clerks, tradesmen and professionals.[103] Almost all Asians who left their country of origin, from the end of the 19th century to the 1940s did so for economic reasons. What they earned helped them in general lead a more comfortable lifestyle than they had had back home, yet part of it was also sent back in the form of remittances. How did they see themselves: as Indians, with ties to the motherland? As British citizens, colonising the vast empire? Or as future Ugandans, Kenyans, South Africans and so on? How did they view the Government of India both before and after independence? Did they expect their mother country to stand up for them in times of need?[104]

It is generally said that overseas Indian communities evolved differently and related to India in their own ways, depending on where they were. They regarded India as their cultural and spiritual home. Ties might have weakened over time, but they were never severed.

> The Indian struggle for independence caught the imagination of them all, both because it promised a brighter day for India and because of its anticipated implications for the rest of the British colonies including their own. Indeed as many of them have remarked they used to feel ashamed of being Indians until the Indian struggle for independence restored their pride and dignity.[105]

The contacts with India increased after India's independence, yet after nearly a century and a half of separate evolution 'the reunion was not always happy'. The expatriate Asians had come to expect more support from their country of origin, once India had gained independence. The speeches of the nationalists had made them believe that India was going to stand up for her children abroad and make sure that all forms of discrimination they faced in their countries of residence would come to an end. The post independence Nehruvian position came as quite a shock.

The fact that the overseas Indians had been economically successful in some societies does not mean that they were a success everywhere they settled. In general they had a difficult life. The expatriate Indians of Fiji, Guyana, Malaysia and Uganda were the victims of state oppression and fierce racist policies at different points in time in the past. (For example early 1960s Guyana, late 1960s Malaysia, 1971 Uganda, 1986-7 Fiji.)[106] There were a number of reasons why in some cases the story of the

Diaspora ended in tears: first they did not integrate with the local population and they were not organised in a way to collectively fight repression. Amongst themselves religious and caste differences were prevalent, and caused internal schisms; they were not a homogeneous group in either language, cultural traditions or religious affiliations. They also felt that first they had done so much for the development of their country of residence and then they had fought side by side with the Africans against the white oppression. They felt that there was a certain amount of injustice when they subsequently became targets of discrimination and oppression by the local population. In fact they had simply become the victims of rising local nationalism. As early as 1965-6 the Asians in East Africa had come to realise that their days were numbered, 'but they were willing to wait and see how fate shaped their destiny.'[107]

In fact it was the lack of integration, which caused both the rift with the host society and the problems with newly independent India. The Diaspora could easily blame the colonial organisation which had kept them segregated from the local population, yet their internal social structure did not allow for Asian-local relations to go beyond the shopkeeper-customer or master-servant level. To the economic barriers one can add the deep differences in culture and ways of life, which did not encourage informal social contacts between the Asians and the Africans. The Diaspora saw its way of life in a pluralistic society that did not require the radical process of assimilation. In that sense the African and Asian publics were usually at odds with each other: one group demanded 'cultural fusion', the other 'cultural separation'.[108] As a result they were seen as foreigners, even legacies of the British imperial system, which made them an unwelcome segment in the host societies. Younger Indians knew that the future would lie in co-operation with the local population,[109] not in the hope for protection from either India or Britain. They knew that the basis for integration has to be sought in common political and economic ideals.[110]

As for nationality, the expatriate Asians felt that the Indian government was trying to confuse them by first advising them to become British, and subsequently asking them to give up that passport for the local East African one. By and large the feeling was that by changing their nationality they would 'allow themselves to be held captive in a land which had given them prosperity but whose people were so unlike their own.'[111] Since they could not maintain dual nationality they looked for comfort in splitting the members of their families into holding different passports: one or two members of the family would register with the East African authorities, whilst the others retained their British passports. In some cases one Indian passport was also maintained.[112]

In fact today many expatriate Indians do not identify with India and its people anymore. Their identification is merely a symbolic one. The fact that they felt abandoned on more than one occasion, and felt rejected by Indian society, which does not regard them as 'real Indians', has created a rift.[113] They felt that it was the responsibility of the Government of India to put pressure on governments of societies where the Diaspora is to be found, to accommodate the interests and aspirations of the Indians living there and give them an equal place in these societies.[114] In that respect the Nehruvian policy failed them miserably. They even felt that India, in its 'anxiety to cultivate African goodwill, was not averse to condoning the injustices being committed against them.'[115] This primarily referred to India closing its doors to the British Asians between 1968 and 1972 in their hour of need when they were first pushed to leave East Africa, and later forcibly expelled.

Conclusion

This chapter has attempted to analyse the change of attitude from pre-independence India to the modern government's attitude with respect to the overseas Indian community. It is obvious that the perception of the expatriate Asian community has changed drastically from being part of the Indian nation, even propagating the traditional Gandhian ideals of independence and non-violence in their country of residence, to simple aliens in their country of origin. Whilst pre-independence behaviour of the Government of India and the nationalists had led the Diaspora to believe that they would be a priority on the agenda of a newly independent India, they were surprised to find out that unless they returned to the motherland to settle, they would simply be treated like any other foreigner. To the Expatriate Asians, lost in the vast legal confusions of the decolonising world this seemed a form of betrayal. Yet to the Indian Government, and especially to Nehru this matter had become of significance with regard to the development of India's 'new' foreign policy and status in the world. If India wanted to make a stand against imperialism it could do so only as a state, and not as a nationalist movement with concern for its Diaspora spread around the globe. Nehru, it has been seen above, and in chapter 3, saw a mission for India: to lead the developing nations in their anti-imperialistic struggle and further lead them as a non-aligned group, to become an independent diplomatic, (and he hoped) economic force in the post second World War world. The Diaspora as he saw it, was an imperial legacy with divided loyalties.

Was this policy the right one for India? With hindsight one can see that India remained in a dilemma when it came to the overseas Indians. Although public interest waned with time the Indian government went through phases where it took a marked interest in the Diaspora's welfare and then there were other times when it categorically shut India's doors in their face.

India's policy of foreign non-involvement slowly changed over the years to allow expatriate Asians to take a certain part in its economic development, but the barriers remained so high that it kept them at bay quite effectively. Why Nehru's policy was maintained for so long despite a shift from idealism to realism within Indian Foreign policy, and why in the mid to late 1980s this position started crumbling, are matters which will be analysed in chapter 6.

Endnotes

1 Twaddle, M. (ed.), *Expulsion of a Minority – Essays on Ugandan Asians*, p.16
2 Grover (ed.), *International Relations and Foreign Policy of India*, 8, p.33
3 Heimsath, C. and Mansingh, S., *A Diplomatic History of Modern India*, p.301
4 Ghai, Y. and Ghai, D., 'The Asian Minorities of East and Central Africa up to 1971', p.281-285
5 Letter to G.K. Gokhale 18.10.1898, quoted in *Indians in East Africa*, Purshotamdas Thakurdav Research Centre, p.22
6 Ghai, Y. and Ghai, D. 'The Asian Minorities of East and Central Africa up to 1971', p.274-247
7 Joshi, P.S., *The Tyranny of Colour*, Durban, 1942, p.303
8 Grover (ed.), *International Relations and Foreign Policy of India*, 8, p.35
9 Twaddle, M. (ed.), *Expulsion of a Minority – Essays on Ugandan Asians*, p.17
10 Further details on South Africa can be found in the case study following this chapter
11 Grover (ed.), *International Relations and Foreign Policy of India*, 8, p.37
12 Sarojini Naidu, 1924, quoted in Heimsath, C. and Mansingh, S., *A Diplomatic History of Modern India*, p.308
13 Ghai, Y. and Ghai, D., 'The Asian Minorities of East and Central Africa up to 1971', p.331
14 Further details on East Africa, especially Uganda in the case study following this chapter

15 Ghai, Y. and Ghai, D., 'The Asian Minorities of East and Central Africa up to 1971', p.281
16 Grover (ed.), *International Relations and Foreign Policy of India*, 8, p.35
17 Twaddle, M. (ed.), *Expulsion of a Minority – Essays on Ugandan Asians*, p.21
18 Grover (ed.), *International Relations and Foreign Policy of India*, 8, p.309
19 Grover (ed.), *International Relations and Foreign Policy of India*, 8, p.38
20 Khilnani, N.M., *Realities of Indian Foreign Policy*, p.58
21 Lanka, S., *India in World Politics – A Historical Analysis and Appraisal*, p.11
22 'That the Imperial War Conference desires to place on records its view that the Resolution of the Imperial Conference of 20 April 1907 should be modified to permit of India being fully represented at all future Imperial Conferences....', 13.4.1917 (Ollivier, M., *The Colonial and Imperial Conferences from 1887 to 1937,* Part 1, p.174)
23 Mr Chamberlain on 27.4.1917 in Ibid., p.252
24 Ibid., p.276
25 Lanka, S., *India in World Politics – A Historical Analysis and Appraisal*, p.29
26 *Indians in East Africa*, Purshotamdas Thakurdav Research Centre, p.24
27 Ollivier, M., *The Colonial and Imperial Conferences from 1887 to 1937,* Vol. III, Part 2, p.15
28 Fraser, T.G., 'Imperial Policy and Indian Minorities Overseas 1905-23' in Hepburn, A.C., *Minorities in History*, p.155-156
29 Ibid., p.166
30 Dr N.B.Khare, member of the Viceroy's executive council, worked infatigably for the welfare of overseas Indians
31 Quoted in Twaddle, M. (ed.), *Expulsion of a Minority – Essays on Ugandan Asians*, p.22
32 Bahadur Singh, I.J. (ed.), *The Other India: The Overseas Indians and their Relationship with India*, p.57-58
33 Sundaram, C., *India in World Politics*, p.231
34 See Chapter 6 of Appasamy, B., (1943), *Indians in South Africa*, p.61-79
35 Ibid., p. 80
36 Heimsath, C. and Mansingh, S., *A Diplomatic History of Modern India*, p.305
37 Jha, S.K., *India and the Commonwealth*, p. 97
38 Miller, J.D.B., *Survey of British Commonwealth Affairs, Problems of Expansion and Attrition 1953-1969*, p.129
39 Grover (ed.), *International Relations and Foreign Policy of India*, 8, p.570
40 Raj, K., *Indian and British Colonialism in East Africa 1883-1939*, p.63-66
41 Chimanlal to Fiji in 1913; Thambi Marakkayar to Malaya and Ceylon in 1917; Sharma and Raju to Fiji in 1920; K.Pillai and V.N.Tiwari to British Guyana in 1924; V.S.S.Shastri to Malaya in 1937; H.N.Kunzru and P.Kodanda Rao to Malaya in 1946; Maharaj Singh, C.S.Jha, and K.K.Husan to East Africa in 1946; in Mahajani, U. 'India and the People of Indian Origin Abroad' in Rajan, M.S. (ed.), *India's Foreign Relations during the Nehru Era,* p.238
42 Ibid., p.240
43 Rajan, M.S., *India and the Commonwealth, Some Studies*, p.20
44 Dutt, S.K., *India's Relations with Developing Countries*, p.13

45 Heimsath, C. and Mansingh S., *A Diplomatic History of Modern India*, p.287
46 Ibid., p.288-89
47 Quoted from Lok Sabha Debates, 8 March 1948
48 Tinker, H., *Separate and Unequal*, p. 93
49 Ibid., p.320
50 Prof. A. Gupta quoted in Bhatia, P., *Indian Ordeal in Africa*, p.121-122
51 Heimsath, C. and Mansingh, S., *A Diplomatic History of Modern India*, p.302
52 Hanson, A.H., 'Power Shifts and Regional Balances' in Streeten, P. and Lipton, M. (eds.), *The Crisis of Indian Planning*, p.43
53 Grover (ed.), *International Relations and Foreign Policy of India*, 8, p.41
54 Quoted in Grover (ed.), *International Relations and Foreign Policy of India*, 8, p.43
55 Heimsath, C. and Mansingh, S., *A Diplomatic History of Modern India*, p.289
56 Twaddle, M. (ed.), *Expulsion of a Minority – Essays on Ugandan Asians*, p.129
57 Grover (ed.), *International Relations and Foreign Policy of India*, 8, p.704
58 Ghai, Y. and Ghai, D., 'The Asian Minorities of East and Central Africa up to 1971', p.297
59 Serpa, E., 'India and Africa' p.187
60 Srivastava in Grover (ed.), *International Relations and Foreign Policy of India*, 8 p.412
61 Ibid., p.418
62 *The Image of Contemporary India Abroad*, p.46
63 Chhabra, H.S., 'India and Africa – Next Door Neighbours', p.47
64 Serpa, E., 'India and Africa'. p.187
65 Ibid., p.188
66 Tinker, H., *Separate and Unequal*, p.339-342
67 Ibid., p.351-352
68 Dutt, S.K., *India's Relations with Developing Countries*, p.22 and 290
69 Ibid., p.23
70 Ibid., p.26
71 Ibid., p.293-294
72 See Appendix, Government announcements - NRI response 1975-1977 and 1980-1982
73 See Appendix Government announcement - NRI response
74 Mahajani, U., 'India and the People of Indian Origin Abroad' in Rajan, M.S. (ed.), *India's Foreign Relations during the Nehru Era*, p.208
75 Heimsath, C. and Mansingh, S., *A Diplomatic History of Modern India*, p.302
76 Ibid., p.302-303
77 Although dual nationality was not allowed, some expatriate Indians managed to obtain an Indian passport after India's independence and to maintain their British citizenship. Dual citizenship was only made impossible with the passing of the Indian Citizenship Act of 1955. See chapter 6 for further details
78 Dutt, S.K., *India and the Third World: Altruism or Hegemony?*, p.134
79 Bahadur Singh, I.J. (ed.), *The Other India: The Overseas Indians and their Relationship with India*, p.61
80 Apa B. Pant quoted in Ibid., p.34
81 Quoted in Ibid., p.38

82 Ghai, Y. and Ghai, D., 'The Asian Minorities of East and Central Africa up to 1971', p.176
83 Ibid., p.177
84 Twaddle, M. (ed.), *Expulsion of a Minority – Essays on Ugandan Asians*, p.23
85 Bahadur Singh, I.J. (ed.), *The Other India: The Overseas Indians and their Relationship with India*, p.170-171
86 Ghai, Y. and Ghai, D., 'The Asian Minorities of East and Central Africa up to 1971', p.178
87 Twaddle, M. (ed.), *Expulsion of a Minority – Essays on Ugandan Asians*, p.24
88 Ghai, Y. and Ghai, D., 'The Asian Minorities of East and Central Africa up to 1971', p.179
89 Figures on how many acquired local citizenship in East Africa can be found in the Uganda case study following this chapter. One should note that although local citizenship was offered in the decolonising countries of East Africa (Kenya, Uganda and Tanzania) the rules governing the acquisition were strict and sometimes impossible to fulfil in the time provided At the time an Indian passport was complicated to acquire since the Indian Parliament had made a six months uninterrupted residence in India a condition for citizenship Bhatia, P., *Indian Ordeal in Africa*, p.32
90 Twaddle, M. (ed.), *Expulsion of a Minority – Essays on Ugandan Asians*, p.130
91 Motwani, J.K., Gosine, M. and Barot-Motwani, J., *Global Indian Diaspora: Yesterday, Today and Tomorrow*, p.124
92 Ibid., p.130
93 Bahadur Singh, I.J. (ed.), *The Other India: The Overseas Indians and their Relationship with India*, p.182
94 Tinker, H., *Separate and Unequal*, p.391-392
95 Tinker, H., *The Banyan Tree*, p.124
96 1955 Citizenship Act
97 Lipton, M. and Finn, J., *The Erosion of a Relationship: India and Britain since 1960*, p.169
98 There was also reluctance from the merchant groups in India such as the Marwaris to let in large groups of Asian traders. See chapter 6
99 Dutt, S.K., *India's Relations with Developing Countries*, p.296-297; Hindu, 24.8.1978
100 Economic Times, 1.8.1988
101 Goswami, D., 'Facilities for NRIs', Financial Express, 8.5.1988
102 'Rules and Methods of Making Investment in India', The Indian, February/March 1981 p.40, Detailed rules on what could and could not be repatriated are explained in detain in the document provided within this article (p.39-46)
103 Motwani, J.K., Gosine, M. and Barot-Motwani, J., *Global Indian Diaspora: Yesterday, Today and Tomorrow*, p.12
104 Chapter 6 expands on the evolution of the profile of the Diaspora to include the Gulf migrants and the Brain drain phenomena in the 1970s and 1980s
105 Motwani, J.K., Gosine, M. and Barot-Motwani, J., *Global Indian Diaspora: Yesterday, Today and Tomorrow*, p.8
106 See case studies chapter 5 for more details on Fiji and Uganda
107 Twaddle, M. (ed.), *Expulsion of a Minority – Essays on Ugandan Asians*, p.132

108 Ghai, Y. and Ghai, D., 'The Asian Minorities of East and Central Africa up to 1971', p.218
109 Ibid., p.272
110 Grover (ed.), *International Relations and Foreign Policy of India*, 8, p.532
111 Bhatia, P., *Indian Ordeal in Africa*, p.38
112 Ibid., p.39
113 Motwani, J.K., Gosine, M. and Barot-Motwani, J., *Global Indian Diaspora: Yesterday, Today and Tomorrow*, p.19
114 Ibid., p.22
115 Twaddle, M. (ed.), *Expulsion of a Minority – Essays on Ugandan Asians*, p.132

5 Case studies

Introduction

The following case studies have been chosen to illustrate the Government of India's policy with regard to the Indian Diaspora explained in chapter 4. The first two describe different crises affecting overseas Indians in Uganda (1972) and Fiji (1986). They show that the Nehruvian policy of non-interference was maintained throughout the time of Indira Gandhi's and Rajiv Gandhi's rule, despite the changing attitudes in foreign policy formulation observed in chapter 3. It is important to note that neither case offered the option of direct intervention. The two studies differ though on several important points: Whilst the Ugandan crisis would have allowed India to offer asylum to the expulsed Asians of non-Indian citizenship, the situation in Fiji did not offer such a possibility. Indira Gandhi chose a showdown with Britain on moralistic grounds over and above extending help towards the Indian Diaspora. The Indian public and press of the time were unconcerned. The Fiji crisis though outraged the Indian population and press, and this stirred the Rajiv Gandhi government into diplomatic action. Rajiv Gandhi protested against the racial discrimination in Fiji on the same humanitarian grounds that India held whilst protesting against the apartheid regime in South Africa. This was in the eyes of the Government of India not protest for an Indian community abroad, but against a particular form of racial discrimination.

The third case study deals with the attitude of the Government of India with respect to the Indian Diaspora in South Africa. India lodged complaints at the United Nations with respect to the discriminatory treatment of the Indian minority before 1947. This policy quickly switched to encompass the black and coloured population of South Africa. India was then no longer speaking for the Indian Diaspora, but protesting against racial discrimination in general. The cutting off of all diplomatic relations and all other commercial and cultural ties between India and South Africa actually brought hardship to the stranded Indian community there rather than help their plight.

This chapter will illustrate the three cases in turn and give a detailed account of the Government of India's reaction in each case.

Ugandan-Asians and the 1972 Expulsions

In August 1972 Idi Amin issued decrees expelling the entire Indian population from Uganda within ninety days. He accused the Asians of economic sabotage and of encouraging corruption. By November 7th 1972 all but a few hundred of Uganda's Indian population had been forced to leave.

Background

In 1971 Idi Amin staged a coup against Milton Obote. He was a welcome change to the Asian population who hoped that the anti-Asian campaign of the post independence years would be scaled down. The Ismailis were especially glad to see a Muslim replace a Christian leader. They had financed mosques and hoped for better treatment under the new leadership. But within less than a year of taking over the leadership of Uganda Idi Amin began to emphasise the misdeeds of the Asians and the 12 000 pending applications for citizenship were cancelled.

> In the first few days after the announcement, Amin vacillated between expelling all Asians or just Asian commercial capital. Publicly this was reflected in his indecision over whether to exempt professionals or not. Another issue resolved in practice was the legal one. An expulsion confined to non-citizens would leave the bulk of big Asian capital untouched; furthermore, it may also leave this section of Asian bourgeoisie in control of the material assets of the entire class once the process came to a conclusion.[1]

On the day of the order the President made no distinction among the Asians on grounds of nationality. Later he amended this to refer only to the non-Ugandan Asians and ordered their confirmation of citizenship by 19 August. He changed his mind again on 18 August, including Ugandan nationals in the decree despite the protests this step provoked at the university. He then once again withdrew the expulsion order against Ugandan Asians and asked those concerned to get their citizenship confirmed.[2] As a result the Asians with citizenship were asked to queue to confirm the validity of their papers, and instead found their certificates and passports torn and destroyed or their citizenship invalidated in other ways through technical faults such as not having renounced their British nationality within the 90 day limit. Eventually there were no Asian citizens left.

Causes of the expulsions

The Ugandan Asians numbered only 74,308 according to an official count in 1969.[3] (There is confusion as to what the exact numbers of Asians in Uganda were at the time of the exodus.[4]) Their number was smaller than in any other East African country. Newspaper reports have put the blame on racism and African nationalism, and the fact that the new Ugandan government was trying to bolster popular support for an unstable regime. However the causes of the expulsion were far more diverse and far more complicated.

At the Commonwealth Heads of State and Government meeting held in Ottawa in August 1973, a year after the expulsions, President Idi Amin Dada defended Uganda's position by stating that the expulsions had been conducted 'From considerations of public interest, social security and the country's economy'.[5] He also maintained that only non-citizens were actually expelled, and that those Ugandan Asians with citizenship left on their own accord, due mainly to the Indian joint family system where you could find several nationalities under one roof.[6]

Colonial rule

Indians had first come to Uganda for the construction of the railways; few of those who survived the railway construction stayed on. Later there had been migration of petty traders and administrators through the British colonial system. Uganda's principal export crop was cotton, which it exported mainly to India and the cotton business was virtually an Indian monopoly.[7]

Soon there emerged a triangular racial system:

> By 1910 the scene in East Africa was more or less set. Administrative and agricultural development were thought to be European occupations; trade and craftsmanship were relegated to Indians; and Africans were encouraged to

work in the European agricultural system and to supply cheap labour in towns that were developing in response to European and Indian activities.[8]

The British colonial system had encouraged a status quo in which the three races inhabiting East Africa were living separated and separately. Each had their economic role in the system. In a way the Asian population represented a 'buffer' between the white colonialists and the indigenous population. They were the middlemen.

Already in 1945 and 1949 had there been anti-Indian riots when local Ugandans protested against the large concentration of Indians in urban Centres. In neighbouring Kenya racial tensions were high in the 1950s, whereas it was relatively quiet in Uganda. In 1956 the Uganda National Congress started a trade boycott of European and Indian shops so that Africans would only buy from Africans. The greatest sufferers were the Indian dukawallas.[9]

This was also the time when African political demands for independence mounted vis-à-vis the British colonial power. A small group of Asian intellectuals tried to push the Indian community to drop their communal attitude and to support the African independence movement. They were called the Uganda Action Group but survived only two years as it became clear that the African leaders had their own agenda for independence. In general the political standing of the Asians remained very low-key and non-involved.

Independence changed the character of the relationship of the tri-level racial policy, as the policy of 'divide and rule' was anti-ethical to the new government. The priority of the new regime was to try and unite the communities, and as a result the Indian element could no longer exist as a separate political entity. What was unacceptable to the new government led by President Obote was the Asian domination of commerce in Uganda and the fact that the Asians were sending money out of the country, especially to the UK.

Indian trade monopoly

Most Ugandan Asians worked in the field of commerce. In the business community there were two great empires owned by Gujarati traders Mulji Madhvani and Nanji Kalidas Mehta. They had branched out from the cotton business into sugar plantations and other businesses such as breweries, hotels, glass and textiles. Around half the Ugandan Asians owned their own businesses, the rest were employees and of these 11% were professionals, 16% were administrative staff, 30% had secretarial or clerical jobs and 30% were skilled manual workers.[10]

In 1952 it was estimated that 5,227 Asian retail traders had an annual turnover of £28.4 million (£5,433 per trader), whereas 11,637 African traders had a turnover of £10.6 million. African traders were 69% of all traders but handled only 27% of the retail trade. The African and non-African traders were largely in non-competing categories, as most African trade arose from the sale of traditional products.[11]

In 1969 Milton Obote followed the Kenyan example and implemented the Immigration and Trade Licensing Act, which was to in time eliminate non-citizens from the economy and advance Africanisation.[12] Certain trade items such as beer, cigarettes, motor vehicles and essential foods were restricted for residents to trade, and all non-citizens were required to obtain work permits.

Another way to attempt to improve the status of African traders was to restrict the Asians from trading in rural areas. As a result they set up shops in towns, and the African traders did not gain, as Africans began to buy at the shops in town because of their lower prices. So the Asian traders doubled their trade, ironically as a result of Africanisation.[13]

The roots of friction lay in the distribution of the Gross Domestic Product. Whatever economic growth had been achieved during the colonial period had enriched the immigrant communities, either the British or the Indians, rather than the indigenous people. In 1963 the monetary income of the Africans was only two and a half times the earnings of the non Africans, whereas the population ratio was 1.4:89.6 and the income ratio was 26:74 (non-Africans to Africans). The per-capita income of the non-African was about 30 times that of the African.[14] The 1966 census revealed that in terms of wholesale trade receipts the Africans controlled 4.6%, Asians controlled 73.6% and Europeans controlled 21.5%.[15] This marked difference in income developed a wide disparity in the standards of living and as a result created friction between the Asians and the Africans.

Another peculiarity was the structure of Indian businesses. Generally they were characterised by relatively close-knit family ties in ownership and management, making them impenetrable from the outside especially for the African population.

As for the allegations of corruption and other malpractice, it is true to say that since the 1968 Kenyan crisis the Indians exported their capital through illegal means such as falsified revenue declarations, overbilling of imports and underbilling of exports and so on.[16] These malpractices had been fuelled by the racial problems in Kenya and the possibility of eviction from East Africa, and since the 1968 British Citizenship Act the Ugandan Asians were in limbo. This created further isolation from the African population.[17]

Citizenship[18]

Apa Pant, India's first High Commissioner to Kenya visited Uganda in the late 1940s and encouraged the local Indian population to take on British citizenship in order to integrate with the local population, at that time still a British colony. This was part of the Nehruvian policy of encouraging expatriate Asians to identify with their host country. The Indian government and Nehru especially expected the Indians to identify with the native population of those countries and in time to support their independence movements from Britain, thus becoming model Kenyans, Ugandans... But things developed differently.[19]

The citizenship issue would fuel the racial tensions as time passed. Most Ugandan Asians were not British subjects; in general they were 'British protected persons'. The Asians felt that having British passports would give them the option to enter Britain freely in times of crisis.

At the time of independence in 1962 the 77,400 Asians were given the option to acquire local nationality upon registration within a grace period of two years, but many, with the exception of the Ismailis preferred to go for a British passport rather than for Ugandan papers. As the grace period drew to a close there was a rush on the Ugandan nationality and 24,212 applications were received. In the late 1960s the breakdown of Asian citizenship was as follows: 36,593 holders of British papers (passports or British protected persons), 8,890 Indian citizens, 253 Pakistani citizens, 1,768 (Indian) citizens of Kenya and 26,657 Uganda citizens, which included the 12,000 whose papers had not yet been processed. In Uganda the process took especially long, as the individuals had to prove that they had forsaken all other nationalities within a specified time period; often that was not the case as Asians tried to maintain some British papers. In many cases the Asians applying for local citizenship were also seen as 'paper citizens', who accepted local nationality only to avoid the consequences of Africanisation.[20] This resulted in more animosity between Ugandans and Indians.

Integration

One of the major criticisms made by the African population was the perception that the Indian population did not integrate or mix with the indigenous population. In part this was because there was no homogeneous African society to integrate into; to an even greater extent this was due to the Indian population not being a homogeneous group themselves. There were no institutions uniting them as 'Indians', and not even 'Hindus' or 'Muslims'. According to Morris in 1954 there were 134 officially registered associations of which the Indian Associations numbered 113. Of those 58 were for any Indian regardless of caste, sect or place of origin. Only 2 associations were meant for the whole Asian Community of Uganda: the Central Council of Indian Associations and the Indian Merchants' Chamber.

> They were controlled by a small group of upper-class men who met one another frequently at social functions and for recreation and informal business at an exclusive club in Kampala. The Merchant's Chamber mainly exercised an economic influence over matters which concerned a large part of all the Indians in the country, but unlike the Central Council, it did not purport to represent the Indian community as such.[21]

The Ismailis remained separate; they seldom were able to put their representatives into influential positions in the Central Council. As a result they organised their sect as an independent community.[22]

In the eyes of the Europeans and the Africans the Asian community was one group. But the castes and sects had by 1955 solidified into formal elements of the structure of Indian society. 'Within the caste and sectarian communities, the leaders did not represent permanent groups recruited on predictable principles whose members held consistent views.'[23]

According to Tandon and Raphael the failure of the Asians was not to have integrated as a tribe into African Society, that ishaving their own ethnicity recognised as a distinct tribe of East Africa.[24]

Outcome of the crisis

India's reaction Around 70% of the total number of the 300,000 Asians in the whole of East Africa were Hindus. As a result it could be assumed that most had retained some ties with India through marriage, visits, and religious organisations or through trading contacts. This was not necessarily the case for the remaining 30% who were Muslims, especially the Ismailis who mostly identified with the host country.[25] During the independence struggle there had been relations between the Indian nationalist leaders and prominent East African Asians. Nationalist leaders had enlisted the financial support of these expatriate Asians to fight the British. But with the passing of the British Empire it had become imperative for India to foster its ties with the new African governments and their leaders. The Asian communities in the region stood in the way of establishing these links. In fact the gulf widened as India started to believe that the Asians were a liability more than an asset in diplomatic relations with Africa.[26] Diplomatically the Afro-Asian camp became of vital importance to India during and after the 1962 China war. China had tried to isolate India's position in the world. At this point India had to show great support for African nationalism and pan-African goals in order to retain their favours.

India was to learn through the Kenyan crisis of 1968 and the Ugandan Crisis of 1972 that African Governments were not necessarily amenable to any outside persuasion on behalf of the expatriate Asians.[27] Instead such attempts were seen as undue interference in internal affairs. This was an eye-opener, as India now had to recognise the leadership of the new African states which varied greatly from country to country, and that Afro-Asian solidarity was not a guarantee that the expatriate Asians would be treated decently.

At home the stereotypes about Asians being exploiters of the local African population were gaining hold: their westernisation, affluence and skills prejudiced public opinion in India towards them. Besides, unlike their counterparts in Burma or Ceylon the East African Asians had no lobbies at the state level to plead their cause.

On 11 August 1972 a statement was made in the Lok Sabha on behalf of the Ministry of External Affairs in which the Asians from Uganda were classified into 4 categories: Ugandan Citizens, British Passport holders, Indian Nationals and stateless persons.[28] The Government of India recognised their responsibility for the Indian citizens only, and also recognised the right of the Ugandan Government to regulate their internal affairs according to their best judgement. India expected that those who had to leave the country would be able to do so under conditions conforming to humane and equitable standards under international law. The government also became concerned about compensation for the properties left behind belonging to Indian nationals.[29] In a statement on 4 September 1972, the Minister of External Affairs S. Singh stated that the Government of India

> considered the present facilities for the repatriation of cash and moveables were wholly inadequate in relation to their long residence in Uganda as well as for starting a new life.[30]

India's insistence that Asians with British passports were Britain's responsibility was closely linked to the fear that India would become a 'dumping ground' for the refugees. In the end India agreed to accept up to 15,000 British Asians, under a similar kind of deal that had been worked out in 1968 for the Kenyan Asians[31] where they could come to India provided Britain had stamped their passports granting them entry at any later date.[32] 'The Government of India have agreed that those UK passport holders whose eventual entry into the UK for permanent settlement has been documented by the UK government could stage through India to visit their relations, etc. en route to the UK.'[33] In the case of the Kenya agreement the option to enter Britain could be exercised only within three months of entry into India, and it was given only after making sure that the applicants were not successful in their attempts to settle in India.[34]

There were cases where Asians were shuttled around several countries against their will, because they were not being granted entry into Britain. In these cases the government of India maintained a hard line by sending them back: in the Lok Sabha debate of 10 August, the deputy minister of the Ministry of External Affairs had to explain that Indians who had arrived in India were not being let into India: 'These persons did not wish to enter India. Under regulations in force international carriers may not bring into India any foreigner against his wishes. On evidence that these British passport holders did not wish to come to India, they were sent back by the same carrier.'[35] In the end 9,622 persons holding various passports or stateless people arrived in India from Uganda between 15 August and the end of 1972.[36]

Why did India not take a tougher line with Kenya and Uganda? Besides being fundamentally in conflict with the Nehruvian attitude of anti-colonialism and anti-imperialism India lacked any sanctions to reinforce such a posture. Besides a belligerent attitude might not have proven beneficial for the expatriate Asians in the long run.[37]

It should also be noted that India was quite offended at allegations that with the help of Zambia she was planning an invasion of Uganda from Tanzania. On 26 September, a military spokesman in Kampala stated that the visit of the President of India to Tanzania and Zambia was to prepare an attack on Uganda.[38]

Despite the expulsions and the false allegations of the Ugandan government with regard to India, the Government of India accepted an invitation for a trade delegation to go to Uganda to help rebuild the national economy less than a year after the incident. The Indian High Commissioner said that 'New Delhi would be delighted by General Amin's desire to improve relations. India, was a firm believer in Afro-Asian solidarity…' [39]

Indian press The Indian press was unanimous in believing that Britain was not going to live up to its responsibility and take in the Asians who were British passport holders. They expected that this burden would be laid onto the Government of India's shoulders.[40]

It was also felt that the African Governments felt that the Government of India had a moral responsibility towards the expatriate Asians, no matter what their nationality, and that as a result of the crisis India's image had suffered. African intellectuals argued that if a power cannot be concerned about its own people it cannot claim to salvage others.[41]

But in general one can say that the Indian press was not very concerned or outraged about the fate of the expatriate Asians. There had been far more press reporting during the Kenyan crisis in 1968, during which the Indian press was less than sympathetic. In the case of the Ugandan crisis the press seemed more concerned with the alleged plans for an Indian invasion, the expulsion of the Indian High Commissioner Mr N.N. Desai and the potential compensation by the Ugandan government.[42] In effect the Indian press upheld the governmental attitude that every country had the basic right to fully control its own economy in the interest of its own people.[43]

Britain's reaction

> Amin's announcement caught Britain in the midst of a controversy over queue-jumping British Asians who were trying to get into the United Kingdom before they could obtain the proper entry vouchers.[44]

The British Government refused to liberalise the immigration controls as the number of vouchers for British Asians had been raised from 1,500 to 3,000 per annum in 1971. It seems the Government felt that resisting appeals for liberalising the immigration controls would strengthen its position against Idi Amin. Besides the British government at first did not take the expulsion decrees seriously, believing that Amin was trying to extract aid from Britain, and as a result handled the Asians' demand for entry certificates into Britain with a deliberate lack of urgency.

At the UN, Britain was heading for a clash with Uganda. Foreign Secretary Sir Alec Douglas-Home addressed the General assembly on the 27th September 1972 with the following words: 'Injustice has to be condemned wherever it raises its ugly head, whether it is perpetrated by Europeans or Africans or Asians or whoever.'[45]

Back home a group led by Enoch Powell, a former senior minister attacked the government's immigration policy, playing on fears of a further increase of coloured population to Britain. He felt that in such a case as the expulsions the whole world had to shoulder the responsibility and that it was not for Britain to handle the crisis alone, especially as this would cause unemployment, overcrowding in schools and housing shortages. There were demonstrations against the 'invasion of Britain', and it is clear that in general the mood was hostile.[46] There was a feeling that the mess of the imperial era had never been completely 'tidied up'.[47]

It was suggested that the natural havens for the Asians from Uganda were India, Pakistan and Bangladesh. If these countries were reluctant to receive them it was suggested in Parliament that overseas aid from Britain could be made conditional on the settlement of the refugees.[48]

As far as local authorities were concerned, they insisted that their schools and housing capacity was filled to its maximum extent. As a result the government created the Uganda Resettlement Board which was given executive powers to organise the reception and resettlement of the refugees. Its main priorities were to have arrangements ready to receive the families, find temporary accommodation and to persuade them not to go to areas under pressure in housing, education and social services.[49]

There was some relief when the Indian government agreed to accept to take on around 15,000 British Asians, granting them temporary abode if let into Britain at a future date. This meant that some of these, especially the elderly, or those who did not want to adjust to a new culture and climate might not enter Britain at all if they decided to remain in India.[50]

On the 30th November 1972 Douglas-Home announced a series of measures of retaliation to Amin's expulsions: the £10 million loan to Uganda which had been frozen was cancelled and the money was to be used instead for the benefit of the refugees; then Britain stopped paying nearly half the wages of about 1000 British experts in Uganda as their contracts ran out, Britain also withdrew its High Commissioner John Hennings from Kampala.[51]

Conclusion

> As a corollary to the main argument it is found that in a politically disturbed environment of a young nation-state, like Uganda, an immigrant minority community howsoever small and important it might be, as an economic asset, and whatever be the timespan of its settlement in the country, it can only survive as a separate identifiable entity if it can establish an equation with the ruling government. Any failure on that score can result in making a scapegoat of the minority community whenever the political inconvenience of the rulers so demanded.[52]

The resident Indian population failed to develop a relationship with the Ugandan elite of the day, and as a result remained mired in political controversy.

The above is the conclusion of anyone studying the minority in its new environment. Yet for the study of the relationship of the minority with its country of origin, it throws open some interesting questions. One of these is that the integration preferred by Nehru of the Asians into African society was perhaps not even possible, no matter how much it was hoped for. This means that official Indian governmental policy actually left all non-Indian nationals of Indian origin around the world in peculiar situations, potentially at the mercy of a political crisis.

The case of Uganda was a clear proof of the Government of India sticking with the original Nehruvian policy of not taking responsibility or even interest in the fate and plight of the people of Indian origin, no matter what their ties were to the mother country. The government of the day put Afro-Indian relations first on the list of priorities, although in this particular case one can argue that India would have gained by opening its doors to the enterprising Asians of Uganda.

Fiji-Indians and the 1987 Coups

In 1993 Fiji-Indians, constituted about 46 percent of the country's 771,000 population. Melanesians, the original inhabitants, made up 43 percent; the rest was made up of Europeans, Chinese and others.

On 14 May 1987, Colonel Rabuka staged a military take over.[53] He ordered the arrest of Prime Minister Bavadra and his cabinet, dissolved the parliament, and dismissed the Governor General Sir Ganilou and his own Commandant who was in Australia at that time. Shortly afterwards, authority was given to a civilian government. Four months later, on 25 September 1987, Rabuka staged a second coup to realise the objectives of the first coup. After 10 days Fiji was declared a republic and a new government was formed under Rabuka's leadership. In effect the Fiji coups unseated an elected government in which for the first time in history the Indian community had held political power. With the abolition of this government went the constitutional rights of the Fiji-Indian population.

Background

The crisis had started of after the victory of the Labour coalition in the general elections on April 1987. The election campaign was the most bitter in the Fijian history and fought on racial, social and economic issues. Soon after the forming of Bavadra's government which included both Indians and Fijians, demonstrations backed by the Alliance Party and the racist Taukei[54] landowner movement, started all over the country. The majority of Indians in the government were seen as a threat to the privileges and powers of the Fijian chiefs. The militant Taukei movement launched a massive campaign of destabilisation and its leaders organised civil unrest called project 'Disobedience'. Alliance leaders mobilised and manipulated the masses by raising racial issues.[55]

In the aftermath of the May Coup Fiji-Indians lost all control and influence over the political process in the country. Rabuka formed a new Council of Ministers that were Alliance parliamentarians and Ratu Mara joined as his political and foreign affairs adviser. However Governor General Ganilou refused to recognise the new regime. To resolve the crisis the Council of Chiefs met on 19 May and an agreement was achieved which replaced Rabuka's Council of Ministers by the Governor General's Council of Advisers. Mara remained the foreign minister. Meanwhile Bavadra and his colleagues were released. Now the protests against the coup started. The coup leaders were criticised by the judges of the Supreme Court and various church leaders. To legitimise its rule, the government appointed a 16 member Constitutional Review Committee that presented its report in early August. The report aimed to ensure continued rule of the oligarchy and gave only little say to Fiji-Indians and Fiji commoners. The coalition and Alliance party agreed to form a joint caretaker government. Rabuka was sceptical about this arrangement and two days later on Friday, September 25th he staged the second coup. This time he abrogated the constitution, dismissed the Governor General and assumed executive authority. In December, however, a civilian government was installed with Ratu Mara as Prime Minister and Sir Ganilou as president of the republic.

Causes of the coup

The coup was the result of racial strife - the age old turmoil and an uneasy relationship-between the two communities whose seeds were sown by the colonial regime in 1879 when the first ship of indentured labourers arrived from India. The coup makers wanted to establish uninterrupted public supremacy of the native Fijians. No doubt race was the predominant factor. But there were other causes as well.

Land Land has long been a contentious issue in the Indo-Fijian relationship. Most of the country's land - more than 83% was owned by the Melanesians. The best agricultural land, about 5.5% was in European hands. Fiji-Indians owned only 2.7% of the total land.[56] The Indians, being an agricultural community, had to depend on Fijians for land and a major portion of leased lands were held by the Fiji-Indians for sugar farming. Land was leased for short terms and Indians demanded more land and for longer periods.

Land ownership was a legacy of the colonial regime. The first Governor Sir Arthur Gordon introduced a policy, which provided that land which had not been acquired by Europeans would remain under Fijian ownership. Indians had no option but to depend on the leased lands. The Native Land Trust Broad (NLTB) of 1940 not only validated all Fijian land claims to 83% of Fiji but also entrenched their land rights by requiring two-thirds of the Fijian council of chiefs in the senate to change the land related aspects of the constitution. But to solve the lease problem the Agriculture Landlord and Tenant Act was passed in 1977 which extended the lease period from 10 to 20 years. In its election campaign of 1987 the coalition of the NFP and FLP promised administrative reforms of the NLTB for greater efficiency and also committed to opening up unused lands to grant national growth and development. As a result of this, the Fijians feared that the new government would try to reduce their control over land and favour Fiji-Indians. It is important to note that the land issue remained an inseparable part of racial strife.

Education and employment Deprived of land, Fiji Indians concentrated themselves in other sectors of employment. They dominated in the universities and schools. In 1968, 464 out of 635 graduates with university degrees were Indians.[57] Consequently in the competitive examinations Fiji-Indians performed better and in the service sectors the largest number of job applications came from Fiji-Indians.

To prevent the Indians from dominating the public services, a policy of balance was introduced. The constitution of 1970 provided that in recruiting to the public service, the Public Service Commission was to ensure that each community in Fiji received fair treatment in the number and distribution of appointments. After independence the government followed a discriminatory policy. Despite poor education the number of Fijians exceeded the Indians in the government services. In 1974 the number of civil service personnel of Fiji origin was 5,414 against 4,716 Indians.[58] In the armed forces discrimination was most overt and Indians had to pay the price for their refusal to join the armed forces during the Second World War. In the 1980s there were only 36 Indians against 933 Fijians in the armed forces. However the situation was somewhat better in the police force when Indian representation was about 40 percent of the total strength. Facing this discrimination Indians turned to the professional sectors and became doctors, engineers, lawyers, teachers and professors.

Business Though Europeans and Australians controlled the largest industries and businesses, Indians have registered notable success in middle sized enterprises. Indians owned the majority of retail and wholesale shops. In the field of trade and commerce Fiji Indians were at least one generation ahead of Melanesians who constituted only 2 percent of entrepreneurs. To reduce this gap the government encouraged the native Fijians to enter into business by providing soft loans and other facilities. But still they were nowhere a challenge to the Indians. Consequently Fiji Indians were seen as a major economic threat to the native Fijians.

Population growth The population growth of Fiji-Indians has long been an issue in the uneasy relationship between the two communities. At the time of independence Fijians were in the minority. The Indian population increased rapidly after 1920. The Birth rate was 2.94% among the Indians against 1.60% among the Fijians.[59] Fiji Indians outnumbered the indigenous population in the 1956 census. The growth of the Indian population was a major concern and it was seen as an attempt by the Indians to occupy the land.

Fijian aristocracy The coup was also the result of tensions between the Fijian aristocracy on the one hand and Fiji-Indians backed by some progressive Fijians on the other. Traditional Fijians saw in their chiefs protectors of Fijian tradition and culture and promoter of their interests. Europeans realised this and during the colonial period they ruled the country through these chiefs and the Bose Levu Vakaturaga (great council of chiefs). They gave them a free hand to rule their subjects. After independence the chiefs' power was recognised by the constitution and they were given the right to interfere in the political affairs of the country. The Fiji-Indians as well as the progressive Fijians, supported the cause of democracy and principles of equality. They championed the course of education and modernisation of society. In the Bavadra cabinet there was not a single minister from the nobility. All this was seen as a threat to the Fijian aristocracy and traditional way of life.

Secondly, Timoci Bavadra, was a commoner from Viscisei situated in the Western part of the island. Compared to Eastern Fiji, the Western part was historically more radical and their ties with the chiefs were not as strong. The Bavadra government wanted to reform the indigenous Fijian institutions, which could deprive the chiefs of their political positions. As a result, the chiefs felt that their traditional positions were threatened and that they could be deprived of their power. The new government was also viewed as an attempt by Indians to gain political power through the back door.

CIA connection Finally, there might have been some CIA involvement. On the 18 May 1987, the Sunday Morning Herald published a news item from sources in Suva linking the CIA with the coup.[60] Later Bavadra himself declared that the CIA masterminded the coup. CIA interest in the area was not unnatural as Fiji is of great strategic importance for the United States. The region had long been a nuclear playground for the West. The new coalition government's anti-nuclear stand was no secret. Moreover the Bavadra government also declared that it would follow a policy of non-alignment and would maintain close relations with both the superpowers. Earlier Fijian governments followed a pro-US foreign policy but the FLP, which had the backing of trade unions, wanted to improve its relations with the Communist countries including the Soviet Union and Libya. It is notable that in a report to the US House of Representatives on the Regional

Security of the South Pacific, the US government does not deplore the coup and expresses satisfaction at the re-establishment of the status quo.[61]

India's response

The Indian response was feeble and delayed. The Government of India criticised the coup of the 14 May on grounds that it was racially motivated and expressed its deep concern over the developments on the islands. India's immediate response was highly disappointing for Fiji-Indians and 'Fiji-Indians living abroad accused the Indian government of total impotency during the crisis.'[62] After initial confusion the Government of India took some diplomatic initiatives. It sent the Minister of State for External Affairs Mr. Natwar Singh and Mr. Eduardo Faleiro to Britain, Australia and New Zealand to discuss the situation in Fiji and to explore the possibilities of sanctions against Fiji to restore the Bavadra government. India appealed to other Commonwealth countries to impose economic sanctions against Fiji. It warned the new Fijian government against any change in the 1970 constitution which could lead to racial hostility and could have for reaching consequences in the stability of the South Pacific region.[63]

India's initial diplomatic initiatives met nominal success and its overall stand was criticised as 'cowardly' by the Indian press. The deposed PM Mr. Bavadra was also 'disappointed and frustrated at the lack of support from the government and people of India regarding the post-coup development.'[64] However when Mr. Jayram Reddy a minister in the deposed government, came to India to rally Indian support for restoration of democracy in Fiji, the Indian government promised to support the deposed Fijian government of Bavadra and promised to do everything within its power to move the Commonwealth Secretariat for early restoration of democracy in the South Pacific island.

In the monsoon session of the Fiji issue was raised in the Lok Sabha. K.Natwar Singh, Minister of State in the Department of External Affairs, clarified the position of Government of India:

> The Government of India has expressed its concern at the overthrow of the elected government and the abrogation of the constitution in Fiji. It was stated that measures towards national reconciliation and a return to democracy should fully take into account the need to consult all section of the population so as to ensure that there is no discrimination against any ethnic group in Fiji's multi-racial society which has lived in harmony for decades.[65]

New Delhi again criticised the leaders of the September coup and said that it was particularly tragic because it took place when the negotiations were in the process of national reconciliation. At the 42nd annual session of the General Assembly of the UN India voiced deep distress over the coup and stressed the South Pacific nations return to democracy and the rule of law.[66] Meanwhile in New Delhi opposition leader A.B.Vajpayee asked the government to take immediate steps to protect the lives and property of persons of Indian origin in Fiji as well as to prevent their forced eviction. On 11 October the Government of India announced the suspension of trade and technical co-operation with Fiji. It was largely a symbolic gesture because of the low level of economic relations between the two countries. However India registered a diplomatic victory at the Vancouver Commonwealth summit in 1987, when India contested Fiji membership and Fiji was expelled.[67] India recalled its envoy from Suva for consultation, though later he was sent back as India's ambassador. In both houses of Parliament in the winter session, both opposition and ruling party members said that the Government should keep up pressure in international fora to ensure that the democratic constitution of Fiji was not changed.[68]

The Fiji issue remained a concern to the Government of India until 1990, as the issue was brought up on several occasions in the Lok Sabha and the Rajya Sabha. When questioned in the summer of 1990 as to what arrangements had been made to provide relief to the people of Indian origin who were victims of racial discrimination the Minister of External Affairs, I.K.Gujral stated that:

> The Government of India has taken up the matter of violation of human rights of Fijians, including people of Indian origin on grounds of race, on a bilateral basis, with concerned countries. India has requested the UN Committee on Programme and Co-ordination to undertake a study of emergence of racism in Fiji in its medium term plan for 1992-97. (...) We will continue to oppose the readmission of Fiji to the Commonwealth till such time as it subscribes to the principles of the Commonwealth which include, inter-alia, non-discrimination on racial basis. We are currently providing moral and diplomatic support to the democratic movement in Fiji. (...) We have instructed our missions in countries neighbouring Fiji to extend long term, multi-entry Visas to people of Indian origin, on request.[69]

All in all the government of India had a response consistent with its general policy regarding expatriate Indians: it protested at the racial discrimination the coup had brought about by ousting an elected government which had Fiji Indian participation, by bringing it up in all possible international fora such as the 1989 Non Aligned Movement Summit, the 1987 and 1989 Commonwealth Heads of Government Meetings and the 1987, 1988 and 1989 sessions of the UN General Assembly. Besides protests were lodged with several human rights commissions and the 1990 Session of the Economic and Social Commission for Asia and the Pacific.[70] India also refused to recognise the unconstitutional 'Interim Government'.[71] But aside from the range of protests lodged by the government there was no specific interference in Fiji's affairs to support or protect people of Indian origin. It remained for the government a purely diplomatic case. Fiji was also mentioned regularly (untill 1992) in the Ministry of External Affairs Annual report as the Fiji government continued to deprive the Indian population of their constitutional rights. The last interaction between the two governments was on the 23rd May 1990 when India was asked to close her mission in Suva because of 'allegedly unfriendly and unwarranted acts'.[72]

Indian press Contrary to its usual stand on expatriate Indians the Indian media gave full coverage of Fiji immediately after the coups. They criticised the military take over, expressed their deep concern over the developments and for the security of Fiji-Indians and advised the Indian government to take all necessary steps for the restoration of Bavadra's government. The Indian Express wrote in its editorial: 'The re-imposition of military rule in Fiji is a tragic blow for democracy in the island nation'.[73] The Hindustan Times warned: 'Fiji can either settle down under a military regime or lapse into protracted ethnic conflict with disastrous consequence for its economy... A Fiji under khaki cannot be expected to dispense justice to the ethnic Indian'.[74] An interesting feature was that the Indian press was highly critical of the British stand on the issue. The Patriot wrote: 'Britain had taken a rather non-committal stand on the May 14th coup despite its intimate links with Fiji and an avowed concern for its constitutional governance'.[75] After the declaration of Fiji as a Republic the Indian Press urged New Delhi to take more vigorous action. The Times of India suggested: 'India should now involve in a vigorous lobbying initiative and make it plain that the failure to democratise Fiji will entail economic sanctions. The Indian and international community's stake in Fiji is sizeable not merely because ethnic Indians constitute a majority of the population there. It is also because of Fiji's critical location in the South Pacific'.[76] Fiji again touched the headlines when Sir Peraia Ganilou accepted the offer of the presidency. Newspapers expressed their disappointment by criticising the world community and Sir Ganilou. The Times of India wrote on 21 November:

> If this is a reflection (appointment of Ganilou) of now little effective pressure of the UK and the other concerned Commonwealth countries namely Australia and New Zealand and India, could bring to bear on the new dispensation in Suva it also means that the situation for an Indian is bleaker than ever.[77] The Hindustan Times called this transfer of power to civilian government a cosmetic 'change' while the Tribune was more bitter and referred to it as another coup: 'the most devastating coup he (Rabuka) pulled off came on Dec.5 when Ratu Sir Ganilou agreed to became the first President of the country.[78]

For the first time in such a crisis there was actually a debate on what the Government of India's role should be vis-à-vis the expatriate Indians and if they had any responsibility at all in light of their plight. The Fiji crisis contrasted sharply with the previous crisis in Uganda where neither the Indian Press nor the Indian people had taken great interest in the plight of the people of Indian origin.

Despite the change in public opinion India's overall response was disappointing and frustrating for the Fiji Indians. Except for the expulsion of Fiji from the Commonwealth, India could not achieve anything substantial. India failed to mobilise international opinion against Fiji and its diplomatic pressure remained ineffective. In fact India was not in a position to do anything concrete for the Fiji Indians. Even prior to the coup Fiji was low on India's foreign policy list. This was clear from the fact that only once had an Indian Prime Minister – Indira Gandhi in 1981-visited this island half of whose population is of Indian origin. Economic relations between the two countries were negligible, so economic pressure could not work. Moreover throughout it has been a declared policy of New Delhi to establish sentimental and cultural but not political relations with the overseas Indians, and Fiji was no exception.

However, in the following months India raised the issue of Fiji-Indians several times in the United Nations and effectively blocked Fiji's re-admission into the Commonwealth to which the Fijians are emotionally attached. It criticised the new constitution and highlighted the racial factors in it. As a result, relations worsened between the two countries. In November 1989 the Indian ambassador was expelled from Fiji and the status of the Indian embassy was reduced to that of a consulate. Finally in

May 1990 Fiji ordered the closure of the Indian embassy and with this ended all official relations between Fiji and India.

South African Asians and Apartheid

In 1989 the South African Indian population was estimated to be around 850,000, that is around 3% of the total South African population of which 80% were in Natal and 40% lived in Durban.[79] There were approximately 5 million whites, 2.5 million coloured and 23 million blacks.[80] Although only a small fraction of the South African population, the Indian community was probably the most diverse in terms of religion, language, place of origin and culture. From the times of first settlements to 1990 the regime in South Africa was based on racial discrimination, which in practice meant the segregation of races. The white race ranked supreme and there was continuous discrimination towards all other races.

In 1990 after over 40 years of struggle initiated by the Government of India within the UN, the system finally came to an end and democracy was installed in South Africa.

Background

This case study is inherently different from the two previous ones, as it does not deal with a crisis as such but with the continuous lobbying of the Government of India against all racial discrimination by the South African regime. Pre-independence the government of India had tried to the best of its ability to protect the expatriate Indian population by lodging protests with the British colonial government.[81] The fight against apartheid as a system was undertaken from India's independence onwards not for the sake of the South African Indian population but for the coloured and black population as a whole. Apartheid had its roots in the colonial system of race separation, but developed a philosophy of its own as dependence from Britain grew weaker. In this case the broad South African population did not want the integration of the Asian population. The plural society, which had been created, was to remain separated by the rule of law, which divided residential areas and work according to race.

South African Indians were encouraged by the Government of India to join hands with the black Africans in their struggle against white supremacy. The South African Indians had a politically sophisticated leadership who fought the apartheid system in the Gandhian tradition on behalf of the politically untutored masses. However the Government of India kept its struggle against apartheid separate from the South African Indians, offering them no direct support.

Colonial rule

British colonial rule allowed two streams of Indian settlers to enter South Africa: indentured labourers and the free passenger merchants. About half of them worked on sugar and tea plantations, whilst the others worked in coal-mines, private farms and railways.[82] They came from all walks of life and not only from the lower castes, in fact a number of them were impoverished landowners.[83] The caste system was imported from India although purity and endogamy could not be strictly adhered to. The social system soon evolved to include the class system of South Africa's competitive individual economy.[84] Emigration from India started with the abolition of slavery in 1833/34. The conditions for indentured labour were not very different from that of slavery. The Cape Colony Governor, Sir George Grey pressed for the introduction of Indian coolie labour to work on the sugar cane plantations in Natal. Serious immigration to South Africa began in 1866. According to the rules for the first five years the Indian labourer was under contract and was assigned to a particular employer, after those five years the Indian labourer could return home or find employment on the local labour market. The indentured workers were followed by free Indians who paid for their passage and sailed to South Africa to pursue occupations ranging from commerce to agriculture. At first the passenger Indians were treated in the same way as the Europeans with full voting rights, but they were disenfranchised in 1896.[85]

The complaints of the first returning Indians in 1871 started an official enquiry into the maintenance of the laws, which were to protect both employer and employee. The Government of India stopped all indentures to the colony and ordered an investigation. The Commission recommended the establishment of the Indian Immigration Trust Board to oversee the importation and repatriation of labour. In 1872 the Commission also recommended that new settlers be given land in stead of a return passage in order to develop the colony. As of 1874 emigration was resumed bringing in a total of 152,184 indentured immigrants (until 1911). Since the immigrant population preferred staying on to returning to India and rarely re-indentured themselves, the Government had to continually replace these Indian workers with new ones and the Indian population of South Africa grew steadily. In 1894 they came to exceed the white population (46,000 Indians vs. 45,000 whites).[86] But racial problems remained and in 1885-87 the Wragg Commission was set up to investigate further irregularities in labour relations.

From about 1890 onwards there was anti-Indian agitation. This was due to the exaggerated claims by the white population that the Indian population was increasingly serious competition on the free labour market and that they were buying up all the land along the coast. Following this political movement the Act of 1895 was passed decreeing that Indians had to return home after their period of indenture and if they decided to stay on without re-indenturing they had to pay an annual £3 tax for women and £4 for men. This penalty later described as a 'penalty upon residence' by Prof. Gokhale and was probably the most unpopular anti-Indian measure ever introduced in South Africa.[87] This resulted in many Indians having to re-indenture themselves in order to go back to India, as most could not afford the tax.

In 1894 the Franchise Law Amendment Bill decreed that all future Indian citizens in Natal would be removed from the voters roll. Gandhi fought the new law and created the Natal Indian Congress to champion the cause of the Indian community. Further discriminating bills were enforced to eliminate the Asian traders. Some states such as the Orange Free State did not allow the settlement of Indians at all on the base of their race. When the Anglo-Boer war broke out thousands of British subjects including Indians left the country. Upon their return further discrimination in the form of new registration awaited them. This aroused protests, which was quite unusual. With the advent of the Boer government led by Botha and Smuts the conflict between the Asian community led by Gandhi and the white population began in earnest. Protest was based on the Gandhian principle of non-violence. Amongst other issues, the Asian population protested against registration certificates, having their fingerprints taken and having to pay for their trade licences.[88]

Gandhi's role in the event remains controversial. The Smuts-Gandhi agreement was seen by some as a sell-out of the South African Indian to the white regime, which brought only temporary relief to the problems of the South African Indians. But Gandhi had stimulated a political awareness amongst the Indian population, he had made the government sensitive to the Indian desire for equal rights, he had raised his voice against injustice and once he left there was a leadership vacuum amongst Indians in South Africa.[89]

In effect the position of the Indians in South Africa deteriorated steadily: after losing the parliamentary franchise in 1896, they lost the municipal franchise in 1924, and later their rights to trade and property were curtailed in order to force them to return to India.[90] But it remains an important fact that the Indians in South Africa were the first non-white group to challenge the unjust legal structure and to challenge white domination.

Apartheid system

Pre-apartheid there had been the suggestion of political representation on a communal basis. In 1946 General Smuts arranged for two Europeans to represent Indian interests in the house of Assembly, and two members, who could be Indian would be elected to the Natal Provincial Council. This split the Indian population into a moderate and a radical camp of which the latter demanded equal rights for all citizens and formed an alliance with the communists and with the other black groups.[91] But in 1948 the National Party won the election and introduced the Apartheid system, repealing the 1946 legislation.

Apartheid meant the four groups inhabiting South Africa were to live separated by law and were under no circumstances to integrate. This included segregated areas for living and working. It also included separations on the busses and trains, in the factories and in the shops.

The Group Areas Act of 1950 allowed the state to further control all non-white citizens. The different races had to move to designated areas, several miles out of town and build new premises. The implementation of the new legislation almost ruined the merchant class mainly composed of Indians. Furthermore other government policies influencing Asian life, were the 'prohibition of Mixed Marriages Act', the 'Population Registration Act' and the 'Reservation of Separate Amenities Act'.[92]

This policy of divide and rule was initiated because of growing alarm at certain developments which included the 1952 Defiance Campaign where all oppressed people had joined in major action to fight the government. The two Indian Congresses had played a major role in the campaign.[93]

Despite all the discrimination the Indian population did rather well for themselves compared to the black population, gaining access to jobs in law and medicine, commerce and industry.[94] They also enjoyed relative prosperity, which marked the Indians out as objects of envy in comparison to the blacks.[95]

Citizenship and political representation

In 1961 the Government of South Africa finally recognised all Indians to be 'citizens of the newly created Republic of South Africa' and created a department of Indian Affairs to take care of all administration concerning the Indian population. Prior to that, the status of the South African Asians had not been very clear. Their recognition as citizens was based on the fact that the government of South Africa wanted to keep its racial policies a domestic and not an international issue. In 1968 the South African Indian Council created for the first time a channel of communication between the Indian population and the government.[96]

By the 1980s things were changing with regard to the Coloured and Indian population. The government introduced the vote for separate houses of parliament, but extra-parliamentary groups sympathising with the banned ANC emphasised that the main part of the population, namely the blacks were still excluded, and intimidated the general public in a way so as not to vote and to cooperage with the state.[97] The objective of the South African government was that the Indian community should run its own affairs and that it should be clear to all in South Africa and the rest of the world that Indian and Coloured communities apart from administering their own affairs had a direct say and participation in matters of mutual concern.[98] In 1981 more than 90% of the elections of the Indian Council were boycotted and in 1984 the first session of the Indian Parliament was not more successful.[99] All Indian political activity was based on two organisations: the Natal Indian Congress and the Transvaal anti SA Indian Council Committees. The former operated from the 1920s to the 1960s and became a member of the ANC-led Congress Alliance. The latter were internally progressive organisations formed in the 1970s and 1980s.[100] It was through these organisations that the Indian South African population contributed to the anti-apartheid struggle.

In February 1990 the African National Congress (ANC), the Pan Africanist Congress (PAC), the South African Communist Party (SACP) and other banned organisations were allowed back onto the political scene. With this and the release of Nelson Mandela the struggle for a non-apartheid democratic regime came to an end for both the African and the Indian population of South Africa.

India's reaction

The Government of India imposed economic and cultural sanctions on South Africa just after the Second World War. This was a severe blow to the local Indian population as it affected commerce and cultural and religious activities. The Indians living in the Diaspora had always maintained cultural and commercial ties with their regions of origin. These links were being severed totally by the actions of the Government of India who at first was protesting against the treatment of people of Indian origin, and later lobbying against the apartheid system as a whole. The local Indian population was expected to identify with the blacks and coloureds and their struggle against the dominating white minority and not rely on India for any kind of support for special treatment.

Post independence India was an ardent supporter of anti-imperialism. Racial discrimination was reminiscent of the colonial system the British had developed. As part of India's support to newly independent states and its anti-imperial foreign policy came the fight against the racially discriminatory system of South Africa. This fight was staged on two levels: bilaterally and in all possible international fora such as the United Nations and later the Commonwealth.

India's policy included a total break of diplomatic relations, including a blanket ban on Indian citizens visiting the Union of South Africa. Indian nationals were only allowed to travel to South Africa in the following cases:[101]

a) In emergency cases like the death or terminal sickness of an immediate relative.
b) If the request came from a relative in the Republic of South Africa and the African National Congress, the Transvaal Indian Congress or the Natal Indian Congress had verified the genuineness of the sponsorship certificate/invitation.
c) If they were invitees, meeting specific religious or cultural needs of bonafide community organisations of people of Indian origin in South Africa.
d) Indian nationals working in Lesotho and Swaziland were given endorsements for the purpose of medical treatment or transit. Indian nationals working in Botswana and Mozambique were allowed endorsements for emergency medical treatment only.

e) Media personnel were granted endorsement on a case by case basis to enable the media to play its role against apartheid.
f) Individuals or representatives of organisations specifically invited by the African National Congress and its affiliates were also permitted to visit South Africa.

This meant that there was an almost total isolation between the Indians in South Africa and the country of their origin. In fact in the eyes of the Government of India the 1 million people of Indian origin were South Africans and had to identify with the national anti-apartheid struggle led by the ANC. When questioned on the problems faced by the people of Indian origin in the republic the Minister of External Affairs Madhavsinh Solanki explained:

> The South African Indian Community has faced the same political, economic and social problems under apartheid as the other non-whites in South Africa. The Indian Government has consistently supported the anti-apartheid struggle. India was the first country to break off trade relations with South Africa in protest against its radical policies and was in the forefront of the campaign for the imposition of international sanctions against that country. We have also given considerable assistance to the African National Congress which we recognise as the representative of the oppressed majority in South Africa because of its multi racial character and its commitment to genuine non racial democracy.[102]

In Parliament the question of South Africa was rarely discussed and when there happened to be questions regarding the Indians living there and how they were treated, the standard answer was that the Government of India had no diplomatic relations with the country and that it was protesting against racial discrimination in South Africa at the UN.

The Ministry of External Affairs report rarely mentioned South Africa, except in cases when India had brought the topic of racial discrimination up at a conference, such as the Commonwealth Heads of Government Meeting at Nassau in October 1985. India in this case was able to achieve consensus among the Commonwealth members for a Programme of Common Action against Pretoria.[103]

At the level of the United Nations India led the struggle against South Africa and its regime of racial discrimination. As early as the 22 June 1946, India addressed a letter to the Secretary General of the UN requesting the inclusion of the question of the treatment of persons of Indian origin in the

Union of South Africa in the provisional agenda of the General Assembly. The General Assembly took note of India's application and stated that

> it is of the opinion that the treatment of Indians in the Union of South Africa should be in conformity with the international obligations under the agreement concluded between the two Governments and the relevant provisions of the Charter.[104]

In India's view South Africa was violating Articles 1(3), 13, 55, 56, 62 and 76 of the UN Charter, provisions relating to human rights.[105] India was also basing its involvement in the matter on the bilateral treaty signed in 1927 called the Cape Town Agreement, which inter alia, provided for the standards of treatment of persons of Indian origin by South Africa and 'obligated South Africa to the application of measures on them so as to aid their conformation to western standards of life.'[106] In South Africa's opinion the treatment of Indians and other races fell into its domestic jurisdiction and it invoked Article 2 (7) of the Charter for the protection of domestic matters.[107] As a result throughout the dispute the South African government refused any kind of negotiations with India, Pakistan, or any committee appointed by the UN to deal with this matter. It even refused to respond to any calls for negotiations coming from either India or Pakistan directly. India kept the issue of racial discrimination on the agenda, switching its concern from people of Indian origin to all races discriminated against by the government of South Africa.[108] The General Assembly of the United Nations disregarded the South African plea of domestic jurisdiction and consistently maintained its own right to discuss the substance of the dispute. It also maintained that South Africa should act in accordance with the purposes and principles of the charter.[109] Throughout the 1950s and 60s the General Assembly resolutions deplored the actions of South Africa and its not complying with the repeated demands of the General Assembly. One of the largest ever sanctions campaigns against one individual state began and South Africa's isolation became almost complete. Calls for the expulsion of South Africa resulted in the Republic being excluded from the annual conferences of the ILO and her withdrawal from the ILO, the UN Economic Commission for Africa and the WHO after being deprived of voting rights. In 1966 South Africa also threatened to leave the UN if her voting powers were curtailed or withdrawn.[110] India strongly supported the moves of the Security Council to expel South Africa from the UN.[111]

In the Commonwealth Prime Ministers' meetings the issue of racial discrimination in South Africa was not discussed until the late 1950s as the agenda required the agreement of all members.[112] The United Nations had become the real fighting ground for countries led first by India and then Pakistan, Ceylon, Ghana and others. The white Commonwealth nations such as Australia, New Zealand and Britain had at first supported South Africa's position in the UN, but that support waned in time. From the point of having coloured member nations in the Commonwealth there developed a concept of multi-racialism as part of the Commonwealth idea. India was particularly clear that remaining in the Commonwealth was based on member countries not adhering to any racially discriminatory practices. After South Africa became a republic the government applied to remain in the Commonwealth, but the approval was not given (although it was given to Ghana) since it was evident that the racial policy was not about to change.[113] Therefore South Africa ceased to be a member of the Commonwealth on 31 May 1961.

But India's insistence went further than the mere exclusion of South Africa. By threatening to boycott the Commonwealth Games in Edinburgh in 1986 the Government of India was supporting the African nations who were trying to force Britain to impose full sanctions on South Africa.[114] This was part of a movement trying to force sanctions on a Commonwealth level against South Africa.

After the dismantling of the apartheid the Indian minority in South Africa, who had not integrated with the black African majority felt left out of the new system. They remained a minority governed by the black majority under a system, which de facto discriminated against them. The government of India retained its ties with the new ANC led government, not supporting the grievances of the Indian minority, in the old Nehruvian tradition. Fears of a 'new Uganda' loomed high, as violence between the blacks and the Indians persisted.[115]

Indian press The Indian press dealt with the South African issue sparsely, although the government stand was reiterated and supported. India was being portrayed as the one country who led the struggle and who called on others to follow suit.[116] The failure of the UN to organise successful negotiations was reported, yet without much emotion.[117] It was also viewed with satisfaction that Pakistan joined India on requesting the reconsideration of the Question of the treatment of People of Indian origin at the UN in 1956.[118] The press also condemned the new deal of an Indian council, which it said could only be an interim arrangement until there was direct representation in parliament.[119] The press also deplored that the black majority was being left out and criticised any Indians who would accept to vote under such conditions.[120]

Despite some criticisms that India's attitude might have slackened vis-à-vis apartheid in the mid to late 1980s,[121] Eduardo Faleiro, the External Affairs Minister maintained in an interview by the Patriot that there would be no compromise on dismantling apartheid.[122]

Conclusion

The three cases described above illustrate clearly the Government of India's position between independence and the mid-1980s. While the Nehruvian policy of non-interference was strictly adhered to during the entire period, it is noticeable that there was a shift in public perception between the crisis in Uganda and the one in Fiji, almost fifteen years later. As time evolved, the Indian public became more aware of the Indian Diaspora abroad, not least because of the Diaspora's changing profile. The treatment and the lot of overseas Indians started to cause public concern as more and more Indians left either for the Middle East or the 'New World' in search for a better life. It is in this light that the differing reaction during the Fiji crisis has to be evaluated. Yet public concern did not alter the governmental position towards the Diaspora. In fact Rajiv Gandhi's campaign against Fiji was held on the same grounds as the mobilisation against apartheid in South Africa. The Prime Minister maintained that if India was fighting against racial discrimination in South Africa, it had the moral duty to do so in Fiji as well. In this way India's protests distanced themselves from speaking out for a section of the Indian Diaspora. A change in public polity was only going to be triggered by the economic crisis in 1991, which is analysed in the following chapter.

Endnotes

1 Mamdani, M., 'Class struggles in Uganda', p.1303
2 O'Brien, J., 'General Amin and the Ugandan Asians', p.94
3 Tinker, H., *The Banyan Tree*, p.151
4 Parson, J.D., 'Africanizing trade in Uganda: The Final Solution', p.59 footnote 3
5 *Speech by Idi Amin at the Commonwealth Heads of State and Government Meeting*, Ottawa, August 1973, p.2

6 Ibid., p.8
7 Tinker, H., *The Banyan Tree*, p.151
8 Parson, J.D., 'Africanizing Trade in Uganda: The Final Solution', p.61
9 Grover (ed.), *International Relations and Foreign Policy of India*, p.577
10 Tinker, H., *The Banyan Tree*, p.155
11 Jamal, V., 'Asians in Uganda 1880-1972: Inequality and expulsion', p.613
12 Tinker, H., *The Banyan Tree*, p.155
13 Jamal, V., 'Asians in Uganda 1880-1972', p.613
14 Ramchandani, R.R., 'The Economic Roots of Friction in Uganda', p.2303
15 Parson, J.D., 'Africanising Trade in Uganda: The Final Solution', p.62
16 Prunier, G., *L'Ouganda et la Question Indienne (1896-1972)*, p.161
17 Tandon, Y., 'The Future of the Asians in East Africa', p.6-7
18 For more detailed explanation of the citizenship question with regards to Britain and the colonies see chapter 4
19 The irony lies in the fact that the Asians were encouraged to take on British citizenship, and expected to lobby with the Africans against the British for the removal of the British colonial system. Later the Government of India maintained that exactly the same Asians were the responsibility of the British government…
20 Motwani, J.K., Gosine, M., Barot-Motwani, *Global Indian Diaspora: Yesterday, Today and Tomorrow*, p.124
21 Morris, H.S., *The Indians In Uganda*, p.106
22 Ibid., p.108
23 Ibid., p.121
24 Tandon, Y. and Rapael, A., 'The New Position of East African Asians', p.8
25 Gupta, A., 'Ugandan Asians, Britain, India and the Commonwealth', p.316
26 Ibid., p.317
27 Ibid., p.319
28 A similar debate had taken place earlier on concerning the fate of the Kenyan Asians in the Lok Sabha debate of the 16 March 1970, with reference to the closure of Indian businesses where again the same categories were used. In this particular case Sri Surendra Pal Singh defended India's non-interference with the view as not to harm the people of Indian origin
29 Press release, *Press Information Bureau Government of India*, 12 August 1972
See also *Lok Sabha Debate,* Q.468; 22.2.1973: 'The Government has been pressing the Government of Uganda for an early and equitable compensation for the assets left behind by Indian citizens. I regret to say that in spite of several such representations the government of Uganda apart from some general assurances against confiscation have not yet enunciated their policy in this regard.' (S. Pal Singh, Minister of State, MEA)
Compensation was finally administered in the form of a cheque of RS 1.44.88.792.60 ($1 627 114.60) given to the Deputy minister in the MEA B. P. Das for the compensation for property left behind by Indian nationals. This was to cover claims on buildings, plants, machinery, Ugandan government stocks, insurance policies, social security funds and blocked bank accounts, but not share holdings, salaries, refunds/dues from governments, baggage claims or the contents of safe deposit boxes. (*Lok Sabha Debates,* 29 January 1976)
30 *Lok Sabha Debates*, Statement Re: Asians in Uganda, 4.9.1972

31 According to Foreign and Commonwealth Office documents in the Public Records Office the 1968 deal between the Indian and the British government was based on the encounter between T.N.Kaul (Secretary, MEA) and the British Ambassador Mr Freeman on the 20.2.1968 whereby it is reported that 'Mr Kaul said there were between 5 and 10 million people of Indian Origin living abroad. The Indian Government could not encourage them to seek refuge in India. She did not maintain an open door, and in no circumstances would India accept large numbers of UK citizens because HMG sought to wash her hands of them. India might possibly give temporary shelter for those who felt impelled to leave East Africa and who were assured of entry into Britain after a short waiting period. But the Indian Government was not committed to this course.' (FCO 37/20, classified secret)

32 Kuepper, W., Lackey, L. and Swinerton, N., *Ugandan Asians in Great Britain*, p.40

33 *Lok Sabha Debates,* Q 763; 16.1.1972

34 Tandon, Y. and Rapael, A., 'The New Position of East African Asians', p.12

35 *Lok Sabha Debates*, Q 1693: 10.8.1972

36 *Lok Sabha Debates*, Q 2414: 8.3.1973

37 Gupta, A., 'Ugandan Asians. Britain, India and the Commonwealth', p.320

38 Amrita Bazar Patrika, 30.10.1972; Delhi Diary by A.N.Das See also 'Uganda Charge against India Ludicrous says Tanzania', Times of India, 29.9.1972; Silk, B., 'Warplot by India says Amin', Daily Telegraph, 27.9.1972

39 *Africa Diary*, New Delhi, 7-13 May 1973, p. 6467

40 Chabra, H.S., 'Asians in Uganda', p.15

41 Gathani, B., 'India's Image in East Africa', The Hindu, 30.9.1972

42 'Explanation sought from Ugandan government', Hindustan Times, 23.12.1972. See also Prem Bhatia, 'An unprecedented Accord', Tribune 19.12.75

43 Hindustan Times, 30.1.1976

44 Kuepper, W., Lackey, L. and Swinerton, N., *Ugandan Asians in Great Britain*, p.4

45 Quoted in Gupta, A., 'Ugandan Asians, Britain, India and the Commonwealth', p.321

46 Kuepper, W., Lackey, L. and Swinerton, N., *Ugandan Asians in Great Britain*, p.43

47 The Guardian, 19 August 1972
See also British Parliamentary Debates, 7.8.1992, Hansard, Vol.842, and 18.10.1972, Hansard, Vol.843

48 Daily Telegraph, 27.8.1972

49 Kuepper, W., Lackey, L. and Swinerton, N., *Ugandan Asians in Great Britain*, p.53-54

50 See footnote 31

51 Statesman, 2.12.1972

52 Ramchandani, R.R., *Uganda Asians The End Of An Enterprise*, p.283

53 India Today, 15.6.1987, p.102

54 Refers to the Fijian land owning aristocracy

55 See chapter 2 for details on the origins of racial problems in Fiji during the colonial period

56 Premdas, R., 'Military Intervention in Fiji: Fear of Ethnic Domination', p.118

57 Ibid., p.124

58 Ibid., p.125

59 Murray, D. in Ashworth, G. (ed.), *World Minorities in the Eighties*, p.42

60 Naidu, G.V.C., 'Crisis in Fiji' p.1106

61 Regional Security Developments in the South Pacific, p.5-10
62 The Hindu, 22. 5.1987
63 The Patriot, 27.5.1987
64 The Statesman, 5.6.1987
65 *Lok Sabha Debates*, 7.8.1987
66 The Indian Express, 30.9.1987
67 Regional Security Developments in the South Pacific, p.7
68 The Patriot, 3.12.1987
69 *Lok Sabha Debates*, Q.509, 9.8.1990
70 *Rajya Sabha Debates*, Q.1700, 22.8.1990
71 *Rajya Sabha Debates*, Q.38, Budget Session 1990
72 *MEA Annual Report 1990-91*, p.18
73 The Indian Express, 28.9.1987
74 The Hindustan Times, 29.9.1987
75 The Patriot, 30.9.1987
76 The Times of India, 21.10.1987
77 The Times of India, 21.11.1987
78 The Tribune, 9.12.1987
79 Kuper, H., *Indian People In Natal*, p.xii
80 Henning, C.G., 'The Indian South African (1860-1989)', in Motwani, J.K., *Global Indian Diaspora*, p.61
81 See chapter 4;
82 Gregory, R.G., *India and East Africa*, p.126
83 Henning, C.G., 'The Indian South African (1860-1989)', in Motwani, J.K., *Global Indian Diaspora*, p.65
84 Kuper, H., *Indian People In Natal*, p. xix
85 Ibid., p.46
86 Henning, C.G., 'The Indian South African (1860-1989)', in Motwani, J.K., *Global Indian Diaspora*, p.66
87 Ibid., p.68
88 Ibid., p.79
89 Ibid., p.84
90 Kuper, H., *Indian People In Natal*, p.48
91 Henning, C.G., 'The Indian South African (1860-1989)' in Motwani, J.K., *Global Indian Diaspora*, p.87
92 Ibid., p.89
93 Hiremath, J.R., 'Indian South Africans A Contemporary Portrait', p.37
94 Henning, C.G., 'The Indian South African (1860-1989)' in Motwani, J.K., *Global Indian Diaspora*, p.85
95 Hiremath, J.R., 'Indian South Africans A Contemporary Portrait', p.39
96 Henning, C.G., 'The Indian South African (1860-1989)' in Motwani, J.K., *Global Indian Diaspora*, p.91
97 Ibid., p.91
98 'Plans for South African Indian Council', The Statesman, 17.2.1975
99 Dumay, C., 'La Communaute Indienne s'inquiete', Le Figaro, 26.12.1993
100 Davies, R., O'Meara, D. and Dlamini, S., *The Struggle for South Africa*

101 *Lok Sabha Debates*, Q1247; 1.8.1991
102 *Lok Sabha Debates*, Q581; 27.2.1992
103 *MEA Annual Report* 1985-86, p.25
104 *Resolution adopted on the report of the joint first and sixths committee*, 'Treatment of Indians in the Union of South Africa', Fifty second plenary meeting, UN, 8.12.1945
105 Raj, G.B.V., *India and Disputes in the United Nations 1946-54*, p.137
106 Ibid., p.147
107 Ibid., p.138
108 In 1952 a separate motion about the rights of the nine million native Africans was submitted (Millar T.B., *The Commonwealth and the United Nations*, p.143). In 1962 there was a change of title of the item in the General Assembly of the UN to 'the politics of Apartheid of the Government of the Republic of South Africa'. This was to include both items of race conflict and treatment of people of Indo-Pakistan origin in the Republic of South Africa
109 Raj G.B.V., *India and Disputes in the United Nations 1946-54*, p.185
110 Millar, T.B., *The Commonwealth and the United Nations*, p.167
111 'India backs move to expel South Africa', Times of India, 27.10.1974 and 'India to work for Pretoria's exit from the UN', Hindustan Times, 22.11.1974
112 Millar T.B., *The Commonwealth and the United Nations*, p.159
113 Ibid., p.161
114 'India now set to pull squad out of Games', The Times, 15.7.1986
115 McDonald, H., 'Minority Blues', Far Eastern Economic Review, 6.2.1992
116 'Racial Persecution in South Africa', The Hindu,4.4.1955
117 'Failure of attempt at negotiations', The Statesman, 28.10.1955
118 'Pakistan Joins India in request to the UN', The Statesman, 15.9.1956
119 'New Deal in Cape Town', Motherland, 20.2.1975
120 Hornsby, M., 'Privileges denied to blacks create divided loyalties', The Times, 23.7.1984
121 'Against Apartheid', News Time, 22.8.1987
122 'No Compromise on Dismantling of Apartheid: Faleiro', The Patriot, 8.1.1987

6 India and the NRIs

Introduction

As seen in chapter 4, India had developed a particular attitude towards Foreign Policy in general and NRIs in particular. Though the Nehruvian doctrine made sense at the time of conception, it failed to provide scope for evolution. As the world developed, changing from a bipolar to a multi-polar place, from a political to an economic focus, India's position proved to be obsolete and obstructed its economic development.

The NRI community itself was changing its profile. During the 1960s and 1970s a further labour exodus took place, this time to the Middle East and Gulf countries such as UAE and Kuwait, but also to Saudi Arabia, Oman and Iraq. Unskilled, semiskilled and skilled labour left in hordes for a promised land where there was a shortage of labour. The salaries promised to be higher than back home and would allow for substantial savings. These emigrants differed from previous expatriate Indians in one fundamental way: their expatriation was to be temporary, as none of the Middle East countries wanted to keep them for good. Still, this system allowed for several years of work and a better life at the end of it back home.

But there was still permanent emigration taking place. The 'brain drain', as it became known commonly, was a phenomenon where young doctors, scientists, lawyers and computer specialists left India for the US, Canada or Australia to have a better life. Often this expatriation started with a further degree in their field of specialisation, which then led them to stay on; for others times it was simply to take a post abroad. There again the gain was phenomenal: huge salaries, good education and health care for the families and after a few years possibly the passport of the chosen place.

All these 'new' categories of NRIs made substantial money and maintained informal family ties with their mother country. Throughout its economic development in the 1970s and 1980s India tried to make some room for the remittances coming from the Gulf, but failed to open up the economy for any serious NRI investment which went beyond the family/state border. It is also interesting to note that the government did not keep separate records for NRI remittances from the Gulf or elsewhere and most statistics were rough approximations. The government's economic difficulties was so great that in the late 1980s the 'hot money' coming from the Gulf was being withdrawn, leaving India with a foreign exchange crisis without precedence. In short the world had changed, the NRIs had expanded to include new communities, and India which remained in its obsolete position.

This chapter sets out to explain the changing global situation and the resulting need for India to change. After describing India's pre 1991 position on remittances and hot money from the Gulf the chapter goes on to describe India's obsolete position and policies in light of the post cold war situation. It further tries to establish that given the New World Order based on economic relations India had no choice but to open up its economy. What exactly those changes were, and how they involved and affected the NRIs and their relationship with India is described in the latter part of the chapter. It concludes with the dilemma that the political rhetoric did not lead to substantial economic action especially where the NRIs were concerned and that India's relationship with the Diaspora remained as convoluted as ever.

India and the NRIs - The Early Years

The government's first moves towards NRI involvement

The early 1970s saw the further export of Indian labour; this time it came in two forms: the temporary expatriation of non-skilled, medium-skilled and skilled labourers to the Middle East, especially the Gulf countries, and the permanent emigration of Indian scientists and technologists to the US, Canada, Australia and Great Britain. They again left India for economic reasons, seeking better opportunities elsewhere.

The Gulf labourers

By 1977 India had become the third largest labour exporter to the Gulf. It increased continuously, from 4 200 in 1976 to 224 000 in 1981 and only slowed down thereafter because of falling oil revenues in the host countries.[1] Yet the remittances that this export of labour brought about were mainly used for consumption and could not as such be considered an investment into India. In fact the remittances created a different 'class' in society where labourer's families could afford certain consumption goods others could not. It also widened the gulf between the regions, as states such as Kerala and Punjab felt the impact of the nouveau riche migrants in their local economy.

Table 6.1: Annual outflow of emigrant workers in the Middle East from India 1976-87

Year	Number of Persons (In Thousands)	
1976	4.2	
1977	22.9	
1978	69.0	
1979	171.8	
1980	268.2	
1981	272.0	
1982	224.0	(93.6)
1983	217.9	(96.9)
1984	198.5	(96.4)
1985	160.3	(98.4)
1986	109.2	(96.1)
1987	121.8	(97.2)

Source: Stock of Indian Immigrants in Gulf Countries, December 1990.

Note: numbers in parenthesis give percentage of emigrants to the Middle East

The Gulf-workers were different from other Indian migrants, as they remained the responsibility of the Government of India. Throughout the 1970s, 1980s and 1990s Indian MPs raised questions about the welfare of the Indian citizens expatriated in that region. For example George Fernandes in September 1991 asked if the Government of India had received complaints of maltreatment of Indian workers in the Gulf countries and what the Government of India was going to do about it. Answers throughout this period were similar to this one:

> Yes, these complaints pertain to charges of contracts and harassment The complaints are first sought to be resolved through the intervention by the Indian Embassy between employer and employee; approaching local labour Courts for redression (sic), failing that the matter is taken up with the local government.[2]

India did get involved when the governments of the UAE and Kuwait announced in 1980 that workers whose permits had expired would be forcibly expatriated, by dispatching an official delegate to persuade the two governments to slow down deportations so as not to strain Kerala's economy.[3] India also arranged for labour agreements to be signed, first with Qatar (1985) and then Bahrain to safeguard the interests of Indian nationals within the parameters of Indian and local labour laws.[4] The government passed a new Emigration Act in 1983 which provides for a compulsory registration of recruitment agents who have to obtain a permit so as to avoid their exploitation of the departing work-force.

During the Gulf War the Indian Government evacuated 1.5 lakh[5] Indians from Kuwait and Iraq following the Iraqi occupation of Kuwait on the 2.8.1990, the work being co-ordinated by the special Co-ordination Unit and the Overseas Indians division.[6] The annual remittances from the region before the war were estimated to have been Rs 3,500 crores.[7] India intensified its bilateral contacts with Kuwait through co-operation agreements and a Memorandum of Understanding to enable the return of 109 000 Indians to Kuwait by November 1992. India also continued her efforts to gain compensation for Indian citizens and Commercial establishments which suffered losses as a result of the Gulf war.[8]

The brain drain

In the early seventies the Indian government became concerned with press reports about the 'brain drain' phenomenon. 'Only 6000 scientists were registered with the government as working abroad, but a 'national Register' of Indians abroad was drawn up which totalled 16,000 - 40% of which were scientists.'[9] A scheme was formulated to attract some of them back to India by allowing them to keep their savings in foreign bank accounts for three years during which time they could also decide to stay or leave. The brain drain remained a problem throughout much of the 1980s and the 1990s. In

1992 the Minister of State in the Ministry of Personnel, Public Grievances and Pensions, Srimati M.Alva enumerated the following list of points which had been developed and undertaken since the 1970s to attract Indian scientists and technologists back:

- Provision for temporary placement of scientists and technologists under the scheme of scientist's pool;
- Provision to create supernumerary posts;
- Facilities to import equipment for returning scientists;
- Special Cell created by the Ministry of Industry to assist NRIs to secure expeditious clearance;
- Programmes launched to pursue research in new and frontier areas of science;
- Delegation of enhanced administrative and financial powers have been made to scientific institutions to improve working conditions of scientists;
- Distinguished professionals of Indian origin are being invited for short-term technical assignments to assist in our developmental efforts in frontier and emerging areas of science and technology.[10]

In 1991 an article in the Patriot estimated that more than 500,000 skilled Indians would be lost to India by the end of the century, that Indian talent worth Rs. 20,000 crores was already abroad and that 8000 trained and qualified young men and women were leaving the country every year.[11]

The role of remittances and hot money

The government facilitated the banking system for the repatriation of foreign exchange in order to help the balance of payments deficit. In fact India's foreign exchange balance was only kept out of the red through these remittances. Later on in the 1980s high interest rates were offered for foreign exchange deposits in order to attract the savings of other NRIs based abroad. The high exchange rates were seen as preferable to possible IMF and World Bank dictates. Yet since these deposits were mostly on a repatriable basis they were nothing more than 'hot money' which could leave the country the instant the economy turned bad or better terms were offered elsewhere.

The main facilities available to NRIs in the late 1970s and early 1980s are summarised below:[12]

1. The Non Resident (external) accounts designated in Indian Rupees (NRE); the advantages of which were the exemption of income and wealth tax, and the freedom to repatriate the balance and the interest.
2. The Non Resident (external) accounts designated in Foreign Currencies (FCNR); the advantages of which were the cover against the risk of any loss arising from fluctuations in exchange rates of currencies and the interest being free of income tax.
3. The ordinary Non Resident account, the balance of which if kept under 50,000 Rs. could be used in India freely without the prior permission of any authority.
4. NRIs could also freely purchase units of the Unit Trust of India, Indian Government securities and National Plan Saving Certificates. If these investments were made by remittances from abroad there are no restrictions for repatriation.
5. Investment in industry on giving an undertaking to the RBI that no repatriation will be sought.
6. Investment in equity issues of the new companies in a wide range of selected industry to an upper limit of 40%.
7. Investment in Priority/Export Oriented Industries up to 74 per cent

The bank deposits were the prime targets for investment as any investment in Industry either prohibited repatriation or made it very difficult. India had in effect 'tapped' some of the revenues coming from the NRIs, yet almost exclusively from those who were temporary expatriates and had remained Indian citizens. In fact the Indian economy had to a certain degree become dependent on 'Hot Money'. Over the years the NRI deposits had come to account for a very high proportion of India's foreign debt (around one-seventh) and they represented a particularly expensive form of borrowing, since their interest rates were on average two percentage points higher than the London bank offered rate. They were volatile and subject to 'panic withdrawals'.[13]

The whole endeavour was quite inefficient and one can certainly not claim that India was looking actively for its Diaspora's participation in the development of its economy. In the early 1990s things started going badly wrong for India. The Gulf war brought about a severe drop in remittances, the Indian workers in the region were fleeing the region. Besides, the end of the Cold War brought about severe global political changes. Both the political and the economic changes of the early 1990s affecting India will be analysed in the course of this chapter. They will also demonstrate why India had to come out of its 45-year pseudo-isolation.

1991 and the Changed Environment

The post Cold war situation

A shift in domestic policy was largely overdue because of the global changes of the early 1990s. With the fall of the Berlin Wall and the subsequent demise of the Soviet Union the only alternative economic model to the capitalist market system had been removed. Economically it disrupted the 'barter system' India had with the Soviet Union, which had allowed for international trade without expending foreign currency. It also resulted in the diversion of Western Aid to the former Communist block, especially Eastern Europe for fear that their collapse might trigger off mass migration to Western Europe.[14]

The collapse of the Soviet Empire had further political and ideological consequences: the traditional Indian stand of non-alignment in international affairs became obsolete. Since there were now no clear-cut blocks of opposing economic and political systems, it made little sense to stand apart as a third group. In fact the world had broken up into a multitude of facets where trade blocs of different sorts were emerging as the dominant grouping. Regionalism determined what bloc one was a part of and South Asia was left high and dry with its regional problems whilst others co-operated to further economic welfare and relations.

Clearly India's moralistic stand on anti-imperialism and other non-economic issues were outdated. These were still issues within the realm of the United Nations, but not within the international fora of economic realpolitik. Most of India's foreign policy relations which went beyond the region, were based on these ideological, moralistic ties. This was clearly depicted in chapter 3. In fact India did not have much of an international economic policy at all since economic nationalism and independence had been on the agenda since 1947.[15] Now that economic and trade relations were taking precedence over ideological ties India had to find a place in a trade group of sorts and consequently had to rethink its international and regional foreign policy.

Over the years India's position in the region had also changed: As seen in chapter 3 India moved slowly from a global, ideological oriented policy towards a more realist regional policy under Indira Gandhi's leadership. India had always been seen as some kind of a hegemon in the region, being territorially the largest country, and militarily the strongest. International relations within the subcontinent have been filled with strife: wars and civil wars, India's regional intervention in Sri Lanka and the insurgency in Kashmir have made the region look unsafe to outside investors. Compared to India the South East Asian region and China who were politically more stable, looked (until recently) far more favourable for investment and funds have been flowing to that region to the detriment of India and the rest of the Subcontinent. The regional animosity has not only led outside investors to view India with suspicion but has also hampered regional trade. India's regional priority was to monitor any instability in neighbouring countries for fear that it might spill over and cause internal disruption; its priority was not to create a trade block to rival China or South East Asia, which would arguably have given it a global place again on the international scene.

In fact regional trade limits itself to SAARC, the South Asian Association for Regional Co-operation comprising India, Pakistan, Bangladesh, Sri Lanka, Nepal, and the Maldives. The World Development report of 1994 defined all the countries in the region as low-income countries.[16] Although the region had over 21 per cent of the total world population, its share of world GDP was less than 2 per cent. Its share of world exports was a marginal 0.90 per cent and of world imports an equally insignificant 1.01 per cent. Analysis of the documentation also shows that while Bangladesh got about 12 per cent of its imports from SAARC and Nepal about 18 per cent, 'the other countries in the region are marginally dependent on each other with regards to imports. Both India and Pakistan get over 50 per cent of their imports from industrial countries while most of the other SAARC countries get about one third of their imports from the developed world.' Exports to SAARC countries as a percentage of exports to the world have been less than 5 per cent for all countries except the Maldives and Nepal.[17] As a result one can conclude that inter-regional trade was of little importance.

Globally India became isolated. This was primarily due to the fact that India had not changed with the times and adapted to a new set of global circumstances.

Yet there were internal changes; it is surprising to note the difference between the reaction to the Fijian crisis in 1986 and the one in Uganda in 1972. Between independence and the mid 1980s one can safely say that ideology prevailed as regards NRIs and that the overseas Indians did not even figure in the minds of the Indian population or on the government's agenda. With Rajiv Gandhi in power 'NRI' became a buzzword and the consciousness of 'another India' abroad started to grip the Indian mind. As will be explained later the basic prejudices against expatriation remained, but at least India took note of its co-Indians abroad. The Fiji crisis exemplified this by bringing in copious press reports on discrimination towards the Indians there and on alerting the Indian government of its responsibilities. The fact that the Indian government did not change its stand concerning overseas Indians not being their responsibility does not diminish the fact that there was a debate going on in the country.

The new economic situation

> For most of the five decades since independence, India has pursued an economic policy of subsidising unproductivity, regulating stagnation, and distributing poverty. We called this socialism. The moment of truth about Indian economic policy - the moment when even its guardians had to accept the old ways had not worked and could be sustained no longer- came in early 1991 when a large part of the nation's gold reserves had to be flown out to London as collateral for a $2.2 billion emergency IMF loan. Without the loan, India would have had to default on its international debt, and the economy would, for all practical purposes, have collapsed. (....) One cannot imagine a greater psychological shock to the average Indian. We have, for millennia, placed our trust in gold as the ultimate security. In the Indian culture, the woman of the house- the embodiment of the family's honour- treasures her gold jewellery both as her soundest asset and as the symbol of her status. The notion that the country was, in effect, pawning its collective jewellery abroad in order to keep paying the rent sent shock waves through the polity.[18]

Besides the global political changes described in the first part of this chapter India's economic system was on the verge of collapsing in early 1991.[19] India had only a billion dollars foreign exchange reserves, which would cover only two weeks of imports. The Gulf war had increased India's oil bills, and deprived her by extension of the remittances from the Indian Gulf-workers who were fleeing the region. The remittances balance laid in front of the Lok Sabha on 19 July 1991, are detailed in Table 6.2:

Table 6.2: The remittances balance laid in front of the Lok Sabha on 19 July 1991

Period	NR (E) Rs crore	NR (E) Rs crore
1988-89 (actuals)	235	2230
1989-90 (Prov. Est.)	4	2179
1990-91 (Prov.)	146	255

The Minister of State in the Ministry of Finance R.Thakur commented: 'Available data shows that there was noticeable fall in inward remittances and perceptible net outflow under NR (E) and FCNR schemes in April-May 1991. The strain on the Balance of Payments was aggravated by the Gulf crisis and this resulted in a sharp drain on the foreign exchange reserves.'[20]

Under normal circumstances such an external shock would not have toppled the country's economy, yet India's economy was extremely weak. India's inflation was at 12 per cent and rising, it had a large public and current account deficit (10 per cent and 3 per cent of the GDP respectively) and heavy foreign and domestic debts. As a result India's credit rating went down and there was a cut-off of private foreign lending.[21] The shortage in foreign exchange had forced a massive import squeeze, which halted industrial growth and produced negative growth rates from May 1991 onwards.[22] Patel sees the origin of the crisis in the age old policies of keeping subsides high in order to placate the voters, financial excesses in the defence sector and in public salaries and perks, and the fact that India relied too much on short term borrowing.[23] Joshi and Little see the roots of India's economic crisis in unsound macroeconomic policies: in the previous oil shock of 1979-81 when the world oil prices doubled, India's account position was changed from a near balance (1979) to a deficit of 2 per cent of the GDP (1981). No current account adjustment followed for the rest of the decade. Besides, the current account deficits persisted due to the stagnation of exports (1982-85), due again to a largely inappropriate exchange rate policy, which in turn was responsible for the heavy accumulation of foreign debt.

India's economic policy had primarily been based on industrial self-sufficiency with a dominant public sector. The reason of a dominant public sector was based on Nehru's conviction that the disinterested 'hands of the state' would take care of the Indian population rather than Indians or foreigners with the intent of making any sort of profit. Tharoor describes the system as a 'compound of nationalism and idealism'[24] It can be argued that Nehru believed he could establish a command economy embedded in a westernised and liberal democratic system.[25]

The Hindu rate of growth The design of economic development, which had been adopted in the 1950s, enshrined a pattern of low growth at around 3.5 per cent for the first three decades after independence. (1950s-1980s) This was not caused by low savings as had been feared in the 1950s but in bad productivity performance, which did not concern the planners.

> Their model ignored matters of efficiency and focused purely on allocative choices: capital investment was directed towards industries protected from competition. (....) The result was a 'control-infested system' that smothered private initiative and encouraged the proliferation of inefficiencies and corruption within both the state controlled economy and the political system as a whole.[26]

In fact Kilnani holds that India's economic destiny and failure was shaped by the belief that the problems and solutions of India's slow rate of growth lay within economic theory; that the 'power of ideas' and an appropriate policy framework were enough to 'produce the economic magic Nehru had wished for'.[27]

Instead this system based on the public sector and controls had led to an economy where industries were kept alive despite low productivity and high losses to prevent job losses, poverty and the resulting political fallout. It cultivated an atmosphere where the corporate houses of the Birlas, Tatas and Kirloskars were being held back by restrictions and regulations because of the mistrusted concept of profit and where any kind of expansion or diversification extensive permits and licenses were required.[28] Bank nationalisation guaranteed the state an easy source of money where the credentials for a loan was not based on efficiency, but priority allocations.

As a result of what the economist Raja Krishna had called the Hindu rate of growth, exports of manufactured goods grew at a rate of 0.1 per cent until 1985 and India's share of world trade fell by 80 per cent after independence. By contrast, India's public sector became the largest outside the Communist bloc. Years of Nehru's socialist pattern of society with its economic nationalism at the base of the structure, though noble in intention, had led to India's biggest economic crisis ever and it required comprehensive reforms to remedy the damage.

Politically the government could do little to stem the crisis. Having come into power in December 1989 the V.P.Singh government fell in November 1990, leaving its place to the minority government of Chandrashekhar, which in turn resigned in March after not presenting the expected budget in February. The summer 1991 elections brought Narasimha Rao's Congress government into power, largely on the back of Rajiv Gandhi's assassination. The unstable political scene contributed to the economic collapse and laid the foundation for a new system, which would disown economic nationalism and favour the opening of the Indian economy. India had in effect to integrate itself into the New World Order where its leitmotiv was terribly outdated. In the words of Finance Minister Dr Manmohan Singh:

> Self-reliance in today's world of integrated global markets cannot be achieved merely by reducing import dependence and insulating the economy from the world. Following that path will only lead to more import controls and promote inefficiency and corruption. It will perpetuate an environment in which the Indian entrepreneurs will not have the flexibility they need to compete with other developing countries in world markets. The resulting inability to export will actually make us more, rather than less dependent on the outside world. Our vision of a self-reliant economy has to be of an economy which can meet all its import requirements through exports, without undue dependence on artificial external props such as foreign aid.[29]

The Need for Change and the Resulting Policies

The new policies

The new government led by Prime Minister P.V.Narasimha Rao and his finance minister, the economist Dr Manmohan Singh, embarked on immediate and extensive reforms. The government's first priority was to stop the slide and restore India's credibility both domestically and internationally: to achieve this, immediate measures to avert defaulting international obligations and restore macro economic balance had to be taken. The medium term objective was to place the economy back on the path of high and sustained growth.[30]

External capital was now allowed into 34 major areas from which foreign capital had previously been excluded. In fact foreign investors could acquire majority share holdings in some Indian companies. The private sector was let into some areas which had previously remained reserved for the public sector, such as road building and aviation; tariffs were slashed (from 300 per cent in 1991 to 50 per cent by 1995) and the rupee was made convertible on the trade account.[31] The government risked two devaluations of the rupee so that India would integrate more easily into the world economy. When questioned in Parliament as to the impact of the devaluation of the rupee vis-à-vis India's balance of payment's position, its foreign currency debt and NRI inflow, the Minister of State in the Ministry of Finance R.Thakur stated that:

> The adjustments effected by the RBI in the external value of the rupee on the 1 and 3rd July 1991 would stabilise the balance of payments situation in the short term and improve the balance of trade situation in the medium term. (...) These adjustments will increase the profitability of our exports, discourage non-essential imports, discourage illegal capital flight abroad and the resulting improvement in our balance of payments will restore the confidence of the NRIs in the Indian economy and encourage the inflow of foreign exchange from NRI sources.[32]

Part and parcel of the reforms was the reduction of bureaucratic processes which had taken so much time for any investment to be approved.

With the reforms, India saved itself from defaulting on its international debt and slowly the open economy started to attract capital investments. The areas into which foreign capital was welcomed broadened over the years to include telecommunications, power and oil exploration. With the sign that India's economy had opened up, further foreign exchange rolled in and the foreign exchange reserves rose to $20 billion in the first few years.

Already in his 1992-93 Budget speech Dr Manmohan Singh could state that the government had achieved its most immediate objective of restoring India's credibility and pulling the economy back from the slide into financial chaos.[33]

The NRI option

There were special concessions for the NRIs to invest their wealth into Indian industry, set up new industrial ventures or simply deposit foreign currency in Indian bank accounts. The initiatives undertaken between July

1991 and April 1992 are well summarised in the parliamentary press report of the 30 April 1992:

1. NRI investment in real estate development: in the areas of development of property, construction of houses, financing of housing development and infrastructure areas such as construction of roads and bridges, up to 100 per cent investment can be made on non-repatriation basis.
2. 100 per cent investment is now allowed in 34 high priority industries including small-scale industries and other industries excepting those reserved for public sector subject to fulfilment of export criteria.
3. The maximum limit for portfolio investment increased from 5 per cent to 24 per cent.
4. Approval of investment and technical collaboration allowed on automatic basis - no need to come to government as clearance is given by RBI.
5. Investment in India Development Bonds to NRIs and investment in Dollars and Pound Sterling in Bonds, which carry 9.5 per cent rate of interest in the case of Dollar, denominated bonds and 13.25 per cent in the case of Pound Sterling bonds. The bonds mature after a period of 5 years and can be gifted to resident Indians. Certain immunities and tax exemptions are available which have made these bonds very popular and the $ denominated bonds have fetched US$1292 million and the Pound Sterling have fetched 180 million. The bonds closed on 31.1.92.
6. Amendment of section 31 of FERA: The RBI have granted general permission under section 31(1) of FERA, 1973 to foreign citizens of Indian Origin to acquire, hold, transfer or dispose of any property in India without having to seek approval of the RBI or Government. Payment for such properties has to be made in foreign exchange remitted through outside India or through purchaser's NRF/ FCNR accounts.
7. Establishment of Chief Commissioner for NRIs: As announced by the finance minister in his Budget speech a post of Chief Commissioner (NRI) has been created and steps are being taken to fill up the post. His office will serve as a focal point for interaction with NRIs and Government Departments, including State Governments.
8. NRIs (whether Indian or foreign citizens) who return to India, either for employment or business, would be granted exemption under various provisions of FERA, from declaring their foreign currency accounts and other forms of foreign currency assets to the RBI provided they

have stayed abroad for at least a minimum of two years and continue to retain professional/business interests abroad.

9. NRIs returning to India for good would be allowed to maintain and operate foreign currency denominated accounts with banks in India without any limit on balance in such accounts, in lieu of the existing Returning Indians Foreign Exchange Entitlement (RIFEE) Scheme.
10. Returning Indians have also been allowed to bring in five kg. of gold by payment of a nominal customs duty in foreign exchange provided they stayed abroad for at least six months.

The above mentioned points show that a great deal of bureaucracy remained in the system and that although this was a step in the right direction, investment procedures had not really been simplified. For NRIs who would have wanted to bring in their savings and invest in industry or buy property, the fact that non-repatriation was still the norm on many investments served as a disincentive.

Besides the incentives listed above the Finance Minister's Budget speech for 1991-92 also proposed that up to 30 November 1991, remittances in foreign exchange could be made to any person in India without disclosing the source, and that if it is gifted it would be free from gift tax, and would not be subject to scrutiny under the Exchange Control and Income Tax Act.[34] This is a typical example of the short term thinking of the government at the time, hoping first of all to get out of the crisis and only then to consider more significant reforms.

Later in 1991 the Reserve Bank announced yet another scheme: the Non Resident (non-repatriable) rupee deposit scheme, where deposits could be opened 'from 6 months to 3 years with authorised dealers out of funds remitted from abroad in free convertible currency through normal banking channel or by payment through existing FCNR/NRE account of the depositor. (...) Income from the deposit will be free from Indian income tax, as also from gift tax for one-time gifting in case of NRIs only.'(...) Both this scheme and the India development bonds scheme brought in US$2.46 billion, as stated in a report dated 5.3.1992.[35]

Furthermore the Foreign Currency (Non Resident) Account scheme was further liberalised by increasing the loan which may be granted from 5 to 10 lakh rupees for the purposes of making direct investment on non-repatriation basis without clearance from the RBI, and by allowing such loans to be repaid in Rupees from the Non Resident Ordinary Account.[36]

It is interesting to note that pre-liberalisation, when the Indian government was working out ways of solving its balance of payments problems, it was, of course, the opposition who most loudly advocated the return of the NRI and the opening of the Indian economy exclusively to the NRIs. They were hailed as the potential saviour of their mother country with their incredible wealth and naturally they owed it to their country of origin: 'BJP leader L.K.Advani said that his party would strive to mobilise enormous resources of Indians abroad to extricate the country from the financial crisis. (...) Mr. Advani maintained that the new Government has to tap the NRIs deposit potential of $70 to 80 billion to repay the country's foreign debt which did not exceed $65 billion.'[37] The opposition saw this as a direct alternative to the reforms and to the IMF loan. 'There is possibly a feeling that instead of going to the IMF and succumb to their conditionalities it would be more prudent to go to the NRIs. All that we need is a mere $5 billion or so and the NRIs, it has been estimated, have more than $20 billion stacked up in banks abroad. A fourth of that should be no problem.'[38] Yet the Government in power held the view that patriotism was possibly the smallest incentive to the NRIs and that in order to attract their funds India had to put its house in order: 'Messieurs Basu and L.K.Advani may be under the illusion that NRIs will send thousands of crores to India out of sheer patriotism, no matter how badly we mismanage our economy and thus threaten our ability to repay the NRI deposits.'[39] In fact there was a feeling that investments in the form of projects were needed rather than more bank deposits which could leave the country at a moment's notice. As put in the following article, further NRI bank deposits were nothing more than a different form of debts: 'In these days of financial crisis, I find that people cannot stop looking towards NRIs for salvation. One proposal after another is made to bribe NRIs into depositing more money with us. (...) This means that NRIs can suddenly withdraw thousands of crores overnight, plunging India into default.'[40]

So the reform process started: after the rupee devaluation and after it had later been made partially convertible, the projected deficit was slashed and some of the regulations which made corruption inevitable and innovation difficult were slashed. A start was also made in welcoming foreign co-operation and joint ventures. But were these reforms enough? According to some the process was somewhat 'half full- half empty'. The Far Eastern Economic Review reviewed what was still needed in the early 1990s:[41]

- $115-130 billion in infrastructure improvements by 2002;
- Slash red tape; expand automatic business approvals;
- Devote more money to primary education;
- Open insurance sector to foreign investment and increase autonomy of state banks;
- Cut consolidated government deficit to 4 per cent of GDP from 6.8 per cent;
- End subsidies on fertiliser, irrigation, and oil products;
- Establish exit policy allowing state companies to privatise and make it easier for private firms to close;
- Make the rupee fully convertible;
- Slash tariffs further, end import controls on consumer durables.

The next part of the chapter will look at the question of political will and in how far India was ready to complete the reforms described above.

What Changes?

'After the initial burst of reforms, the absence of any overall economic design or strategy, and consequent inability to explain the logic of government actions to the citizenry became uncomfortably clear.'[42] The government was caught trying to pacify as many demands as possible, without any clear goal in sight, and this remained the case throughout the 1990s as coalition government after coalition government (first two United front governments, then the BJP coalition) struggled with the economic condition of India. It seems as if the discourse of liberalisation had simply replaced the discourse on planning in the political fora. It remained a debate of good versus bad, without any clear direction and as a result the implementation in general and with respect to the NRIs in particular severely lagged behind the rhetoric.

The debate

The argument that 'national economic sovereignty' was threatened by liberalisations that opened India to the world and not only to the NRIs, was the standing argument of the political left and the Hindu nationalists.[43] They argued that the reforms only touched a fraction of the Indian population and that the masses had nothing to gain but everything to lose.

Indian industrialists complained of the reforms, as it took away the protectionism they had become used to and exposed their weakness to competition. The outside investor was still the economic predator who wanted to take advantage of the Indian economy for his own benefit. He was relying too much on imported machinery, rather than using the indigenous options and did not reinvest the profits made into the country, but took it all abroad. At the base of the debate were the effects of the reforms on Indian society and the resulting changes on the population. Growth which was not to help solve India's poverty, illiteracy, poor health and inequality problems would widen the gap between the rich and the poor, the urban and the rural areas, and the different regions in the country.

Yet the leading criticism of the liberalisation was that it had not brought about the growth expected, did not improve the country's credit rating, did not upgrade the technological level of Indian industry, and did little for the masses of poor and unemployed.[44] The Indian democratic system was at the base of such a debate. For 45 odd years India had lived within the parameters of the Nehruvian vision: fundamentally socialist and not intent on profit and performance. Now that that system was being shed it put much of India's 'raison d'être' into question.

The reality

The resulting reality was that the rhetoric of change did not all translate into action. India in 1991 had been forced to open its economy in order to save it from collapsing, but once saved, the process of liberalisation started to stagnate. Policy implementation is always slower than the rhetoric preceding it, especially when the country is as large and diverse as India. But in India's case the willingness to break with the Nehruvian tradition and to jump head over heels into a new system where outside capital would dictate the Indian state of affairs did not exist among the majority of the population or the politicians, no matter what they said. As a result the structural changes in the administration became painfully slow and the public sector was not dismantled. There was simply not the political will to cut the umbilical cord with Nehruvian tradition. His system had come as a package and now that it was time to dispense with some parts and leave others there was no one willing to do it. As a result the gap between the getting things done and the existing know-how/skills remained and the system was stuck.[45]

Perceptions of India

The opening of India's economy had a serious effect on India's perceived and real position in the world. After 1991 India was just like any of the other Asian countries competing for foreign investments. The appeal of a stable democracy was offset by the disorganised bureaucracy, the stagnating reforms keeping the public sector and rules and regulations in place (in fact kept in place by that very democracy). As a result it took longer to set up any new project or to invest in an existing one, than anywhere in Asia. The fact that it was potentially the largest middle-class market was offset by the fact that this particular middle-class was poorer than its SE Asian equivalent and would not bring in the expected profits for international brands. In a global context India was not the investment haven it could be. India was now no longer percieved as the aloof moral values keeper where profit and the like were unimportant, but the country with the largest poor population.

Change and the NRI

Political will vs. political action: reasons for lack of economic actions

When India was forced to open up its economy it did so with considerable resistance from the mainstream politicians and the population at large. Opening India went against the Nehruvian tradition of independence and self-sufficiency. This system cultivated for the best part of 45 years had left an incredible bureaucracy making any investment, expansion and development difficult, sometimes impossible. For India to have really opened up, all red tape should have been cut and in effect it was not. Some regulations were removed but enough was left to 'protect' the local industry from facing too much competition too quickly, and the public sector was not dismantled. The local industrialists were part of the lobbies which wished for India to remain closed, as competition would soon show the inefficiencies which had been allowed to develop. In particular the trading class of the Marwaris disagreed with potential competition, especially if it came from NRIs who had certain advantages over other foreign investors.[46] Their hegemonic position within India was threatened.[47] Besides the Marwaris there was a fair amount of local prejudice towards the NRIs and their real motives for investing in India. The population at large still held the Nehruvian attitude that these Indians had left for a better life and were now only back for economic benefit. This attitude will be analysed in the next section of this chapter. There was also the long standing prejudice towards foreign direct investment (FDI) in general. This attitude gets only a brief mention here but was further analysed earlier in chapter 3 and is contrasted with post 1991 FDI trends in chapter 7.

Did the government of India really have the political will to push these reforms through? The discourse promised to reform the system but the above mentioned obstacles show that political action did not necessarily follow political discourse, and here one might question India's sincere political will.

The principal obstacles are analysed below under three headings:

Prejudice towards foreign investment The experience of colonialism and memories of post independence neo-colonialism as well as that of the Gandhian principles of Swadeshi had influenced Indian thinking about foreign investment. The colonial economic structure of India can be best explained in terms of exploitation and dependency. Exploitation refers to the kind of economic structure under which the relationship between producer and consumer was determined by a powerful intermediary whose interest was of prime importance; it was invariably the colonial government. The peasants of rural India stuck in a feudalistic social structure and a property-less industrial labour class suffered at the hands of the powerful intermediaries. To counteract that colonial experience after independence, the Industrial Policy Resolution of 1949 adopted a mixed economic pattern of planning, categorising the industries into 4 groups that were then reduced to 3 in the Industrial Policy of 1956. The basic Idea was the inculcation of a value system based on Indian thinking or Gandhian philosophy, towards the upliftment of the downtrodden and moderation of the upper echelon of the society through a democratic parliamentary system.[48] These ideological legacies included an apparent dislike of foreign investment. As a result, India made a choice in favour of planned development soon after gaining political independence. The Planning Commission was constituted in February 1950. A detailed account of the development of foreign investment in India has been given in Chapter 3. It follows that the prejudice towards foreign investment was historically ingrained, and that this led to the kind of planning and development of the public sector which was later almost impossible to dismantle.

Bureaucracy A wide network of administrative and legal regulatory instruments evolved to curb monopolies and the concentration of economic power, restrict diversion of the limited national resources to low priority areas, regulate prices of essential goods and conserve foreign exchange resources. The government undertook the direct responsibility to ensure the rapid expansion of the public sector in areas which were strategic for the long-term interests of the Indian economy. The choice of planned development was undertaken after long and intensive deliberation and with the realisation that a country of India's size, with scarce resources could not be dependent upon foreign resources for her development in general and for the building of basic and capital goods industries in particular, and had to set priorities. This meant that state controls ensured that permits were needed for everything and that no industry could expand, diversify or change course quickly according to market demands. The 1991 reforms changed little of the bureaucracy as heavy regulation remained in place and the public sector was not dismantled.

Industrialists and local industry The worries of the local industrialists were already voiced in 1989 by K.K.Birla in the Rajya Sabha:

> The recent happenings in the industrial and other fields in the country which seek to oust the existing management through sheer money power are disturbing. To corner the shares of a company and to dislodge its management or to grab the property of others may be an acceptable mode of business for an entrepreneur in western countries, but it is contrary to our philosophy and culture.[49]

This quote recalls the debate about Swaraj Paul in the early 1980s when his companies bought majority share holdings in Escorts and DCM and the management of the company later refused to transfer the shares.[50] Government regulation concerning portfolio investments by non-Indians had to be changed subsequently. Most feared were NRI empires such as the Hindujas from Europe and the Chhabrias from Dubai, because they could challenge the Birlas, Goenkas and Modis from the Marwari caste of traders and industrialists.[51] As a result there was some kind of 'conspiracy' against NRIs whereby clearances took years and project costs would go haywire.[52] The Marwaris who had any influence were presumed to try and hamper any foreign investor who came in their way, since that would mean competition if not a threat to their own sphere of influence. This was encouraged by the presumption that the NRI industrialists who had successfully competed abroad would have no problems dominating India's closed markets. Unlike other multinationals they had a high degree of knowledge of the Indian market and mentality, which gave them an edge in both production and marketing strategies.

By inviting FDI into the country, the 1991 reforms brought back the danger that the economically strong NRIs would come and buy up local industry and oust local management which big houses such as the Birlas and the Tatas vehemently opposed.

The other danger to local industry was that the competition the long time protected industry of India would be exposed to. Local manufacturers were not up to international quality standards and this posed the danger of losing market shares.

Political will?

As mentioned earlier it seems clear that there was a lack of political will to go all the way in the reform process. The Nehruvian state had come as a package and those who held political power in the 1990s seemed incapable and unwilling to break with it. The above mentioned obstacles could and should have been tackled in order for the reform process to kick in and let the Indian economy seriously profit from outside investment. To date India is embroiled in the debate of whether the path taken in 1991 was truly the right one. This is not simply a practical problem of swift implementation where the vastness of the country and its complexities complicate the process; it is the lack of public and political will.

The NRI Relationship

Above it has been seen that economic action did not follow the government's discourse and that the real obstacles to the opening of the Indian economy with respect to the world in general and the NRIs in particular was based essentially on the bureaucracy, the stalling of local industrialists and local prejudice towards outside investment, especially with respect to the NRIs. The Government of India did what it had promised to do up to a certain point and then the reforms stalled. Although verbal encouragement continued with respect to the NRIs, practical action was lacking.

Why did the relationship between the Indian government and the NRIs not change with the 1991 economic reforms? Of all the investors who rushed to India when the economy opened up, the NRI contingent was the slowest. Their demands till today are still opposed by policy makers and other interest groups.

The NRI demands

These are frequent demands seen throughout the reform period in the press, and all of them have little to do with special treatment; they are requests for the reforms to be seen through so that investment is made not only possible but efficient. They include better terms and conditions for investment, streamlining the procedures so that confusion about how to invest is reduced;[53] the bureaucracy be reduced; [54] FERA to be reviewed; the RBI being given full autonomy to formulate interest, monetary and exchange rate policies; and all quantitative restrictions on imports to be abolished.[55]

The question of dual nationality was probably the most contentious one. The request was given even more emphasis with the opening up of the Indian economy and the calls to the NRI community to invest in India. The NRIs felt that giving Indian citizenship would make investing in India easier, as under NRI regulations they were not allowed to remain in the country for longer than 180 days at a time. There was great press speculation during the early reform period and even in Parliament there was quite a debate which also involved the issues of representation and franchise. Right from the pre-reform period in 1990 when the Patriot reported on the proposals and packages involving dual nationality to save the country's industrial investment problems,[56] to the definite 'NO' by PM Narasimha Rao in May 1994,[57] the issue came up regularly. Some suggestions involved charging the NRIs $5000 each for an Indian passport,[58] others a sort of Green Card which would allow the NRIs free access to India to work and stay without the right to vote.[59]

Within a matter of months contradicting statements were published as the government semi-officially announced granting dual citizenship to the NRIs: in July 1991 the Minister of State for External Affairs, Eduardo Faleiro stated that the government was considering offering dual nationality;[60] in early December it was reported that dual passports were ruled out by the union government;[61] then again in December 1992 the Minister for Water resources V.C. Shulka said that in principle the government would grant dual citizenship.[62]

Yet although the issue was debated the Government of India ultimately retained its position, as described by the Minister of State in the Ministry of Parliamentary Affairs and the Minister of State in the Ministry of Home Affairs M.M.Jacob: 'In recent months the demand for dual citizenship has been raised in different fora and various considerations have been advanced justifying the granting of dual citizenship. The concept of dual citizenship is not consistent with the Constitution of India and the Citizenship Act, 1955.[63] Any move to dual nationality would have required amending the constitution.[64] Besides, there was the issue of which NRIs would be entitled to the Indian passport; the regulations would have had to shut out Indians who left before Independence, since citizenship was not clearly defined before the passage of the Independence of India Act.[65] In fact the Government took the view that such a step would be hazardous to national security as Pakistani citizens could in effect claim Indian citizenship.

> The Overseas Indian Economic Forum, UAE has suggested in a letter to Prime Minister P.V.Narasimha Rao that an NRI representative be nominated to Parliament and an exclusive ministry set up to deal with expatriate affairs. (....) The suggestions include: holding consultations with NRI bodies before preparing the Budget; nominating and NRI to the Rajya Sabha; setting up an exclusive ministry for NRI affairs; privatising the public sector and offering its shares to overseas Indians; relaxing the gold import rules; allowing NRIs to hold dual citizenship; and setting up a free port in India.[66]

Representation was also suggested in Parliament during a Lok Sabha debate which in the end was voted out, since the members were afraid that the rich NRIs would come and take over their constituencies. Besides the fear that NRIs might be interested in buying votes with all their money, there was also a threat of corrupting the Indian culture:

> (...) if they are given the right of getting elected here and are given the citizenship the culture of this country will be changed. Everywhere we will hear pop music and see peep shows. God knows what else will be seen here. We will be finished and they will dominate. We will not be able to stop that situation.[67]

The above demands, some simple, economically sound requests, others specifically tailored to the NRI status, arise out of the myriad of problems NRIs face and have faced when investing in India. The fact that property owning is restricted, or that money gets stuck in non-repatriable accounts if a business fails, are added to the simple inconveniences of water, electricity and infrastructure problems which they do not have to put up with in the country of their adoption.[68] From the NRI point of view, investing in India is difficult: 'Once here, they come up against business partners who fleece them of their money, land deals that often turn out to be fraudulent, arrogant bureaucrats, corrupt officials and red tape. Multinational Companies have a system of PR agencies to deal with these kind of blocks. But for an individual NRI, the signal reads: You are not welcome.'[69]

Indian attitudes

There is evidence to show that the Indian perception of the NRI is at the base of the indifferent, sometimes difficult relationship between the Diaspora and the government. In effect all those who left India did so for economic gain, to live a better life elsewhere. As a result, the relationship is based on a fair amount of mistrust.

The government Before independence there was a certain amount of responsibility and solidarity towards those who had left India. It was, after all, colonial rule which had sent them abroad. In the light of the independence movement the unity of the Indian people was important. At that time the solidarity was mutual as funds from abroad supported the Indian National Congress in the struggle against British colonial rule. Post independence they were expected to come home if they were going to take part in the building of a new India. If they did not, they were expected to integrate into their host society. Nehru made this a national policy, advising expatriate Indians to adopt the nationality of the country they had chosen and to partake actively in the development of that society expecting nothing from 'Mother India'.

Before independence India was a political nation (as opposed to a cultural one) held together by the British Raj. Territorial unity and hence political identity were created by the Raj. In 1947 the new Indian government took over most of the infrastructure and many of the Raj's governing attitudes, and consequently transformed India into a 'nation-state project'.[70] The union of India had to be on political grounds as culturally India is so diverse; it has many civil societies - not one. In fact Nehru believed that an Indian identity could only be created by creating an Indian State - nothing else would link so diverse a population.[71] As a result, post independence the NRIs' links are primarily to their region/state of origin via their family, which in turn made them a difficult entity for the central government to deal with.

So the official policy was carved out according to Nehru:

> It is the consistent policy of the Government that persons of Indian origin who have taken foreign nationality should identify themselves with and integrate in the mainstream of social and political life of the country of their domicile. The government naturally remains alive to their interests and general welfare and encourages cultural contacts with them. As far as Indian citizens residing abroad are concerned, they are the responsibility of the Government of India. (....)[72]

This statement is repeated in similar forms annually in the Ministry of External Affairs Annual Report.

The NRIs were not primarily seen as a source of foreign exchange. Few held the view that:

> ...It would only be natural for us to turn to the one resource on which we have a national claim. This resource is the large funds, which are at the command of people of Indian origin overseas. Sentimentally they also would like to give first preference to India. Unfortunately, however, we have not been able to cash in on their sentiment. We have failed to create a climate in which they can bring in their funds and repatriate them at will.[73]

As seen earlier, this was also the view of the opposition at the time of India's balance of payments crisis in 1991: the NRIs had the means to bail India out of its economic crisis and had the duty to rescue their mother-country.

The Indian government had only twice asked the expatriate Asians for help. Firstly contributions of the Diaspora were welcome to boost the defence efforts during India's dispute with first China and then Pakistan.[74] Nehru was reported to have said that Indians overseas had a dual loyalty,[75] although this ran contrary to the policy he had been propagating. One can safely say though that although Nehru wished the emigrants to integrate into their host society, he believed that they would do nothing to harm India.

The people In ancient old tradition an Indian who went overseas lost his caste and with it his place in society. This was ancient Hinduism's way of protecting Indian society from change. There is still a feeling of superiority among those who were born and raised in India as opposed to those who were not.[76] It is a question of perception.

Modern Indians still look at the Indian Diaspora as some sort of twisted outcasts. Their money is welcome but they are not. They are essentially not Indian anymore; corrupted by the civilisation they have chosen to settle in. In fact there is a fear that if let back in through the back door, such as by giving them Indian citizenship and allowing them to settle freely, there would not only be an economic sell-out of the country but they would corrupt the Indian culture. They are also seen as cowards and to a certain degree as traitors: Cowards because they have avoided living within India's difficult economic circumstances and have by extension deprived India of their skill; Traitors because they have abandoned their parents, leaving them to age alone.

In addition there is also a feeling that when Indians went abroad they exploited the local people there in order to make plenty of money; once unwanted in the host country they seek to come back to India.[77] This attitude is especially common when one deals with parts of the Diaspora which experienced hardship in times of crisis such as the Ugandan and Fijian Asians; they made the choice of becoming foreign and now must face the consequences of their choice.

When they come back to India, it is solely for the purpose of profit, not for the gain of the country. Whatever profit is made will in turn be taken out and not be reinvested into the country so that it might grow and develop. This in turn will maintain not alleviate the disparities, which exist in Indian society. Their motivation is selfish which encourages mistrust.

Of course there are Indians who have realised that the stereotypes of the low caste expatriate who left his mother country for material gain is not accurate and that many of the of the original migrants had left India reluctantly and made their fortunes through hard work and entrepreneurship. More often than not they include those middle class Indians who have sent their children abroad to make a better life for themselves. But they are few in absolute numbers. It is not in the consciousness or perception of most ordinary Indians that the Diaspora have retained their cultural roots and traditions despite the odds.

The Importance of NRIs

Besides all the debate on how much the NRI community can/ should invest, what their rights are, and what are legitimate demands and which are not, a fundamental point is lost. NRI investment is linked in more than one way to foreign direct investment. The debate to let them invest in the country throughout the 1980s paved the way for the Indian public to accept the idea of further foreign investment through the reforms. Multinationals or international companies such as Dupont, Motorola or General Electric often turn to an NRI management person for assessment on the country and the market.[78] They serve as middlemen who get sent to India to head the opening and development of such corporations. Alone in that position they yield a great deal of influence.

The Diaspora's point of view:

> The perception by East Indians (sic) from India that they are necessarily superior to East Indians from other societies has in a very real sense come back to haunt them. Because of their perception that they are intrinsically better than East Indians from other societies, the latter have tended to treat them with disgust and contempt. In fact, today many East Indians from societies of the Diaspora do not identify with India and its people. In addition their identification with India is merely a symbolic one. Perhaps one of the basic reasons for this is that they see India as doing nothing to help them. More importantly is that they regard ways of life in India as too traditional and one dimensional and therefore do not help them much in their adjustment to the new societies they have taken up residences in. (...) Indeed the East Indians' quest to survive in societies of the Diaspora is something that the East Indians from India have yet to understand. Moreover it is such a lack of understanding by the latter that leads them to see East Indians from societies of the Diaspora as not being true East Indians.[79]

This view expresses the distance which has evolved between India and its Diaspora. It shows what the Indian policies have achieved over the years, namely a relationship based on mutual distrust and contempt which will have great difficulties evolving into something mutually beneficial in the future.

The India-NRI is a case of 'mutual abandonment'. While the 'mother-country' disowned its children abroad, not even coming to their rescue in times of crises, the Indian Diaspora has in turn disowned its land of origin. While that does not mean that they shed their Indianness and their traditions, quite the contrary, 'little Indias' are created wherever the migrants go, it does mean that they feel responsibility for India and India's position in the world.

Conclusion

It has been argued in this chapter that global changes required India to change politically and economically. India's discourse did change in light of the international and national events that preceded the summer of 1991. Its actions which followed, went only half way and were never really completed. To a certain degree there was continuation of the past policy with other means. This was due to several things: For one, the ingrained Nehruvian approach to economic and foreign policy in general and towards the NRIs in particular. The government once saved from defaulting on its international debt did not have the political muscle to push through the totality of the reforms. As a result, the difficulties faced by NRI and other investors remained prominent. These were principally linked to an overbearing public sector and insurmountable bureaucracy. Besides, the population at large remained highly prejudiced towards the NRIs. They felt that the returning NRI did so for personal profit alone and not for the good of the country of his origin. The situation created was one where, despite India's desperate need for NRI involvement, the two sides stood at loggerheads over issues of reform, citizenship and representational rights.

The next chapter will explore India's relationship with Foreign Direct Investment (FDI) over the years and then analyse the economic results after the reforms, showing that even after the opening of the Indian economy NRI involvement and investment remained pathetically low.

Endnotes

1 Naidu and Reddy, 'Stock of Indian Emigrants in Gulf Countries', p.25

2 Minister of State in the Ministry of External Affairs, E.Faleiro, *Lok Sabha Debates*, Q.6952, 12.9.1991

3 Weiner, M., 'International Labour Migration from India: a Macro Economic Analysis' in Amjad, R. (ed.), *To the Gulf and Back; Asian Employment Programme*, p.131

4 *MEA annual report 1985-86*, p.23

5 One lakh = 100 000

6 *MEA annual report 1990-91*, p.82

7 One crore = 10 000 000
8 *MEA annual report 1991-92*, p. 48,50
9 Dutt, S.K., *India and the World: Altruism or Hegemony?*, p.141
10 *Lok Sabha Debates*, Q. 6648, 8.4.1992
11 Agrawal, D., 'The Malaise of Brain Drain', The Patriot 6.9.1991
12 Bahadur Singh, I.J. (ed.), *Indians in South East Asia*, p.166-170
13 'Perils of 'Hot' Money', Times of India, 25.10.1991
14 Khilnani, S., *The Idea of India*, p.96
15 See chapter 3 for details
16 Mehta, A., 'Global Trading Practices and Poverty Alleviation...', p.29
17 Ibid., p.30-34
18 Tharoor, S., *India from Midnight to the Millennium*, p.159-160
19 It should be noted that this was not the first time the Indian economy was at the verge of collapse, it had happened for example in 1964. Yet this time there was no alternative but to open up the economy to outside investments. During the previous crisis, India had reformed parts of the economy, yet it had never led to serious liberalisations
20 *Lok Sabha Debates*, Q. 392, 19.7.1991
21 Joshi, V. and Little, I.M.D., *India's Economic Reforms 1991-2001*, p.14-15
22 Manmohan Singh, in 1992-93 General Budget, *Lok Sabha Debates*
23 Patel, I.G., 'New Economic Policies: a historical perspective' Economic and Political Weekly, 4 -11.1.1992
24 Tharoor, S., *India from Midnight to the Millennium*, p.160
25 Hanson, A.H., 'Power Shifts and Regional Balances', in Streeten, P. and Lipton, M., *The Crisis of Indian Planning*, p.43
26 Khilnani, S., *The Idea of India*, p.97
27 Ibid., p.98
28 Tharoor, S., *India from Midnight to the Millennium*, p.163
29 *Lok Sabha Debates*, Budget speech, 29.2.1992
30 Manmohan Singh, 1992-93 Budget, *Lok Sabha Debate*, 29.2.1992
31 Tharoor, S., *India from Midnight to the Millennium*, p.171-172
32 Lok Sabha Debates, Q.101,19.7.1991
33 1992-93 Budget, *Lok Sabha Debates*, 29.2.1992
34 *Lok Sabha Debates*, Q.271, 2.8.1991
35 *Lok Sabha Debates*, Q. 2999, Pre-budget session 1992
36 *Lok Sabha Debates*, Q. 260, 13.3.1992
37 'BJP Stand on NRI Funds', Financial Express, 12.6.91
38 Panandiker, P.D.H., 'What to choose - IMF or NRI?', Hindustan Times, 18.7.1991
39 'NRIs will not Rescue Us - Bogus Alternatives of CPM, BJP', Times of India, 15.7.1991
40 Aiyar, A.S.S., 'Say Good-Bye to Hot Money', Times of India, 21.7.1991
41 'Life in the Slow Lane', Far Eastern Economic Review, 21.8.1997, p.71
42 Khilnani, S., *The Idea of India*, p.99
43 In this case the BJP was referring not only to NRI investment which it had appealed for earlier, but to the fact that opening the Indian economy had let in various multinational companies, which the BJP disliked intensely
44 Tharoor, S., *India from Midnight to the Millennium*, p.181

45 As an alternative view one can speculate that the reasons for stagnation might lie in the lessons the Government of India learnt in watching the speed of transition to a market economy in the Soviet Union and the social and political consequences the change brought with it. India with over 950 million people could not afford such social and political risks and might have thus shrunken away from full liberalisation

46 See Appendix: Government announcements - NRI response, a few articles in newspapers mention the trader class protesting against the liberalisation which brought in fierce competition, e.g. 27.10.1987; 22.4.1983

47 See two pages ahead

48 Nevertheless this system was also part of a Nehruvian idea to industrialise India's rural economy as quickly and as effectively as possible. Although it might seem that the Nehruvian principles contradict the Khadi economy advocated by the Mahatma, both policies actually had the same goal, namely to uplift the poor strata of Indian society

49 *Rajya Sabha Debates*, 3.4.1989

50 See Appendix of NRI responses in the Chronology; Swaraj Paul was the first NRI to challenge the alleged Indian reforms of the 1980s by buying a large number of shares of both DCM and Escorts through various companies of his own. This sent a chill through the industrialists' community, as they saw that a simple transaction on a stock exchange could make them lose control of their company. There were lobbies to the government to outlaw such transactions and although Swaraj Paul fought this case for years in the Indian courts he ultimately lost and the shares were never transferred to his name

51 Elliot, J., 'Survey of India: Competitive Modern Caste', Financial Times, 25.11.1987

52 Goel, L.N., 'Sadder and Wiser', India Today, 31.7.1989

53 'Serving Motherland from abroad', Hindustan Times, 30.3.92

54 'Cut More Red Tape: NRIs', IN, 19.9.91

55 'NRIs for FERA Review', Hindustan Times, 18.1.92

56 'Dual Citizenship', Patriot, 28.3.90

57 'Rao Opposes Dual Citizenship for NRIs', Statesman, 18.5.94

58 'Trapping NRI Millions', Times of India, 23.7.91

59 'Green Card for NRIs Under Consideration', BP, 20.6.92

60 'Delhi Considers Dual Nationality for NRIs', SWB, 10.7.91

61 'India: Government Rules Out Dual Passport for NR Citizens', SWB, 7.12.92

62 'Dual Citizenship for NRIs', SWB, 31.12.92

63 *Lok Sabha debates*, Q. 1548, 5.3.1992

64 See 1955 Citizenship Act

65 'Dual Citizenship for NRIs likely soon', The Telegraph, 10.3.92

66 'NRI representative in Parliament sought', BP, 8.7.91

67 Dr G.S.Rajhans speaking on the 25.7.1986, *Lok Sabha Debates*, Resolution Re: Conferment of same rights as enjoyed by Indian Citizens on Persons of Indian Origin living abroad

68 Chanran, P., 'Citizens of Two Worlds', Indian Express, 27.10.91 and 'Harsh Realities Discourage Indians Abroad from Investing in India', The Indian, October/November 1977

69 Khan, N.H., 'Home, Sweet Home', 26.4.1998 (Internet)

70 See Chapter 1 and Chapter 4 for details on creating a new Indian identity on the basis of shared history as opposed to a religious or cultural value system
71 Kilnani, S., *The Idea of India*, introduction and chapter 4
72 *MEA Annual Report 1991-92*, and see chapter 4 for details
73 View expressed in Bahadur Singh, I.J. (ed.), *The Other India: The Overseas Indians and their Relationship with India*, p.217, who also believed that the Indian Diaspora was part of India and should not have been ignored by the Government of India
74 Twaddle, M. (ed.), *Expulsion of a Minority – Essays on Ugandan Asians*, p.134 and Bhatia, P., *Indian Ordeal in Africa*, p.124
75 Twaddle, M. (ed.), *Expulsion of a Minority – Essays on Ugandan Asians*, p.134
76 Motwani, J.K., Gosine, M., Barot-Motwani, *Global Indian Diaspora: Yesterday, Today and Tomorrow*, p.18
77 Bahadur Singh, I.J. (ed.), *The Other India: The Overseas Indians and their Relationship with India*, p.42
78 'Large NRI Funds May Flow in with Offer of Dual Citizenship', Economic Times, 9.7.92
79 Motwani, J.K., Gosine,M., Barot-Motwani, *Global Indian Diaspora: Yesterday, Today and Tomorrow*, p.19-21. Quote shows that the mutual mistrust and contempt is not a recent phenomena, but has been part of both the Indian and the Diaspora's psyche for a long time

7 Foreign investment and the NRIs

Introduction

This chapter deals with the development of foreign investment in India and the nature of NRI investment after the 1991 reforms. In the previous chapters the political and theoretical side of external non-involvement in general, and India's position towards NRIs in particular has been explained. The political will to change the Indian attitude towards foreign investment, and especially towards the status of the NRIs after the 1991 reforms, was not very strong. In part this was due to historically ingrained attitudes towards foreign investments,[1] in part it was due to the Indian attitude towards the Diaspora.[2] After the 1991 reforms the relationship of the Indian government with its Diaspora was no longer an issue to be seen in the context of India's nation state building project, which had excluded the Diaspora at independence. It had become a question of Indian economic development and what part the NRIs could play in it. As a result of the government's unchanging attitudes, the NRI involvement in India's post reform development was particularly slow and remained low both in relative and absolute terms of foreign investment.

India traditionally disliked the concept of relying on foreign capital and chose the self-sufficient path based on planning instead. The Planning Commission was installed to this effect in the 1950s. In order to implement the development plans the state was obliged to mobilise financial resources through a variety of fiscal measures. The various plans and their attitude towards FDI have been described at length in Chapter 3. The following table illustrates the composition of foreign assistance authorised and utilised by the public sector according to the economic plans.

Table 7.1: Composition of foreign assistance authorised and utilised: percentage share

	Authorisation			Utilisation		
Plan period	**Loans**	**Grants**	**Other assist-ance**	**Loans**	**Grants**	**Other assist-ance**
First Plan	59.4	36.4	4.4	62.7	34.8	2.5
Second Plan	50.2	4.9	44.9	50.7	11.2	38.1
Third Plan	79.7	4.6	15.7	66.6	3.7	29.7
Annual Plans	73.7	5.5	20.7	69.9	7.2	22.9
Fourth Plan	92.8	4.8	2.4	91.9	4.1	4.0
Fifth Plan	80.3	19.7	-	79.1	20.9	-
1979-80	64.4	35.6	-	74.7	25.3	-
Sixth Plan	87.6	12.4	-	80.8	19.2	-
Seventh Plan	93.1	6.9	-	89.2	10.8	-

Source: Economic Survey, 1996-97, Government of India, p.197.

As can be seen in the table foreign assistance was very much part of Indian economic development right through the various plans, yet it was closely monitored by the government and for many years subject to the public sector's idiosyncrasies. Private FDI as such was almost unheard of until the mid 1980s.

The public sector, which was created at the time, brought with it an immense bureaucracy, which even the 1991 reforms have not managed to dismantle sufficiently. The Planning Commission also encouraged an attitude towards economic development based on allocation to priority sectors rather than profit engineering strategies, and with it mistrust towards all forms of profit. Consequently India's relationship with FDI and its sources is a curious one. The effective changes brought about by the 1991 liberalisation reforms and globalisation and their effect on FDI, especially from NRI sources will be analysed here.

This chapter is divided into three parts. The first part reiterates the main reforms of 1991 and describes the NRI contribution to FDI and to India's economic development. The second part looks at the reasons for low NRI investment and investor problems in general. The third briefly describes why China has been more successful in attracting and using investment to build up its economy. The chapter concludes that although economic reforms have led to improvements in the Indian economy, the development is not as satisfactory as could have been expected. It also ascertains that the specific involvement of the NRIs in the post 1991 period was in relative and absolute terms small and insufficient to have made a difference on its own.

NRI Contribution to India's Economic Development

The new industrial policy

The 1991 reforms set out to change the country's economic system by removing the hurdles for outside investment and by creating a new investor-friendly economic climate in the country.[3] The Industrial Policy of July 24, 1991 reduced the long entrenched industrial licensing system. It drastically reduced the number of industries reserved for the public sector from 17 to a mere 6. These are Defence, Atomic Energy, Coal & Lignite, Minerals, Mining, and Railway Transport. India still retained a positive list of 15 industries requiring compulsory licensing.[4] These accounted for only 15 per cent of value added in the manufacturing sector in 1994-95. In addition, there were some restrictions on location of industries within the specified boundaries of 23 Indian cities with a population of more than one million, as per 1991 census of India. The Government of India allowed 'automatic approval' of FDI up to a maximum of 51 per cent equity in selected 'high priority industries' which numbered 35 industries. The Government also relaxed certain policies and procedures to motivate the NRIs and the Overseas Corporate Bodies (OCBs) to invest.[5]

Recognising the need for modernising India's industrial and export infrastructure, not only for promoting and sustaining higher growth, but also to facilitate larger inflows of FDI into hi-tech. export oriented and employment generating manufacturing sectors, the Government offered packages of special incentives to foreign investors in selected infrastructure sectors. These included (i) power; (ii) telecommunications, (iii) petroleum exploration, (iv) refining and marketing activities, (v) transportation (vi) ports and shipping, and (vii) air taxi operation.[6] The Government also liberalised its polices for the participation by foreign investors in the drugs and pharmaceuticals and the in banking services sector.

Figure 7.1: Foreign exchange reserves

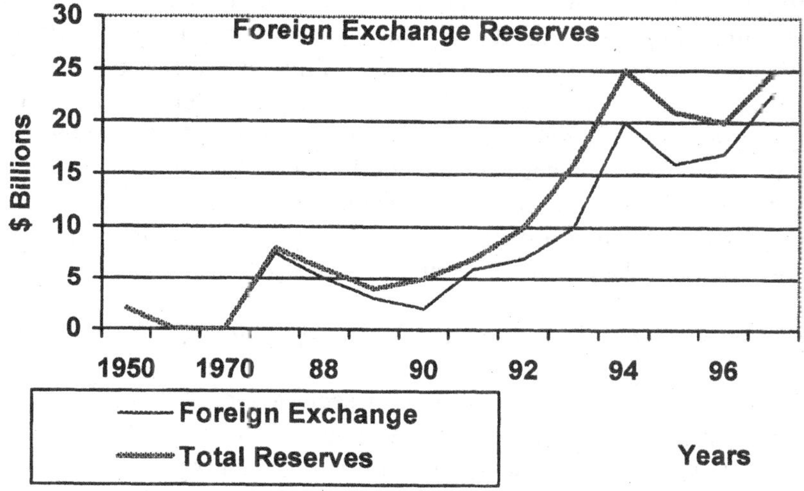

Source: Business India: Anniversary Issue 15 August 1997.

Figure 7.2: Foreign trade

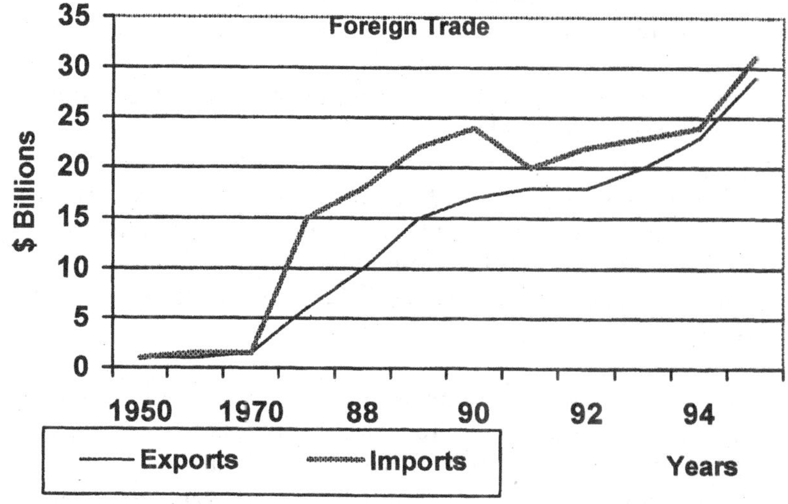

Source: Business India: Anniversary Issue 15 August 1997.

The two graphs above illustrate the foreign exchange reserves and foreign trade situation pre- and post-liberalisation. The 1990-91 crisis is well illustrated by both the imports graph and the graph of foreign exchange reserves dipping sharply. It should be noted that both the foreign exchange reserves and trade picked up sharply after the 1991 reforms, vindicating the opening up of the Indian economy. At this stage one can argue that NRI investments had a good chance of making a major impact on the Indian economy, yet as this chapter shows, the absolute and relative amounts of NRI investments remained very low and did not contribute substantially to the growth evident in the two graphs.

NRI contribution to India's economic development

Who are the NRIs? Sub section 1 of section 2 of the Foreign Exchange Regulations Act, 1973 (FERA) defines the term 'Persons Resident in India' as those who come under any of the following category:

- All Indian citizens who have been staying in India after the 25 March 1947;
- Foreign citizens who stay in India for employment, or carrying on business in India or circumstances indicating an indefinite period of stay;
- Foreign citizens who come and stay in India with their spouses, if the spouses are resident in India.

Indian citizens who proceed abroad for higher studies, short business visits, training, medical treatment etc. are treated as residents of India even during their temporary absence from India.

Non Resident Indians (NRIs) fall under the following broad categories:[7]

- Indian citizens who stay abroad for employment or for carrying on a business or vocation or for any other purpose in circumstances indicating an indefinite period of stay outside India.
- Indian citizens working abroad on assignment with foreign Governments /Government agencies or International/Regional agencies like the UNO (including its affiliates), the International Monetary Fund, the World Bank etc.

Officials of the Central and State Government and public sector undertakings deputed abroad on temporary assignments or posted to their offices (e.g. Indian Diplomatic Mission) abroad.

Non Resident Indians become residents of India only when they come back to the country for employment or for any other purpose indicating an indefinite period of stay in India. They are not regarded as persons residents in India during their short visits to India say for holidays, business, etc. Indian citizens who take up jobs on completion of their higher studies abroad are regarded as Non Resident Indians only from the time they take up jobs abroad.[8]

PIOs: A person is deemed to be of Indian origin if he at any time held an Indian passport or he has either of his parents or any of his grand-parents was an Indian and a permanent resident in undivided India at any time. A wife of a citizen of India or of a person of Indian origin is also deemed to be of Indian origin even though she may be if non-Indian parentage.[9]

OCBs: Overseas Corporate Bodies include overseas companies partnership firms, trusts, societies and other corporate bodies which are owned directly or indirectly to the extent of at least 60 per cent by individuals of Indian nationality or origin, resident outside India, as also overseas trusts in which at least 60 per cent of the beneficial interest is irrevocably held by such persons.[10]

As from July 1991, the facilities specially available to the Non Residential Indians were as follows:

1. NRIs are permitted to acquire shares/convertible debentures of an Indian company through a stock exchange in India under the portfolio investment scheme of up to 24 per cent. Subject to the conditions that the total investment of all NRIs on repatriation/non-repatriation basis will be within an overall ceiling of:

   (a) 24 per cent of the total paid up equity capital of the company concerned; and

   (b) 24 per cent of the total paid up value of each series of the convertible issued by the company concerned.

   Investment made on repatriation basis by any single non residential investor in equity/performance shares and convertible debentures of any listed Indian company should not exceed 1 per cent of its total paid up value of each series of convertible debentures issued by it.

2. NRIs may own up to 100 per cent equity on repatriable basis in the revival of sick industry.
3. NRIs may pay income tax at a flat rate of the 20 per cent on dividends occurred from investment made in foreign exchange, whereas foreign companies are to pay tax at a rate of 25 per cent.
4. It is open to NRIs to invest up to 100 per cent equity in the service industry sector on repatriation basis in specified sectors and on non-repatriation basis in others.
5. NRIs are allowed to invest on repatriation basis in existing new companies engaged or proposing to engage in the following activities, namely:
   (a) Financing of house development;
   (b) Real estate development; and
   (c) Infrastructure areas such as construction of roads, bridges etc.
6. NRIs may give a gift to an Indian relative free of gift tax.

Added to the above were options to invest in Government securities, units of UTI etc.

Basically NRI investment can be divided into two categories: repatriable and non-repatriable.

> The repatriation benefits include, not only the initial amount of investment, but also of the interest and dividend income, as well as the maturity or sale proceeds, inclusive of the appreciation on the initial investment. (…) NRIs not keen on repatriation, would enjoy a much wider choice of investments.[11]

On the basis of non-repatriation NRIs may invest in proprietary/ partnership firms, the issues of new Indian companies and deposit certain sums with public or private limited companies.[12]

NRI investment and other FDI

In July 1991 the Government of India reformed the Foreign Exchange Regulation Act (FERA) and Monopolies and Restricted Trade Policies (MRTP) and allowed foreign investors to invest upon 51 per cent in industries and other sectors without any prior approval from any Indian financial institution. During the years 1994 and 1995, NRI contributed 7.0 per cent and 8.0 per cent respectively to total investment.

The liberalisation of the Indian economy attracted substantial foreign portfolio investment, thus stock markets received foreign portfolio investment at the tremendous rate of four million dollars per day.

Table 7.2: Foreign investment flows by category (US$ million)

	1991 -92	1992 -93	1993 -94	1994 -95	1995 -96	1995 -96 (Apr-	1996 -97 Dec. [b])
(A) Direct Investment [a]	150	341	586	1314	2133	1500	1710
a) RBI automatic route	--	42	89	171	169	76	83
b) SIA/FIPB route	87	238	280	701	1249	872	1181
c) NRIs (40% & 100%)	63	61	217	442	715	552	446
(B) Portfolio Investment [a]	8	92	3649	3518	2214	1121	2343
a) FIIs[c]	--	1	1665	1503	2009	1002	1511
b) Euro equities[d]	--	86	1602	1839	149	64	812
c) Offshore funds[2] & others [c]	8	5	382	239	56	55	20
Total (A+B)	**158**	**433**	**4235**	**4895**	**4347**	**2621**	**4053**

Source: Economic Survey, 1996-97, Government of India, p. 98.

a) Figures shown are based on actual inflows. These may differ from foreign investment flows.
b) Provisional.
c) Represents fresh inflows of funds by FIIs.
d) Represents the amount repatriated to India by the corporates from their GDR proceeds.

As seen in the table, total foreign investment surged from $0.4 billion in 1992-93 to $4.2 billion in 1993-94, and rose further to $4.9 billion in 1994-95. Total foreign investment approved during the year 1995 has been Rs. 37,489 crores, but actual inflow was limited to 6720 crores, i.e. only 19 per cent of the approved value. (See Table 7.6.) However, in 1995-96 there was a modest decline in investment flows to US$ 4.3 billion due mainly to a sharp fall in the issue of Euro-equities abroad.

After the economic reforms of 1991, the Government of India has been offering high interest to attract foreign investors. As a result there was large NRI investment in India under the portfolio scheme which was highly fluctuating by nature.

Due to the growth of NRI investments and other FDI since 1991, India's foreign exchange reserves had risen. Gold holdings of the RBI rose steadily and peaked at $ 25.2 billion at the end of March 1995, then declined to $ 21.7 billion at the end of May 1996. However resources rose steadily in subsequent months to reach $ 24.0 billion by January 1997.

The 1991 reforms also improved and diversified the non resident bank accounts/deposit schemes. Under these schemes, persons of Indian origin resident abroad can open bank accounts in India freely out of funds remitted from abroad or out of funds legitimately due to them in India. There are five types of non resident accounts which can be maintained by authorised dealers:

i. Foreign currency non resident Accounts FCNR(A);
ii. Non Resident (External) Rupee accounts NR(E)RA;
iii. Foreign currency non resident (Banks) Accounts. FCNR(B);
iv. Non Resident (Non-repatriable) Rupee Deposits NR(NR)RD;
v. Foreign currency (Banks & Others) Deposits FC(B&O)D.

The total net flows, including occurred interest, into various non residential deposits account remained subdued in 1993-94 to 1995-96. (See Table 7.3.)

Table 7.3: Outstanding balance and net flows under various NR deposits schemes

A. Outstanding Balance Under Different Schemes (1) (US$ million)

Schemes	**(end of) March '93**	**(end of) March '94**	**(end of) March '95** (Revised)	**(end of) March '96** (Revised)	**(end of) Nov. '96** (PE)
FCNR(A)	10617	9300	7051	4255	3460
FCNR(B)	----	1075	3054	5723	6805
NR(E)RA	2862	3590	4556	3916	4646
NR(NR)RD	610	1797	2479	3544	5079
FC(B&O)D	1044	533	----	----	----
Total	15133	16295	17140	17438	19990

B. Net Flows Under Non Residential Deposits (1)

Schemes	**1992-93**	**1993-94**	**1994-95** (Revised)	**1995-96** (Revised)	**1996-97** (PE Apr. -Nov.)
FCNR(A)	-825	-1317	-2249	-2796	-795
FCNR(B)	----	1075	1979	2669	1028
NR(E)RA	335	728	964	-208	894
NR(NR)RD	610	1187	628	1280	1704
FC(B&O)D	350	-576	-558	0	0
Total	**1220**	**1097**	**818**	**945**	**2885**

Source: Government of India, Economic Survey, 1996-97, p. 101.

* P.E. Provisional Estimates.
(1) All figures are inclusive of accorded interest

As calculated from Table 7.3 (A&B) there is a net outflow of $825 million in the 1992-93. However during 1993-1994 and 1994-1995 there was again a net outflow of $1,317 million and $2,249 million respectively. Under the NR(E)RA scheme, there were inflows of $ 335 million, $ 728 million and $964 million during 1992-93, 1993-94 and 1994-95 respectively. As a result, the outstanding balance under the scheme rose to $ 4,556 million as at the end of March 1995.These flows gained momentum during the first half of 1996-97 in response to the relaxation of reserve requirements and the rationalisation of interest rates on deposits. During April-November 1996, net inflows reached on all time high of about US$ 2.9 billion while the inflows under FCNR(B) account increased moderately during April-November 1996 compared to 1995-96. The flows under NR(NR)RD sustained the upward trend of the total outstanding balances under all the non residential deposit schemes increased from US$ 17,438 million at the end of March 1996 to US$ 19,990 million at the end of November 1996. Excluding the balances under NR(NR)RD accounts, which are liabilities in domestic currency, the external liability on acccunts of non residential deposits at the end of November 1996 amounted to US$ 14.911 million.

As a comparison to post 1991 bank account deposits Table 7.4 provides the figures between 1984 and 1991.

Table 7.4: Inflows under NR (E) RA and FCNRA schemes (Rs crores)

Fiscal Year	Non Resident (External Rupee Account)[a]	Foreign Currency (Non Resident) Account	Total	Total Out-standing Liabilities (Rs. crores)[c]	Total Out-standing Liabilities ($ Mn)[c]	Share of NRI Out-standing to total external debt%[b]
1984-85	604	275	879	3819	3075	9.6
1985-86	616	1151	1767	5650	4590	11.0
1986-87	477	1173	1650	7847	6074	13.8
1987-88	477	1363	1840	10054	7769	15.5
1988-89	235	2230	2465	14154	9049	16.9
1989-90	277	2165	2442	17831	10363	18.2
1990-91	156	255	411	20754	10584	15.9
1991-92	-44	-3641	-3685	21679	7847	10.7

Source: The Economic Times, New Delhi, 17 December 1992.

a) Excluding the estimated accrued interest
b) The last two years figures are not comparable with the rest as they include short term debt.
c) Inclusive of NRI deposits.

With the amendment of the Foreign Exchange Regulation Act of 1973 announcing major concessions to FERA companies in November 1991 and January 1992, further NRI investment was attracted. The ordinance removed a large number of restrictions on companies with more than 40 per cent non residential equity, removed FERA controls on Indian firms setting up joint ventures abroad and allowed Indians to hold immovable property abroad, subject to certain conditions stipulated by the Reserve Bank of India. Other major concessions announced in November 1991, January 1992 and January 1993 were as follows:

- Companies with foreign share holding could increase foreign equity to 51 per cent by remittances in foreign exchange in the 35 high priority industries.
- NRIs are permitted to make direct investment in partnership/ proprietor concerns in India and by way of subscription to shares/debentures of private/public limited companies. They are also permitted to place funds in company deposits. Similar facilities are available to OCBs where the investment are allowed with the repatriation benefits if the funds are received the NRE or FCNR accounts.[13]
- NRIs are permitted to subscribe to and take up shares of Indian companies for the purpose of its incorporation, and the company is to issue shares to NRIs on the condition that the total face value of shares to be taken up by the NRI should not exceed Rs. 20,000/-.
- 100 per cent NRI investment on full repatriation basis will be allowed in export trading and star trading houses at par with other high priority industries. NRIs and OCBs were permitted 100 per cent investment in high priority industries on repatriation basis.[14]
- The restriction sales/transfer of shares /bonds and debentures were amended.
- The Government has allowed non residential industries and OCBs predominantly owned by them, to hold up to 100 per cent foreign equity in all sectors of industries including the small scale sector, but barring those reserved for the public sector.
- NRIs are allowed to gift close relatives in India shares held by them in Indian companies.[15]

To attract NRI investments the Government of India also liberalised the MRTP Act of 1969, the object of which was to curb the monopolistic behaviour of large business houses. By the end of March 1990, 1854 undertakings were registered under the MRTP (Monopolistic Restrictive Trade Practices) Act of these 1787 belonged to large industrial houses and the remaining 67 were 'dominant' undertakings.

In an important liberalisation measure announced on June 30, 1988, the Government freed dominant undertakings from the industrial licensing policy restrictions applicable under the MRTP Act. With this decision, companies which were termed 'dominant' could take advantage of the relaxation in the industrial licensing policy announced for non-MRTP and Non-FERA companies. The new industrial policy scrapped the assets limit for MRTP companies altogether. The MRTP Act was amended and chapter

II on the monopolies dropped, so that now a company no longer needed prior permission of the commission for investment decisions for the establishment of new undertakings. The Government hoped that this would enable Indian firms to become large enough to compete effectively on the global market.

Foreign collaborations

One of the major objectives to India's economic reforms was to build a self-reliant economy through better utilisation of its human and material resources with the help of foreign technology. Foreign collaboration agreements were made between Indian companies and foreign parties if the following conditions were satisfied:

1. Foreign equity investments should be by way of cash without being linked to tied imports or machinery equipment or payments for know how, trade mark etc.
2. The Indian collaboration should be free to sub-license the technical know how / engineering design to another Indian party on mutually agreed terms to which the foreign collaborator would also be a party.
3. The royalty is calculated on the basis of the selling price of the product, net of excise duties minus the cost of components, brought out or imported.
4. There should be no payment of a minimum guaranteed royalty.
5. There should not be any restriction on the export of that product to any country.
6. The Indian party should have the right to produce the items even after the expiry of the collaboration, without making additional payments.[16]

Table 7.5: Foreign collaboration approvals - comparative figures

	1991	1992	1993	1994	1995	1996	1997*	Total
1. Total No. of Foreign Collaborations.								
i. SIA	760	585	307	382	593	410	67	3104
ii. RBI	188	736	676	702	799	719	253	4073
iii. FIPS	2	199	493	770	945	1174	420	4003
Total	**950**	**1520**	**1476**	**1854**	**2337**	**2303**	**740**	**11180#**
2. Total No. of Foreign Collaborations (Technical)								
i. SIA	514	342	248	290	428	311	40	2173
ii. RBI	147	485	441	501	552	424	138	2638
iii. FIPS	--	1	2	1	2	9	35	50
Total	**661**	**828**	**691**	**792**	**982**	**744**	**213**	4911
3. No. of FC Approvals involving Foreign Investment.								
i. SIA	246	243	59	92	165	99	27	931
ii. RBI	41	251	235	201	247	295	115	1385
iii. FIPS	2	198	491	769	943	1165	385	3953
Total	**289**	**692**	**785**	**1062**	**1355**	**1559**	**527**	**6269**
4. Total amount of Foreign Investment.								
i. SIA	3.6	4.2	1.6	3.2	3.0	11.8	1.7	29.1
ii. RBI	1.4	7.8	6.6	5.3	5.4	12.5	17.3	56.3
iii. FIPS	0.3	26.9	80.4	133.4	312.3	337.2	205.1	1095.6
Total	**5.3**	**38.9**	**88.6**	**141.9**	**320.7**	**361.5**	**224.1**	**1181.0#~**

Source: Government of India, Economic Survey, 1996-97.

Note:

(i) 1 Billion = 100 Crores.

(ii) '#' -- Includes 45 proposals for global depository receipts (GDR)/Foreign currency convertible bonds (FCCBs) involving investments of Rs. 150.18 Billion.

(iii) '*' -- Figures for 1997 updated up to 30/4/97.

(iv) '~' -- The amount of Foreign Direct Investment (FDI) Approved =US$36.0 Billion. Approx.

Automatic approval was given by the reserve Bank of India (RBI) for Foreign Direct Investment with up to 51 per cent foreign equity in the 35 high priority industries and for up to 50 per cent in the mining sector. The foreign investment promotion Bond (FIPB) cleared the approvals which were not in conformity with the automatic approval system within a period of four to six weeks. The secretariat for industrial approval (SIA) placed in the Ministry of Industry also had powers to clear the projects under certain circumstances. It has to be noted that in the post-policy period most foreign collaborations were made in the technical sector.

FDI (Foreign Direct Investment) response

The positive signals generated by the new policies and a more supportive administrative infrastructure since 1991 have considerably improved the investment climate for FDI in India. This is apparent when one compares India's experience in this regard to the 10 years prior to the liberalisation. Table - 7.6 provides data regarding the response to the favourable changes made towards attracting FDI in the period of 1991 to 1996. It may be noted that aggregate FDI approvals have made a quantum jump from the expectedly low base level of Rs. 739 crores ($ 325 million) in 1991 to Rs. 29513 crores ($ 8367 million) in 1996 (up to September).

Table 7.6: Foreign direct investment: Actual inflows vs. approvals

	1991	**1992**	**1993**	**1994**	**1995**	**1996**	**Total 91-96***
Approvals							
Rs. Crores	739	5256	11189	13591	37489	29513	97777
US $ Million	325	1781	3559	4332	11245	8367	29608
Actual Inflows							
Rs. Crores	351	675	1786	3009	6720	5877	18418
US $ Million	155	233	574	959	2100	1670	5690
Actual as % of approval	48	13	16	22	19	20	19

Source: Government of India, Economic Survey, 1996-97, p. 99.

* Up to September 1996.
Note: The approval and actual figures include NRI direct investment approved by RBI.

Yet actual FDI inflows were only US$2.1 billion in 1996 out of the US$11.2 billion approved and the share of actual inflows declines in comparison to the approved amount again in 1996. Despite these large discrepancies between actual and approved figures, the actual inflows of FDI have shown high rates of annual growth. Thus, Table 7.11, shows actual inflows of FDI almost doubled every year in the post-reforms period. In Dollar terms, India used to attract an average annual inflow of FDI of $150 million during the 1980 to 1990 period. The actual inflows of FDI increased to $233 million in 1992 and further to nearly $1 billion in 1994 and 1.5 billion in 1995, 1.7 billion in 1996 (up to September). A major share of such direct investment was flowing into the engineering sector, electrical and electronic equipment sector, manufacturing sector and into finance companies.[17]

Reasons for Low NRI Investment

Post liberalisation analysis by the Government of India and by the Indian Press have given the impression that NRI investment has been an important factor in the Indian economy's recovery:

> NRIs are emerging as important investors in India according to the India Investment Centre (IIC). There has been considerable increase in investments made by NRIs in different projects during the post liberalisation period. The total NRI investment committed in 1990 was a mere 52.4 million rupees and this went up to 197 million rupees in 1991 (...) Between August 1991 and February 1993 the total approval given by the government, including the RBI aggregates to 67.9 billion rupees and out of this NRI approvals amount to 5.38 billion rupees – nearly 8% of the total investment approved. During this period the NRIs emerged as the 4th largest investors only behind the USA, Switzerland and Japan.[18]

But actually looking at the exact figures gives quite another picture. NRI investment after 1991 can only be considered high if one compares it to the period before liberalisation, where it was indeed minute.

Table 7.7: Investments made by NRIs (amount in Rs Crores)

	31.3.87	31.3.88	31.3.89	31.3.90
I Direct Investment on Repatriation Basis (proposal approved)				
a. 40% Scheme	829.31	989.33	1186.22	1373.49
b. 74% Scheme	54.55	72.53	83.17	92.07
II Direct Investment on Non-repatriation Basis	138.38	202.30	254.16	302.68
III Portfolio Investment (Actual Purchase of Shares/Debentures)				
a. Repatriation	53.03	64.32	70.99	73.20
b. Without repatriation	0.95	1.91	1.75	2.63
IV Deposits in Indian companies	26.10	26.29	27.43	27.43
V Bank Deposits (outstanding balances in NRE/FCNR Accounts)	7847.31	10170.00	13971.00	17831.00

Source: Lok Sabha debates, Question No. 1435, Winter 1990.

Note: Figures are cumulative.

Direct investment amounted to only Rs 1465 crores in 1990. Since the liberalisation NRI investment has indeed increased to average 7-8 per cent of all foreign investment. For example in 1993 the Indian government had approved foreign investment worth Rs 79.9bn for the first 11 months of the year, out of which NRI contributed Rs 6.82bn or 8 per cent.[19]

The table below the percentage of NRI investments at an even lower rate since the reforms: between 3.7 per cent in 1991 to 11 per cent in 1992, the average being about 5 per cent. As a percentage, this is rather low, considering the expatriate Chinese account for around 80 per cent of their country's foreign investment (see next section).[20]

Table 7.8: Non Resident Indians are an important source of investment

India	India's total foreign investment approvals ($ millions)	Share by NRIs (%)
1983	61.3	10.5
1984	99.5	13.0
1985	101.9	15.1
1986	84.8	7.4
1987	82.1	19.3
1988	173.2	7.4
1989	195.1	6.7
1990	73.3	4.1
1991	234.9	3.7
1992	1267.2	11.6
1993 (Jan-May)	1046.9	5.6

Source: Far Eastern Economic Review 26 January 1995.

The reasons for low NRI involvement have to be traced back to their relationship with their country of origin and to the structure of the Diaspora. In an article in the Financial Times G. Piramal suspects that the 'lack of seriously wealthy people flourishing outside of India' is just one factor. There is also lack of industrial entrepreneurship added to a general lack of interest in India among second generation immigrants.[21] The Indian Diaspora is actually rather small compared to the size of the Indian population. Estimates are around 14 million, many of which are professionals. There are though a substantial number of expatriate Indian industrialists and traders who have money to invest, know how to propagate and industry to expand. But it has been seen in chapter 6 that despite the reforms the basic relationship between the Indian government and the NRIs has not changed. Although the Government of India has set out specific incentives to promote NRI investments and has instructed the Indian Investment Centre to encourage the NRIs interest in their country of origin, it has not been perceived as enough by the NRIs concerned. The Government still expects them to put up with the petty hassles of Indian bureaucracy, besides having limited rights on residency periods, they are expected to build new industry with new technology and know-how despite having limited property and importing rights. The NRIs in turn feel that they are given no special concessions and that they are not treated on par with resident Indians. For any transaction the NRIs need to go through major paperwork such as forms for RBI approval. The most common forms are listed below:

Forms for seeking RBI approval with official acronyms[22]

1. Investment in proprietorship/partnership concern by NRIs Non - repatriation basis, (FIN)
2. Purchase of shares of companies in India, (FNC)
3. Fresh acquisition and holdings of immovable property in India, (IPI1)
4. Sale & Transfer of immovable property in India, (IPI2)
5. Issue of shares/Debentures to Non Residents, (ISD)
6. Investment in Shares/Debentures through stock exchange by NRI on Non repatriation basis, (NRI)
7. Investment in Shares/Debentures through stock exchange by NRI on repatriation basis, (RPI)
8. Transfer of Shares by Non Residents, (TS1)
9. Transfer of Shares through stock exchange acquired by NRI/OCBs under direct investment scheme with repatriation benefits, (TS4)

Main investor problems in India

The problems faced by companies and foreign investors are of varied nature. They affect NRIs as well as all other investors such as multinational companies and other private foreign investors. Among the major reason for the delays in implementing projects are:

- Non co-operation of Government officials;
- Inconsistency in Government policies;
- Delays in obtaining clearance from the Pollution Control Board;
- Lack of co-ordination between the central and state policies;
- Getting electrical power connections, loan problems, poor infrastructure and lack of professionalism in handling the cases;
- An excessively zealous and time consuming judiciary systems;
- Corruption among officials; and
- Strong reactions from local people and opposition parties regarding the set up of new industries.

The Indian Investment Centre, a Government of India organisation, operational for the last 30 years gives long lists of complicated do and don'ts to the potential investor. Despite advocating an open economy and promising to facilitate the bureaucracy, the Indian system is actually still bogged down by complex regulations which in turn waste precious time and money.

Despite the moderate success of the economic reforms since 1991, there were some negative reactions and criticisms either by the public or through media reports. The BJP emerged as a strong political party in the 1990s and part of its agenda was 'economic nationalism.'[23] One view from the BJP has been that India should be more self-reliant a familiar policy of the earlier days. In its view, foreign companies were not to be allowed to invest in consumer goods, which would bring in elitist goods and further increase social tension. Their investment was to be limited to infrastructure and to improve the technological level of India's industry. A regular BJP slogan in the early 90s was 'No potato chips, only microchips'. The BJP lived up to its ideals when they threw out the Enron contract in 1996 after taking over from the Congress in the state of Maharashtra. The deal was later re-negotiated, but left a specific impression on how a future BJP government was going to handle the Indian economy. No doubt this attitude deterred foreign investment.

Reforms Under the BJP Government

Since 1997 there has been a new government in power led by the BJP party. It is though a coalition government, largely reliant on smaller parties of the extreme right and regional parties. As a result of the nature of the alliance, any new policies take a very long time to push through, since the agreement of many different parties is needed. The reform process has continued, albeit at a very slow rate.

> While foreign investment is welcomed in wide-ranging activities, simultaneous measures have been introduced in the form of dividend balancing, foreign exchange neutrality, foreign equity cap, etc. based on sectoral sensitivities with a view to providing a level playing field to the domestic industry as also protect national interest.[24]

The BJP government has officially recognised the growing importance of FDI as an instrument of technology transfer and the augmentation of foreign exchange reserves and made it a part of the New Industrial Policy.[25] The liberalised foreign investment policy provides for *automatic* approval of up to:

- 100 per cent equity in 2 categories of industries: electricity generation (non-nuclear) and construction of infrastructure (roads, bridges etc.);
- 74 per cent equity in 9 categories (new in 1997): includes mining services, basic metals, other manufacturing industries, construction etc.;
- 51 per cent equity in 21 categories (expanded by 14 in 1997): includes Agriculture, plantations, manufacturing of food products, of textile products, paper, basic chemicals, rubber non metallic mineral and metal products, machinery and equipment, restaurant and hotels, business and health services etc.;
- 50 per cent in 3 categories: Mining of iron ore, of metals and of non-metallic metals.

The industries which were deliscenced in 1998 and 1999 were coal and lignite, petroleum and its distillation products and sugar. All other industries are assessed on a case by case basis by the Foreign Investment Promotion Board.

Trade and other policy initiatives[26]/[27]

Amongst other things the BJP government simplified import control policy with the abolition of import licensing, except for consumer goods and a small negative list of banned and restricted items. The duties on capital goods have been reduced further for export schemes and certain project imports.

Most importantly certain restrictions imposed by FERA have been reduced so as to reduce the constraints for firms operating with foreign equity. The requirement of prior/final approval by the RBI for bringing in foreign investment or the allotment of shares against proposals duly approved, has been dispensed with. New companies will now only have to file the required documents with the RBI regional office within 30 days of issue of shares. This means that the RBI has delegated powers to its regional offices for granting automatic approval in respect of foreign collaboration.

In case of shortfall in NRI contributions in private sector banks, multilateral financial institutions are now also allowed to contribute foreign equity to the extent of the shortfall in NRI contributions up to 40 per cent.

Besides selected infrastructure projects of Rs. 100 crore and above have been taken up for detailed monitoring to remove bottlenecks and expedite implementation. The government has also decided to set up a Foreign Investment Implementation Authority (FIIA) in the Ministry of Industry to ensure quicker implementation of FDI approvals.[28]

The BJP's other liberalisations include:

- The credit card business and money changing business have been included in approved non-banking financial activities for FDI.
- Protection of intellectual property rights is being ensured by India acceding to the Paris Convention.[29]
- The insurance sector is in the process of being opened to private investment.

PIO cards[30]

As for special incentives for the NRIs, the Person of Indian Origin (PIO) Card scheme was launched on the 31.3.1999. This was the answer to the long-standing request of dual nationality by NRIs/PIOs who were interested in investing in India. The PIO card allows for some special economic, educational, financial and cultural benefits besides acting as a long-term visa for the cost of $1000 for the duration of 20 years. They include:

1. No registration with the FRRO if the stay does not exceed 180 days.
2. For acquisition, holding, transfer and disposal of immovable properties PIO cardholders would be given parity with NRI nationals.
3. Children of PIO card holders will be treated at par with children of NRI nationals with respect to admission to educational institutions in India.
4. They would be eligible for NRI nationals housing schemes.
5. The PIO card though excludes any political rights.

Apart from the PIO card there have been no further special incentives for NRI investments. In both the 1999 and the 2000 budget they get barely a one line mention. The current policies do not reflect a particularly strong courting of the NRIs. Yet in contrast to the budget speeches, the Chennai declaration of the BJP included an interesting paragraph in the section on 'strengthening our mooring in our basic beliefs':

> We believe that the vast community of NRIs and PIOs also constitute a part of the Great Indian Family. We should endeavour to continually strengthen their social, cultural, economic and emotional ties with their mother country. They are a rich reservoir of intellectual, managerial and entrepreneurial resources. The Government should devise innovative schemes to facilitate the investment of these resources for India's all-round development.[31]

This particular statement is the absolute rejection of the Nehruvian doctrine which was at the heart of Indian policy for close to 45 years. However it has to be noted that till now this remains part of the rhetorical discourse the different governments have been giving since 1991 and where implementation is still lagging severely behind, as will be seen in the next section.

The current status of India's economy[32]

India's GDP at current prices is US$ 372 billion for 1998 and US$ 421 billion for 1999 (provisional). The Foreign Exchange Reserves are at US$ 29.52 billion (March 1999) which covers approximately 7 months of imports. Total foreign debt as a share of GDP has declined to 26 per cent.[33]

Table 7.9: FDI approvals v/s actuals

Year	FDI approvals (Rs billion)	FDI inflows (Rs billion)
1991	5	4
1992	39	7
1993	89	18
1994	142	33
1995	321	68
1996	361	101
1997	549	155
1998 (Aug)	229	73

Source: India means business, Perspectives, Ministry of External Affairs, November 1998, p.13.

To this date actual FDI inflows are a fraction of the approved amounts. This has not changed under the BJP government despite the fact that the

BJP promised speedy implementation of all proposed industrial and other projects based on FDI.

Table 7.10: NRI inflows as a part of FDI (US$ million)

Year	NRI Inflows	FDI Inflows (including NRIs)
1991/92	63	133
1992/93	51	559
1993/94	217	4153
1994/95	442	5138
1995/96	739	4971
1996/97	639	6133
1997/98	241	5385
1998/99	62	2401

Source: Reserve Bank of India Bulletin, October 1999.

NRI investments touched a high in 1995/96 and have been falling ever since. As a result special permission was given for domestic mutual funds to seek NRI investments, NRIs were given permission to invest in air taxi operations and to transfer by way of gift immovable property held by them to charitable organisations in India. The Non Resident (Special) rupee-deposits (replacing the FCNR(A) deposits) which were introduced in April 1999 are yet to attract investments.[34]

Still NRI inflows remain a small fraction of the actual FDI flowing into India despite further reforms. They oscillate around the 8% mark, only reaching 10% in 1996. Political instability, India going to the polls three times in only a few years, and fluctuation in the value of the rupee also have a stringent impact on FDI, as seen in the figures for 1997 and 1998.

Comparison of India's Position with China with Regard to FDI

Although FDI flows to India increased ever since the announcement of the new industrial policy in 1991, India still lags behind other developing counties in investment terms. Notably, India has not been able to attract as much foreign investment as China, which has also introduced structural reforms and has been following a policy of liberalisation. G. Etienne, a

Swiss economist, who wrote extensively on both India and China, commented that though India scores over China in respect of its legal system, political institutions and system of higher education, China on the other hand scores over India in the area of FDI.[35] According to him the Chinese seem more open towards FDI and unlike India do not have any kind of inhibition towards it. Although China's combination of a dynamic market economy with a communist dictatorship seems an absurdity, the Chinese government in 1978 switched to a policy of gradually introducing market mechanisms and introducing foreign firms. As a result the economy's efficiency went up. India on the other hand only cautiously reformed its socialist system in the 1980s, but even in the more radical 1991 liberalisations the Indian economy's efficiency did not improve much.[36] China's FDI strategy has been based on an area specific approach. This approach has ensured that the limited infrastructure and respective policy vis-à-vis labour did not have its effect on the free play of the market forces within the stipulated region.

Table 7.11: FDI inflow country wise (billions of US dollars)

Country	1991	1992	1993	1994	1995
India	0.1	0.2	0.3	0.6	1.8
Taiwan	1.3	0.9	0.9	1.4	1.5
Korea	1.2	0.7	0.6	0.8	1.5
Thailand	2.0	2.1	1.7	0.6	2.3
Singapore	4.9	2.4	5.0	5.6	5.3
South East Asia	20.8	27.2	46.5	53.6	56.0
China	4.4	11.2	27.5	33.8	37.5
Developing Countries	41.3	50.4	73.1	87.0	99.7
World	157.8	168.1	207.9	225.6	314.9

Source: United Nations Trade and Development Report, 1995.

It can be seen in Table 7.11 that China has attracted much larger amounts of FDI than India. In 1995, India attracted a $1.8 billion increase, whilst China received about $37.5 billion, which is almost 30 times more than India. In fact between 1979 and 1993 China already received $60 billion FDI while India received a mere $2 billion.[37]

There are certain advantages to China as compared to India: First of all 'China does not have a strong legal tradition',[38] secondly the domestic market in China consists of about one billion customers. China has exhibited a very high rate of savings resulting from its austerity policies. Its savings and investment rates are around 35 per cent of the GNP compared to the Indian rates of only two thirds as high.[39] Thirdly Chinese enterprises have a strong performance record. China also has a strong infrastructure. Compared to China, India's power, transport, and seaports still leave much to be desired. And, there is no political instability in China. The lack of a complicated bureaucratic system and a certain amount of transparency in economic policies are the main reasons behind China's success. Furthermore China has no private property and no large indigenous private enterprises.[40]

But a major difference lies in the respective countries relationship with its Diaspora: Looking at the expatriate Chinese one notices that China has a Diaspora of overseas Chinese both near and far.

> Taiwan with 25 million have $40 million to invest. Hong Kong with 4 million Chinese have an equivalent amount to invest. They are the major investors in China.[41]

Then there are all the other expatriate Chinese in South East Asia, the US, Canada, Australia and Europe. All of them are still considered Chinese by the Government in Beijing with inherent rights to return to the country of their ancestors. Including Hong Kong and Taiwan they total around 55 million. They retain links with their ancestral land through a network of associations prominent in the cities they inhabit.[42]

Historically Beijing's policies towards their people abroad have been one of inclusion: China's 1949 Common Programme pledged to protect 'the legitimate rights and interests of Chinese residing abroad'. In 1954 the Draft Constitution even provided for Overseas Chinese representation in the National People's Congress, and later China pledged to resolve problems of Overseas Chinese through negotiations with the governments with which it had diplomatic relations.[43] In fact Beijing pursued a politically motivated activist policy which offended the elites of the various countries. From 1954-55 onwards Beijing tried to cultivate newly emerging nations by making the settlement of problems relating to the overseas Chinese conditional on political recognition.[44] China's problem with its Diaspora was more complicated than the overseas Indian one as overseas Chinese could hold dual nationality. The traditional Chinese attitude was that a child born to a Chinese father or mother either in China or elsewhere was looked upon as Chinese.[45] In India there was no concept of nationality before the British arrived. The main exception was the agreement reached with Indonesia where the Chinese population had to chose between one or the other nationality. There emerged a pattern that regimes friendly with Beijing would not have Chinese interference when it came to the Diaspora. Beijing turned a blind eye to the massacre of the Chinese population at Sukarno's death, whilst similar massacres in Malaysia were severely condemned. Malaysia was anti-Communist and not on friendly terms with Beijing.[46]

Besides China's attitude towards the Diaspora, there was and is among the Chinese a deep-rooted attachment to Chinese culture. This attachment was fortified by the existence of a commonly accepted culture.

> Thus the phenomenon of one country, one culture and one ruler gave the Chinese a coherent whole from which they could draw inspiration and identity.[47]

It created a kind of 'ethnic solidarity' unknown to the Indians and their counterparts abroad.

India's Diaspora on the other hand is made up largely of professionals such as lawyers and doctors, who have less interest in investing back in their country of origin. According to T.Thomas they may have less than 5 per cent of what the Chinese Diaspora has as investible funds.[48] Besides there is a smaller degree of affinity to India, as India is a multi-cultural, multi-lingual, multi-religious amalgam with more than one civil society. In general the NRI identifies with the state of his origin more closely than with the country as a whole. Most importantly though is that there is no Hong Kong/Taiwan or equivalent offshore and that the Indian Diaspora is smaller and more dispersed than the Chinese equivalent.

Though often China and India are compared with each other, much to the detriment of India, the points above have shown that the parameters are too different to draw any useful parallels between the two Asian giants. Yet it has to be stressed that India could do more to attract investments from the NRIs. It is evidently not enough for India to have the makings of a modern financial system with stock-markets, banks and courts (and 'lawyers, who know at least in theory that not all commercial disputes are before them because foreigners have done wrong'[49]). In order for the government of India to attract more FDI, especially from the NRIs, it would have to work on the bureaucracy and follow up the 1991 reforms with more de-licensing and a general simplification of the system.

Conclusion

In conclusion, it can be said that, although FDI inflows into India substantially increased since the announcement of new industrial policy, the overall economic development has not been as satisfactory as expected. As mentioned in chapter 3, from 1948 to the mid-1980s the rate of FDI inflow was very poor. During that time, the Government allowed very limited foreign direct investments, tariff rates were high, and there were restrictions on imports and exports. In those days no difference between NRIs and other foreign investment were made; and the NRIs in general stayed clear of investing in India.

The 1991 reforms opened the Indian economy to foreign investments. The NRIs were targeted as a specific group with special incentives which included high interest rates and reduced tax rates. There was some NRI investment both in FDI and portfolio investment. The Government of India's repatriation policy attracted some NRI investment in both the consumer and social sector in India. But as the data has shown NRI investment remained painfully low.

India seems to have had a problem attracting foreign investment as opposed to other countries such as China. The main source of its problems lie with the fact that even the 1991 reforms did not go far enough. Furthermore the problem lies with the country's relationship with its Diaspora. Unlike China, India did not court its expatriates and offered limited special incentives for the section of NRIs who had the means and the interest to invest. With all the skills of the NRI community India could have tapped into the resources of a rich and successful community settled abroad who had a good reason to help India develop. This chapter has exposed that even after the 1991 liberalisation the actual investments from the NRI community have remained low and that the relationship between the government of India and the Diaspora did not substantially change between 1947 and 1999 despite a change in the government's rhetoric first in the 1980s and more so in the early 1990s.

Endnotes

1 See chapter 3, foreign economic policy
2 See chapter 5
3 The reasons, which forced India to open-up, have been looked at in chapter 6

4 Coal and Lignite; Petroleum (other than crude) and its distillation products; Distillation and brewing of alcoholic drinks; Sugar; Animal fats and oils; Cigars and Cigarettes of Tobacco and manufactured tobacco substitutes; Asbestos and Asbestos based products; Plywood, decorative veneers, and other wood based products such as boards; Raw hides and skins, leather, chamois leather and patent leather; Tanned and dressed Fur skins; Motor cars; Paper and Newsprint except bagasse-based units; Electronic aerospace and defence equipment: All types; Industrial explosives including detonating fuse, safety fuse, gun powder; nitro-cellulose and matches; Hazardous chemicals; Drugs and Pharmaceuticals; Entertainment electronics (VCRs, Colour TVs, CD Players, tape Recorders); White Goods (Domestic Refrigerators, Dish Washing machines, Programmable Domestic Washing Machines, Microwave ovens, Air Conditioners);
Source: Economic Survey 1996-1997, Annexure 3A, Government of India
5 See chapter 5
6 *Facilities and Incentives for NRIs*, Indians Investment Centre, p.2-3
7 This definition is evidently linked to holding Indian citizenship. It is the only official definition given by the Government of India but is meant for tax purposes only. Investments in the various schemes open to NRIs are generally open to people of Indian origin irrespective of their nationality. Yet this specification is consistent with Indian foreign economic policy which tried to limit outside involvement. See chapter 1 for more details
8 *Facilities and Incentives for NRIs,* Indians Investment Centre, p.2-3
9 Ibid., p.3
10 Ibid., p.3
11 Sing, R. and Pal, K. 'Investment Planning for NRIs', Financial Express, 22.5.1994.
12 Ibid.
13 *110 investment opportunities available to NRIs*, p.69
14 Ibid., p.224
15 Chacko, B.J., *NRI: Guide on Taxation, Investment and Incentives*, p.220-241
16 Chacko, B.J., *NRI: Guide on Taxation, Investment and Incentives*, p.266
17 *Government of India, Economic Survey, 1996-97*, p. 97-99
18 SWB, Press Trust of India, 12.5.1993
19 Shiraz Sidhva, 'Foreign Investment on the Rise', Financial Times, 31.12.1993
20 Wolf, M., 'The Markets: A Tale of two Giants', FT 29.5.95
21 'Survey of India: Where are the expatriates?', G.Piramal, Financial Times, 30.9.1993
22 'NRI Portfolio Management - An Overview', Financial Express, 11.2.1992
23 Krishna Ananth, V.,'Swadeshi and Left', The Hindu, 18.10.1996
24 *Survey of Important Developments During 1998-1999 – Achievements and Future Prospects*, Annual Report, Ministry of Industry, Chapter 1
25 *Foreign Investment Policy of the Government of India*, Indian Investment Centre, New Delhi, July 1999, p. 1 and 2;
26 Ibid. p.2
27 *Survey of Important Developments During 1998-1999 – Achievements and Future Prospects*, Annual Report, Ministry of Industry, Chapter 1
28 Ibid.
29 'Foreign investment in India', Indo-German Economy, 4/99

30 *Ready Reckoner for NRI Investment*, Secretariat for Industrial Assistance (SIA), Department of Industrial Policy and Promotion, Government of India, May 1999, p. 23-24
31 'Chennai Declaration', BJP News Report, 28th - 29th December 1999
32 *Foreign Investment Policy of the Government of India*, Indian Investment Centre, New Delhi, July 1999, p.3
33 'Foreign investment in India', Indo-German Economy, 4/99
34 'NRI inflows crossed $21bn. In March 1999', The Indian Express, 7.7.1999
35 The Hindu, 29.12.1993
36 Rohwer, J., 'Measuring up the Giants – China First, India Next', The Economist, 30.10.93
37 Wolf, M., 'A Tale Of Two Giants', Financial Times, 29.5.95
38 Perkin, D., 'Completing China's more to the Market,' Journal of Economic Perspective, Spring 1994, p. 34
39 Rohwer, J., 'Measuring up the Giants – China First, India Next', The Economist, 30.10.93
40 Wolf, M., 'The markets: A Tale Of Two Giants', Financial Times, 29.5.95
41 Thomas, T., 'Comparison Of China and India For Investments', Reuters News, 10.8.1993
42 Financial Times, 27.6.1996
43 Ram, M., 'The Heritage of the Raj', Far Eastern Economic Review, 23.11.1979
44 Bahadur Singh, I.J. (ed.), *The Other India: The Overseas Indians and their Relationship with India*, p.229
45 Bahadur Singh, I.J. (ed.), *The Other India: The Overseas Indians and their Relationship with India*, p.225
46 Ghai, Y. and Ghai, D., 'The Asian Minorities of East and Central Africa up to 1971', p.319-324
47 Bahadur Singh, I.J. (ed.), *The Other India: The Overseas Indians and their Relationship with India*, p.226
48 Thomas, T., 'Comparison of China And India For Investments', Reuters News, 10.8.93
49 Rohwer, J., 'Measuring up the Giants – China First; India Next', The Economist, 30.10.1993

8 Conclusion

At independence and for the subsequent years India was economically quite weak. India remained a democracy shunning any form of radical dictatorship, yet chose ideology, not national interest to guide her foreign policy path over the next 40 odd years. Despite economic and development problems the government made the conscious choice for ideological reasons to exclude from its development its rather rich Diaspora. The expatriate Asian was a victim of this form of government and what could have been a mutually beneficial relationship did not develop. As a result of these policies India's development suffered.

To this day the ties between India and its Diaspora are of a curious nature: they are mainly based on trans-national family relations and private interests the individual expatriate might have in the region/state of his origin. The actual dialogue between the central government and the Diaspora as a whole remains governed by the old ideals of non-interference and suspicion, despite rhetorical change. Since the 1991 reforms the word 'NRI' has come to symbolise the liberalisation of the Indian system. This means that the government presented various schemes in order to attract FDI. Information for the NRIs specifically was streamlined in the India Investment Centre to which any query was referred, yet there was no specific mobilisation through the embassies or High Commissions to recruit investment on a large scale. Rhetorically the NRIs have been courted so that they might come and support their mother country, yet the actual policy changes still looked like the Indian government was intent on keeping FDI in general and NRI investment in particular out of India.

The problem which has been addressed in this book, is the failure of the Indian government to develop a relationship with its Diaspora throughout the post-independence years and to use this asset to assist Indian economic development. Furthermore it is noted that since Diasporas in general are important and powerful non-state actors which can influence policies in both their home and host countries, the case of India is an unusual one.

What Does the Diaspora Mean to India?

To the pre-independence Indian government the expatriate Indians were victims of the British colonial system, having been forced to leave India for economic reasons. They were a product of the British system of exploitation. As a result they were very much regarded as part of the Indian nation which had to fight off colonial rule. In fact the general idea was that until India was independent from Britain, the Indian government could not properly defend the interests of the expatriate Indian. As has been seen in chapter 4, there was a major anti-imperial rallying campaign going on in different parts of the British Empire. There, the richer parts of the Indian Diaspora, located mainly in East Africa were called upon to fund the anti-colonial struggle and to support by whichever means the fight in India.[1]

Post-independence India regarded the expatriate Indian very differently. As anyone living in India would quickly recognise, the Diaspora is viewed as a group of people who abandoned India for their own and their family's economic benefit. They did not contribute to India's struggle or to India's growth. They left for selfish reasons and for selfish reasons they did not return. By abandoning their mother country they have in fact lost their Indianess. Whatever reasons makes them or their money come back is to be mistrusted, as they will not do anything for the sake of India, but only for the sake of financial gain. They are not considered representatives of India, but rather a legacy showing the bad side of India. Being a product of the imperial system they have exploited the local population of the developing countries they inhabit, taking over the position the British held before the demise of the colonial system.

The government's position is echoed by the public opinion. There are few Indians who do not look at returning NRIs and their investment with suspicion. Since they have abandoned their mother country once, it is likely that they have only returned for their own benefit, and not that of India. Although private family ties are maintained and private financial contributions are not frowned upon, there is a general mistrust when it comes to NRIs being given equal rights with respect to investment and property.[2]

There are three major conclusions addressing India's foreign policy development, India's early relationship with the Diaspora and the changed scenario after the 1991-liberalisation reforms.

The framework used for analysis was foreign policy analysis. The third chapter concluded that as long as Indian foreign policy was ideologically driven, it was consistent; regional policy on the other hand was not based on ideals and was consequently reactive.[3] Issues concerning the Diaspora were international not regional problems. Therefore they fell into the policies governed by ideals and morals. As Indian foreign policy priorities developed the NRIs were excluded totally and did not become part of foreign policy formulation at all. Besides self-sufficient economic development hindered NRI participation. Post imperial-India was economically weak; but self-sufficiency, not interdependence had been chosen as the route to development. It was precisely the ideological framework which India developed that was to hinder a state-Diaspora relationship from developing. Yet whilst these ideals faded and changed over time, the exclusion of the Diaspora remained a constant.

India's foreign policy choices after Nehru were based on realist assumptions of power and regional stability. Unlike her father Indira Gandhi did not look at India's image in the world as one of her priorities, but pushed for a hegemonic position in the region. Her regional and international decisions were based on the facts that India had severe regional problems with both Pakistan and China. There was further international friction with the US who supported both Pakistan and after the Sino-Soviet split, also China. It was in India's interest to remain friendly with the Soviet Union, who in turn had problems with China and the United States, not least because of the Soviet invasion of Afghanistan. The origins of Indo-Soviet friendship are complex and are part of pre-Indira Gandhi policy formulation, yet it is safe to say that the geopolitical outlook of Mrs Gandhi was based on the framework mentioned above.

The switch in foreign policy perspectives between Nehru and Gandhi was tremendous, Nehru being interested in large international issues, Gandhi in bilateral and regional issues. The foreign policy change did not extend into the economic front. Indira Gandhi remained suspicious of foreign direct investment which smelt of outside interference, and did not look for active support from the Diaspora. She made herself particularly unpopular during the East African crisis of 1968-1972 when she clearly endorsed the Nehruvian attitude of non-involvement and put India's relations with the African States first. In the bargain came a public showdown with Britain where India could publicly force Britain to live up to its colonial responsibilities, by having to let all Asians with British passports into the country. This was to Indira Gandhi a sign of India's strength.

The chapter shows that from independence onwards the issues concerning the Diaspora were excluded by Indian foreign policy and that even when there was a switch from idealism to realism with Indira Gandhi, there was no change with respect to the Diaspora. Economic foreign policy was based on similar ideals of self-sufficiency and the limitation of external involvement and therefore the Diaspora remained excluded.

The fourth chapter on India's relationship with expatriates, shows that in pre-independence times there was an intense relationship, as it was under the British colonial system that the labour expatriation started. The Indian government during the British period took great interest in the fate of the expatriate Indians, their rights and how they were treated. Later when the independence campaign was growing the Diaspora was called upon to contribute financially to the cause. The plight of Indians abroad was a major issue for the independence movement. The Government of India felt it could only offer proper protection once it was an independent government. Then only would it be able to take up the cause of fellow Indians abroad with the respective governments. Especially the Indian communities in East and South Africa were concerned and involved in India gaining independence. Therefore it came as a shock to most expatriate Indians when the Nehruvian attitude was adopted after independence.[4] Nehru developed a policy which encouraged the expatriate Indians to identify and integrate with their host society and not to look at India for help. This major attitude shift took place in light of India's change of perception of the country's role and structure within the new, post Second World War society. India switched from being a nationalist movement trying to break free from imperialism to a nation-state project.

The nationalist movement, one can argue, was geographically very vague and had as main objectives the riddance of the colonial power. Within this nationalist movement the Diaspora was included. With the advent of the nation state with firm borders and Statist priorities such as national integration of the diverging civil societies, came the exclusion of the Diaspora. Not being a homogeneous group made their integration within the new state structure virtually impossible. Nehru believed that an Indian identity would be created through the act of creating a state. This identity would not be based on race or religion, but would adhere to more modern, secular values. Nehru's new state was based on a group of such values including democracy, religious tolerance and cultural pluralism. This new state with a new concept at its base could not endorse fierce nationalism which would have to rally itself around religion or a political personality for stability and which could have included the Diaspora. For India there was only a shared historical past which could bind people. The Diaspora was not part of that past. Nehru needed to find a framework into which India's many civil societies could be fitted. If India was to survive in the modern world and remain a unity; a well-defined nation-state and a new, but vague identity were essential. Sunil Khilnani expresses the development of the Nehruvian model most accurately in his book *The idea of India*:

> Nehru's idea of Indianess emerged through improvised responses to constrained circumstances: its strength was not its ideological intensity, but its ability to steer towards an Indianess seen as layered, adjustable, imagined, not as a fixed property. While Nehru was attracted by the political and economic examples of the modern West, he was far less taken by its cultural models. It was fundamental to him that Indian nationalism could not fashion itself after European examples. In contrast to the academic analysts who see nationalism as the diffusion of a standard form devised in the industrialised West - whether in the Gaelic version of a community of common citizenship or the Voelkish idea of a shared ethnic or cultural origin - Nehru self consciously rejected the idea that Indian nationalism was compelled to make itself in one or other of these images. To that extent Nehru agreed with the two men whose influence he acknowledged as most important to his thinking about this matter, Tagore and Gandhi. But unlike Tagore and Gandhi, for who the state was a dispensable nuisance, Nehru believed that an Indian identity could emerge only within the territorial and institutional frame of a state.[5]

The state created would be committed to protect the cultural and religious difference rather than imposing a stereotype of Indianess.

What is further discussed in this part of this book is that by a nation simply changing its perception and definition of itself in the world, it can not necessarily annihilate its past history. The Indian Diaspora was very much a product of the subcontinent's history. Nehru's new age policy which suddenly cut the ties between those who had expatriated themselves and their mother country, could not reduce those ties at a family and private level. The expatriate Indians would always in one way or another be tied to their country of origin, not least because they would be classified as an ethnic minority within their host country. That classification of being Indian bound them to India. By turning itself into a nation state project with Statist priorities, India did not manage to rid itself of an uncomfortable and at the time perhaps embarrassing group of people. This again was due fundamentally to the diverging civil societies that make up India and which were not erased with the new Statist concept. This meant that the individual expatriate or expatriate group would continue to maintain relations with its state and region of origin no matter what official policy was. So the part of Nehru's Statist policy of non-responsibility towards people of Indian origin was not necessarily a success.

But in time India needed to change as the post cold war world made its idealistic foreign policy framework obsolete and economic development was urgent. Chapter 6 showed that the 1991 reforms brought about a certain measure of change. There was change at all levels: the NRI community, itself now quite different from the communities excluded at independence, were called upon to invest and participate in Indian economic development. Yet although some obstacles for investments were removed, the incentives for investment in general and NRI investment in particular are to this day not very good. Whilst multinational corporations could take financial risks when investing, the structure for the average NRI to set up an independent small to medium size venture and bring his know-how and new technology to the country was not available. Buying property remained restricted to specially reserved areas until the mid 1990s and the bureaucratic processes at state and national level remained fundamentally too long and complex. The government of India and the people in general maintained their suspicion towards foreign investment, and the relationship between the government and the Diaspora did not fundamentally change. This was particularly evident in the government refusing to offer any substantial concessions such as dual nationality to the expatriate Indian community despite repeated demands. To a great extent the unchanging relationship was due to a certain awkwardness of the government having to go with a begging bowl to a community that it had previously ignored. In fact there had been a certain pride in distinguishing oneself from the NRIs who had no real home but still tried to remain Indian. Pride had to be swallowed when asking those for money who had treated you as 'poor country cousins'. This can be particularly understood if it is remembered that a great deal of national pride rests in the fact of being an Indian from India with an intact caste. The 1991 reforms required a swallowing of this national pride at a personal and national level since it involved begging from a community of people on whose very ostracisation lay a certain degree of national identity and pride.

A further issue to be addressed at this point in the analysis of State-Diaspora relations is education. A large part of the problem in the case of India was due to the following facts: Education is seen in India as a means to liberate the individual not to advance society. Formal education is only around 150 years old. It liberated the benefiting individuals, normally middle class and castes from the shackles of Indian societal structure. This in turn prompted a move outward, from the village to the town, from the town to the city, from the city to the metropolis... to abroad. With education came not an embetterment for society, but a loss to society. Hence further education has not been a priority with the government because its results are not ploughed back into the system. Education, especially further education is not what makes Indian society grow. Indian society adopts norms that have not been developed locally, but thought out elsewhere. Further education plays a role in the relationship between the NRI and the Indian Government. In fact it was to a great extent the further education received which allowed for the creation of a sophisticated expatriate community. Education again is an issue which creates resentment on the part of the Indian population, as they do not see why doctors and engineers locally educated should go out to have a better life elsewhere. Till the early 1990s only the immediate family benefited from remittances from the overseas Indians and that in turn divided society further. Since 1991 investments from those abroad were facilitated, yet still rare and the Indian population at large feels that local talent is not integrated back into the Indian system.[6] The education issue creates more resentment in the Diaspora community, as they see that India does not encourage the development of home-grown talent yet expects NRI contributions in order to acquire the necessary ideas and tools which have been developed elsewhere. So one can see that another issue of contention between the Diaspora and the government of India is that of education and how the Diaspora's view on Indian development differs from that of the state.

The last chapter concluded that as a result of unchanging attitudes, NRI investment remained painfully lows, around 7-8 per cent of all FDI. There was a move by the press to show that measures to attract NRI investment have been a great success, but this can only be accepted in relations to the pre-1991 figures, when there had been next to no NRI foreign direct investment at all. The only thing which increased are the deposits in special bank accounts with which the government of India attempted to attract large sums of money at very high interest rates for short periods in order to help smooth over a chronic cash shortage. Unfortunately the high interest rates which attracted a lot of NRI hot money forced the government of

India to borrow from other sources in order to be able to pay for the interest rates.

The brief comparison with China and its expatriates showed that there are other kinds of possible relationships, since China attracts over 80 per cent of FDI from its expatriate community.

A Missed Opportunity

These three conclusions lead to the following thoughts: Since India excluded the Diaspora in its post independence development it did so at a certain cost. One can only speculate how much the economic cost has been over the years. What is certain is that this was truly a missed opportunity as from independence onwards the different communities of the Diaspora could have contributed to India's economic growth. Their profile throughout the past 50 years is that of a rather rich and successful community who never lost interest in India. Their ties to their home regions could have been exploited without altering the centre's policy of building relations with the Diaspora's host counties. The opportunity was missed at several stages and times. Whilst it is unlikely that Nehru would have actively courted NRI involvement in post independence India, change was possible from the mid 1960s onwards. Indira Gandhi could have maintained a closed economy, yet allowed NRI investment especially after having shown India's strength internationally with the victory of the 1971 war against Pakistan. At that particular point India's foreign policy was being reformulated along realist lines and this could have been a point for starting a dialogue with the Diaspora. Yet as is seen in the Appendix[7] no policy for the Diaspora was in place until much later. Again, in the mid to late 1980s an opportunity was missed when Rajiv Gandhi tried to move India's foreign policy priorities away from the region to inter-third world co-operation. The NRIs and their financial capabilities could have been welcomed to help India grow in light of the development taking place in South East Asia in the same period. After all China invited non resident Chinese investments right through the 1980s. Yet the question of NRI money and other capabilities only became a political issue when India's economy almost collapsed in 1990. It was then that the curious calls for NRI investment and donations to save the mother country were heard. Suddenly politicians speculated that if only each and every NRI gave a small percentage of his or her income for the benefit of India, the national debt would be recovered and India would grow like some of the South East Asian tigers. How such calls could be made in light of years of Nehruvian policy is difficult to understand. Yet even despite those calls the actual policies never allowed for intensive investments. Was India's caution after the first success of liberalisation due to the experiences faced by other countries such as Russia and other post soviet states? After all these countries went through enormous political change and at huge social costs which India might have felt she could not afford. Was it simply because the Indian bureaucracy, not slashed to the bare minimum, still blocked the process of reforms? Why the reforms after 1992/3 stagnated, one can only speculate. What this stagnation in effect meant for India was that to the mid 1990s optimal growth rates were not reached, and further investment from the NRIs in particular stayed away.

For matters to change today there would have to be a major change in Indian public and governmental attitudes. A paradigm shift of this magnitude could only come about if the Indian population could quickly and effectively feel the benefits of economic liberalisation. In other words the population would have to experience not only the inflation which inevitably comes with the opening up of markets, but a distinct rise in standards of living. For many this would be particularly difficult to measure, as there is no Indian equivalent to the American dream of owning a car, a house etc. With these goals missing in the average Indian psyche it is difficult to explain to the average Indian family what to expect from a growing economy. Only with an understanding of the benefits of globalisation in the Indian economy could public attitudes change. Unfortunately India's size and enormous population is hardly in a position to go through such changes smoothly. At present the general feeling is that it is the NRIs and other multinationals who benefit from the Indian markets whilst the local population has to put up with staggering price rises, and more goods on the shelf a majority cannot afford. This is where the popular support for the more nationalist BJP came from. Their call for investments, which would only help develop India's infrastructure, yet leave multinationals such as Coke and KFC at the door (only micro chips, no potato chips) struck a chord with the broad public. There has been significant NRI support for the BJP and its not clearly formulated policies.[8] It has to be noted for instance that the BJP prior to its election did not clearly enunciated its policies towards giving the NRIs more rights in India, be that in the field of investments, property acquisition or nationality/voting rights. Since 1997 the BJP has headed the new coalition government made up of various regional parties. Although the reform process has continued the general problematic trend of actual FDI inflows being only a fraction of the approved amounts has continued. The same goes for NRI investments. They remain a fraction of the FDI flowing into the country. This the case despite the BJP introducing a PIO card, giving the NRIs a certain legal status, which they had been asking for, for years.

In general one can say that the case of India is unusual to the extent that an economically powerful Diaspora which was part of the general public consciousness was excluded on purpose from taking part in India's development. Diasporas as such are powerful entities. They regroup in their chosen host countries and in many instances do not fully integrate with the host society. Amongst Diaspora societies, Indians, along with the Chinese are notorious for non-integration. As a group they maintain relations with their home country, be it through family ties and marriage, through business and commerce relations with their hometown or region, or simply by maintaining local and religious traditions. Such a group can be of help to the country of origin in more than one way. Despite not maintaining the nationality of origin the expatriate group could act as representatives, even as a political lobby in the host country, as the Jewish lobby so effectively does in the United States of America. In this way they could lobby for the national interests of their home country. The other way of supporting the mother country is clearly by contributing to the economic development, especially in the case of developing countries. The money and know how they bring with them is often crucial to their place of origin.

It has been seen in the previous chapters that a strong State-NRI bond did not exist in India for most of the time after independence. India did not court its Diaspora; it actively dissociated itself from it.

This work has not addressed the issue from the point of view of the Diaspora. It has rather sought to give an analysis of how the problem between India and the Diaspora evolved, and why despite the obvious advantages that would have followed from the relationship, it failed to develop. The issue is addressed briefly from an NRI point of view in Shashi Tharoor's book: *India - From Midnight to the Millennium*. In a chapter on NRIs [9] Tharoor states that:

> Most of the contemporary world's emigrants are people who left their homelands in quest of material improvement, looking for financial security and professional opportunities that, for one reason or another, they could not attain in their own countries. Many of them left intending to return: a few years abroad, a few more dollars in the bank, they told themselves, and they

> would come back to their own hearts, triumphant over the adversity that had led them to leave. But the years kept stretching on, and the dollars were never quite enough, or their needs mounted with their acquisitions, or they developed new ties to their new land, and then gradually the realisation seeped in that they would never go back. And with this realisation, often only half acknowledged, came a welter of emotions: guilt at the abandonment of the motherland, mixed with rage that the motherland had somehow - through its own failings, political, economic, social - forced them into this abandonment. The attitude of the expatriate to his homeland is that of the faithless lover who blames the woman he has spurned for not having sufficiently merited his fidelity.[10]

Tharoor goes on to explain that India's policy has not only bred resentment amongst the Diaspora, but that expatriation has in some cases bred extremist political attitudes. In trying to define himself vis-à-vis the host society the expatriate needs an identity. Often this comes in the form of being over assertive of values he remembers from back home, which in an oversimplified version reduce to family, caste and religion. This in turn leads to the financial and moral support of right wing ultra nationalist Indian parties such as the Vishwa Hindu Parishad (VHP) or the Rashriya Swayamsevak Sangh (RSS). Such support is according to Tharoor doubly gratifying, as it appeases the sense of guilt and it vindicates the decision to have left the mother country. This kind of support is highly controversial as it does not help India's developmental needs, yet increases the political turmoil at a time when economic development should be on the forefront of the debate. Furthermore it is important to note that such NRIs take the liberal system of the country they have chosen to live in for granted whilst actively supporting movements which will destroy the liberal structure back in India.

In the case of India there has been little analysis on the State-Diaspora relationship from the Diaspora's point of view.

There has been little research on State – Diaspora relations in general, and no research in the case of India in particular. Yet it has been shown that the case of India is a curious one, defying all logic and contrasting sharply with other State – Diaspora relations.

Endnotes

1 See chapter 4 for details

2 See chapter 6 for details
3 This is true with exception of China till 1962
4 It only dawned on many East African Indians that India was no longer their security net when British immigration legislation limited their entry to Britain and they tried to find alternative support by turning to the Government of India in light of East African independence. Their being told that they were in effect the British government's responsibility came as quite a shock since it was evident that Britain did not want them
5 Khilnani, S., *The Idea Of India*, p.167
6 Based on discussions with Professor Sachin Maheshwari, Dean of the Indian Institute of Technology, New Delhi, summer 1998
7 See Appendix, 'Government offers, NRI response'
8 Tharoor, S., *India From Midnight to the Millennium*, pp.139-143
9 See chapter 6
10 Tharoor, S., *India - From Midnight to the Millennium*, p. 142

Bibliography

'110 Investment Opportunities available to NRIs', New Delhi, 1997.

'Discussing Economic Reforms: Achievements and Further Intent', *Economic and Political Weekly*, 28(31), Bombay, 31 July 1993.

'Facilities and Incentives: For NRI's', *Indian Investment Centre*, New Delhi, 1995.

'Facilities for Non Resident Indians', RBI, New Delhi, June 1999.

'FDI Flows to India: Pre and Post Scenario', *Quarterly Economic Report*, 1994

'FDI: No Looking Back Now', *Press Trust of India*, New Delhi, 8(14), September 1996.

'Foreign Direct Investment', *Quarterly Economic Report*, Indian Institute of Public Opinion, 30(3), New Delhi, September 1996.

'Foreign Investment in India', *Indo-German Economy* 4/99, New Delhi, 1999.

'Foreign Investment Policy of the Government of India', *Indian Investment Centre*, New Delhi, 1995.

'Happy Anniversary', *The Economist*, London, 6 August 1997.

'Harsh Realities, Discourage Indians Abroad from Investing in India', *The Indian*, Hong Kong, October-November 1977.

'India means business', *Perspectives*, Ministry of External Affairs, November 1998.

'Indians Abroad Praised for Anti-Emergency campaign', *The Indian*, Hong Kong, August 1977.

'Indians Abroad', *The Indian*, Hong Kong, July-August 1978.

'Indians Abroad', *The Indian*, Hong Kong, September 1978.

'India's next 50 years', *The Economist*, London, 6 August 1997.

'Investment Opportunities Available to NRIs', *Indian Investment Centre*, New Delhi, June 1997.

'Investments', *Monthly Reviews of the Indian Economy*, Centre for Monitoring Indian Economy, New Delhi, July 1997.

'La Communaute Indienne s'inquiete', Le Figaro, Paris, 26 December 1993.

'NRI Deposits: Why this coyness', *Economic and Political Weekly*, 30 September 1989.

'NRI Inflows crossed $21bn. in March 1999', *The Indian Express*, 7 July 1999.

'Rules and Methods of making Investments in India', *The Indian*, Hong Kong, February-March 1981.

'The Approach of the second Five Year Plan', *Second Five Year Plan*, The Publication Division, Ministry of Information and Broadcasting, Government of India, New Delhi, October 1956.

'The Indian Ideal - The end of the 3rd Way', *Far Eastern Economic Review*, Hong Kong, 21 August 1997.

'Which NRIs?', *Economic and Political Weekly*, 14 July 1990.

A Compilation of Foreign Collaboration Approvals Prepared by the National Register of Foreign Collaboration, Department of Scientific and Industrial Research, New Delhi, 1995.

Africa Diary, January-June 1973.

Agarwal, Rakesh (1986), *Foreign companies and Foreign collaborations*, Nabhi Publishers, New Delhi..

Ali, Ahmad, 'Aspects of Fiji Indian History 1879-1939', *Economic and Political Weekly* 12 (42 and 43), Bombay, October 1977.

Ali, Ahmad, 'Fiji Indians and the Politics of Disparity', *India Quarterly* 4(32) October-December 1976.

Ali, Ahmad, 'The Indians of Fiji', *Economic and Political Weekly*, 8(36), Bombay, 1973.

Ali, S.S., 'Fiji Institutionalised Racial Discrimination', *Mainstream*, 10(30). New Delhi, December 1991.

Alley, Roderic, 'The Military Coup in Fiji', *The Round Table* 304, Commonwealth Journal of International Affairs, London, October 1987.

Amjad, Rashid (1989), *To the Gulf and Back: Studies on the Economic Impact of Asian Labour Migration*, UNDP, Geneva.

Anantakrishnan, S.V., 'The Brain Drain dilemma', *Indian Review*, 75(8), New Delhi, November 1979.

Appadorai, A. and Rajan M.S. (1985), *India's Foreign Policy & Relations*, South Asian Press, New Delhi.

Appadorai, A. (ed.), *Select Documents on India's Foreign Policy & Relations 1947-72*, volume II, Oxford University Press, New Delhi.

Apparsamy, B. (1943), *Indians of South Africa*, Padma Publications Ltd, Bombay.

Ashworth, Georgine (ed.) (1980), *World Minorities in the Eighties*, Quatermaine House Ltd., Sunbury, UK.

Backmann, R., 'Diaspora Chinoise: l'Empire du dehors', *Le Nouvel Observateur*, Paris.

Bahadur Singh, I. J. (ed.) (1982), *Indians in South East Asia*, Sterling Publishers, New Delhi.

Bahadur Singh, I. J. (ed.) (1979), *The Other India: The Overseas Indians and their Relationship with India*, Arnold-Heinnemann, New Delhi.

Balachandran, P.K., 'An Embattled Community: Asians in East Africa Today', *African Affairs*, 80, 1981.

Balakrishna, Pulapre, 'Waiting for Private Investment', *Economic and Political Weekly*, 29 (16 & 17), Bombay, 16-23 April 1994.

Bandyopadhyaya, J. (1970), *The Making of India's Foreign Policy - Determinants, Institutions, Processes & Personalities*, Allied Publishers, New Delhi.

Bandyopadyaya, J. (1980), *The Making of India's Foreign Policy*, Allied Publishers, New Delhi.

Berghe, Pierre, L. van den (ed.) (1970), *Race and Ethnicity*, Basic Books, New York.

Bharati, Agehananda (1972), *Asians in East Africa: Jai Hind & Uhuru*, Teen Murti Library, New Delhi.

Bhatia, D.P., 'Tuning the Economy for a steep Rise in FDI', *Economic Growth and Social*, March 1996.

Bhatia, Prem (1972), *Indian Ordeal in Africa*, Teen Murti Library, New Delhi.

Bhushan, Kul, 'New Indians are Innovators', *The Indian*, Hong Kong, May 1978.

Bhutani, S.K., 'Fiji: self-inflicted Wounds', *World Affairs* 3, Lancer International, New Delhi, December 1991.

Biers, Dan and Sidhva, Shiraz, 'Life in the Slow Lane', *Far Eastern Economic Review*, Hong Kong, 21 August 1997.

Bradnock, R.W. (1990), *India's Foreign Policy Since 1971*, RIIA - Pinter Publishers, London.

British Parliamentary Debates (1972-73) *Hansard*, London, UK.

Budget Speech 1998-99, Economic Times, New Delhi, 1998.

Budget Speech 1999-2000, Economic Times, New Delhi, 1999.

Budget Speech 2000-01, Economic Times, New Delhi, 2000.

Buissoondayal, U. (ed.), *Indians Overseas*, Mahatma Gandhi Institute, Moka, Mauritius.

Cameron, John, 'Fiji, the political economy of recent Events', *Capital & Class* 33, Conference of Socialist Economists, London, Winter 1987.

Carrim, Y., 'Indian South Africans in the Transition to a Post Apartheid South Africa', *Africa Quarterly*, 32(1-4), ICCR, New Delhi, 1992-93.

Chako, B. J. (1994-1995), *NRI: Guide on Taxation, Investment and Incentives*, Wadhawa and Company Law Publishers, Agra.

Chattopadhyaya, H. (1970), *Indians in Africa, a Socio-Economic Study*, Bookland, Calcutta.

Chauhan, I. S., 'India & Politics in Fiji', *Eastern Anthropologist* 44(1), Ethnographic and Folk Cultural Society, Lucknow, January-March 1991.

Chennai Declaration, *BJP News Report*, 28-29 December 1999

Chhabra, H.S., 'Asians in Uganda', *Mainstream*, New Delhi.

Chhabra, H.S., 'India and Africa - Next Door Neighbours', *New African*, January 1981.

Chopra, Prem (1993), *The Crisis of Foreign Policy - Perspectives and Issues*, Wheeler Publishing, Allahabad.

Chopra, S. (ed.) (1983), *Studies in India's Foreign Policy*, Guru Nanak Dev University, Amritsar.

Choucri, Nazli, 'A New Immigration in the Middle East : A Problem for Whom?', *International Migration Review*, 11(4), Winter 1977.

Citizenship Act, 1955 (1956), Universal Law Publishing Co., New Delhi.

Clarke, C., Peach, C. and Vertovec, S. (eds) (1990), *South Asians Overseas - Migration and Ethnicity*, Cambridge University Press, Cambridge.

Damodaran, A.K. and Bajpai, U.S. (eds) (1990), *Indian Foreign Policy - The Indira Gandhi Years*, Sangam Books, New Delhi.

Das Gupta, Surajeet, 'NRI Industrialists: Quiet Success', *India Today*, New Delhi, 15 November 1989.

Datt, Ruddar, 'Multinational Versus Swadeshi', *Mainstream*, Annual, New Delhi, 1993.

Davies, R., O'Meara, D., Dlamini, S. (1944), *India in World Politics - A Historical Analysis & Appraisal*, Sultan Chand & Co., Delhi, Lahore.

Davies, R., O'Meara, D. and Deanini S. (1988), *The Struggle for South Africa*, Zed Books Ltd., London.

Don Nanjira, D.D.C. (1976), *The Status of Aliens in East Africa*, Praeger Publishers inc., New York.

Dubey, Ajay Kumar, 'Indo-African Economic Relations 1965-85 - a Case of South-South Interaction', *Africa Quarterly* 27(3-4), 1987-88.

Dutt, Srikant Kumar, 'India and the Overseas Indians', *India Quarterly*, 36(3-4), New Delhi, 1980.

Dutt, Srikant Kumar (1984), *India and the Third World: Altruism or Hegemony?*, Zed Books Ltd., London.

Dutt, Srikant Kumar (1981), *India's Relations with Developing Countries: A study of the Political Economy of Indian Investment, Aid, Overseas Banking & Insurance*, PhD Thesis, London School of Economics, London.

Dutt, Srikant Kumar (1988), *Viewpoints on the Third World*, Allied Publishers, New Delhi.

Dutt, V.P. (1990), *India and the World*, Sanchar Publishing House, New Delhi.

Dutt, V.P. (1984), *India's Foreign Policy*, Vikas Publishing House, New Delhi.

Economic Survey 1996-97, Government of India, Ministry of Finance, Economic Division, New Delhi, 1996-1997.

Foreign Direct Investment on the Asian and Pacific Region, Paper Presented and Summary of the discussion 25-27 January 1988, Asian Development Bank, Manila, May 1988.

Foreign Investment Policy of the Government of India, *Indian Investment Centre*, New Delhi, July 1999.

Foreign Press, Selected Articles, *Economist*, London, April 1982-September 1995.

Foreign Press, Selected Articles, *Financial Times*, London, April 1982-September 1995.

Foreign Press, Selected Articles, *Reuters news*, London, April 1982-September 1995.

Frankel, F., 'Play the India Card', *Foreign Policy* 62, 1986.

Freund, B., 'The Rise & Decline of an Indian Peasantry in Natal', Journal of Peasant Studies, 15(2), London, January 1991.

Gen. Idi Amin Dada, *Speech at the Commonwealth Heads of State & Governments Meeting*, Ottawa, August 1973.

General Assembly - 5th Session - Plenary Session and Annexes, Official Records UN, New York, 1950.

General Assembly - 7th Session - Plenary Session and Annexes, Official Records UN, New York, 1952.

General Assembly - 9th Session - Plenary Session and Annexes, Official Records UN, New York, 1954.

General Assembly - 10th Session - Plenary Session and Annexes, Official Records UN, New York, 1955.

General Assembly - 12th Session - Plenary Session and Annexes, Official Records UN, New York, 1957.

General Assembly - 13th Session - Plenary Session and Annexes, Official Records UN, New York, 1958.

General Assembly - 14th Session - Plenary Session and Annexes, Official Records UN, New York, 1959.

General Assembly - 15th Session - Plenary Session and Annexes, Official Records UN, New York, 1961.

General Assembly - 16th Session - Plenary Session and Annexes, Official Records UN, New York, 1961.

General Assembly - 17th Session - Plenary Session and Annexes, Official Records UN, New York, 1962.

General Assembly - 27th Session - Plenary Session and Annexes, Official Records UN, New York, 1974.

General Assembly - 27th Session (General Committee), Official Records UN, New York, 1974.

Ghai, Y. and Ghai, D. (1971), 'The Asian Minorities of East and Central Africa up to 1971', *Minority Rights Group Report*, no.4, London, April 1971 (reprinted 1979).

Ghai, Y. and Ghai, D. (eds) (1970), *Portrait of a Minority - Asians in East Africa*, Oxford University Press, Nairobi.

Global Trading Practices & Poverty Alleviation in South Asia, UNIFEM Regional Seminar, UNIFEM, New Delhi, India, 30 January-1 February 1995.

Goswami, Omkar, 'The Fall & Rise of India's Companies', *Business India* (50th Anniversary Issue), Bombay, 11-24 August 1997.

Govinda Raj, B.V. (1959), *India and Disputes in the UN 1946-54*, Vora & Co. Publishers, Bombay.

Gregory, G.R. (1993), *South Asians in East Africa*, Westview Press, Oxford.

Gregory, R.G., 'Cooperation and Collaboration in Colonial East-Africa - The Asians Political-Role, 1890-1964', *African Affairs* 80(319), London, 1981.

Gregory, R. G. (1971), *India and East Africa: A History of Race Relations within the British Empire 1890-1939*, Oxford University Press, Oxford.

Grosse, R.E. (1980), *Foreign Investment Codes and the location of Direct Investment*, Praegers Publishers, New York.

Grover, V. (ed.) (1992), *Africa and India's Foreign Policy*, Deep and Deep Publications, New Delhi.

Grover, V. (ed.) (1992), *International Relations and Foreign Policy of India*, volumes 1, 7 and 8, Deep and Deep Publications, New Delhi.

Guha Thakurta, P. and Protap, A., 'NRI Entrepreneurs - A Mixed Homecoming', *India Today*, New Delhi, 31 July 1989.

Gupta, A., 'India and Fiji - Faulty Perspective', *Economic and Political Weekly* 23(44), Bombay, 1988.

Gupta, A., 'India, Fiji and South Pacific', *Economic and Political Weekly* 22(25), Bombay, 1987.

Gupta, A., 'Trouble in Fiji: The External & Domestic Factors', *Review of International Affairs* 38(898), Socialist Alliance of Working People of Yugoslavia, Belgrade, September 1987.

Gupta, A., 'Ugandan Asians, Britain, India and the Commonwealth', *African Affairs* 73(292), London, July 1974.

Gupta, A. (ed.) (1971), *Indians Abroad: Asia & Africa*, Report of an International Seminar, Indian Council for Africa, Orient Longman Ltd, New Delhi.

Gupta, I.D. (1995), 'FDI in China and India: Planning & Development Strategy', Paper Presented at International Seminar at Osmania University, Hyderabad.

Gupta, M.G. (1985), *Indian Foreign Policy - Theory & Practice*, Y K Publishers, Agra.

Gupta, S.P. (ed.) (1993), *Liberalisation, its Impact on the Indian Economy*, Macmillan India Ltd, Delhi.

Hagan, Stephanie, 'Race, Politics & the Coup in Fiji', *Bulletin of Concerned Asian Scholars*, 19(4), Boulder (USA), October -December 1987.

Haksar, P.N. (1989), *India's Foreign Policy and its Problems*, Patriot Publishers, New Delhi.

Handbook of Industrial Policy and Statistics 1993, Office of the Economic Advisor, Ministry of Industry, Government of India, New Delhi, 1993.

Handbook of Statistics on Indian Economy, RBI, New Delhi, 1999.

Heimsath, C. and Mansingh, S. (1971), *A Diplomatic History of Modern India*, Allied Publishers, Bombay.

Hepburn, A.C. (1978), *Minorities in History*, Edward Arnold, London.

Hiremath, J.R., 'Indian South Africans - A Contemporary Portrait', *Africa Quarterly* 32(1-4), ICCR, New Delhi, 1992-93.

Historical Relations across the Indian Ocean, Reports and Papers of the meeting of experts organised by UNESCO at Port Louis, Mauritius, 1980.

Howard, M.C., 'State Power and Political Change in Fiji', *Journal of Contemporary Asia* 21(1), Manila, Philippines 1991.

Huttenback, R.A. (1971), *Gandhi in South Africa*, Cornell University Press, London.

IIC Monthly Newsletters, New Delhi, 1998-2000.

India 1999, CD-ROM published by the Ministry of Information and Broadcasting, Government of India.

India and the United Nations, Report of a study group set up by the ICWA, Manhattan Publishing Group, New York, 1957.

India: Bilateral Treaties and Agreements 1947-1970, 1-6 Policy Planning and Research Division, MEA, SIBA EXIM Pvt. Ltd., New Delhi, 1994.

Indian Press, Selected Articles, *Business Standard*, Calcutta, India, 1975-95.

Indian Press, Selected Articles, *Daily Bombay*, Bombay, India, 1975-95.

Indian Press, Selected Articles, *Deccan Herald*, Bangalore, India, 1975-95.

Indian Press, Selected Articles, *Financial Express*, Bombay, India, 1975-95.

Indian Press, Selected Articles, *Hindustan Times*, New Delhi, India, 1975-95.

Indian Press, Selected Articles, *Indian Express*, New Delhi, India, 1975-95.

Indian Press, Selected Articles, *National Herald*, New Delhi, India, 1975-95.

Indian Press, Selected Articles, *News Time*, Hyderabad, India, 1975-95.

Indian Press, Selected Articles, *Observer of Business & Politics*, New Delhi, India, 1975-95.

Indian Press, Selected Articles, *Patriot*, New Delhi, India, 1975-95.

Indian Press, Selected Articles, *Sunday Observer*, New Delhi, India, 1975-95.

Indian Press, Selected Articles, *The Economic Times*, New Delhi, India, 1975-95.

Indian Press, Selected Articles, *The Hindu*, Madras, India, 1975-95.

Indian Press, Selected Articles, *The Pioneer*, New Delhi, India, 1975-95.

Indian Press, Selected Articles, *The Statesman*, New Delhi, India, 1975-95.

Indian Press, Selected Articles, *The Telegraph*, Calcutta, India, 1975-95.

Indian Press, Selected Articles, *The Times of India*, New Delhi, India, 1975-95.

Indian Press, Selected Articles, *Tribune*, Chandigarh, India, 1975-95.

Investment opportunities available to NRIs, *Indian Investment Centre*, New Delhi, April 1999.

ISG, 'Non-Resident Control & National Interest', *Economic & Political Weekly*, New Delhi.

Jain, P. C. (1989), *Racial discrimination against overseas Indians*, Concept Publishing Company, New Delhi.

Jain, R.K. (1993), *Indian Communities Abroad*, Manohar, New Delhi.

Jamal, Vali, 'Asians in Uganda, 1880-1972: Inequality and Expulsion', *Economic History Review*, 2nd Series 29, 1976.

Jefferson, H.G. and Rawski, G.T., 'Enterprise Reform in Chinese Industry', *Journal of Economic Perspectives* 8(2), Nashville, Spring 1994.

Jenkins, Rhys (1987), *TNC and Uneven Development: The Internationalisation of Capital and the Third World*, Methuen, New York.

Jha, S.K. (1984), *India & the Commonwealth*, Mohit Publications, New Delhi.

Joshi, P.S. (1942), *The Tyranny of Colour*, Durban.

Joshi, V. and Little, I.M.D. (1996), *India's Economic Reforms 1991-2001*, Oxford University Press, New Delhi.

Kapila Uma (ed.) (1996), *India's Economic Reforms* 1& 2, Academic Foundation, New Delhi.

Kapur, Aasha (ed.), *Industrial Policy - Critical Issues*, 3 week training program for IAS Officers, Indian Institute of Public Administration, New Delhi, India, 2-20 November 1992.

Kapur, Harish (1994), *India's Foreign Policy 1947-92 Shadows and Substance*, Sage Publications, New Delhi.

Kaul, Man Mohini, 'The Developments in Fiji: An Alternative View Point', *Strategic Analysis*, 13(12), Institute for Defence Studies and Analysis, New Delhi, March 1991.

Kaul, T.N. (1988), *Ambassadors need not lie*, I, Lancer International, New Delhi.

Kaul, T N. (1989), *Ambassadors need not lie*, II, Lancer International, New Delhi.

Keys, I. B., Edge, A. G. and Wells, R.A. (1992), *The Multinational Management Game: A Global Strategy*, IRWIN, Boston.

Khilnani, N. M. (1984), *Realities of Indian Foreign Policy*, ABC Publishing House, New Delhi.

Khilnani, S. (1997), *The Idea of India*, Hamish Hamilton, London.

Kojima, Kiyoshi (1978), *Direct Foreign Investment: A Japanese Model of Multinational Business Operation*, Croom Helm, London.

Kuepper, W.G., Lackey, G.L. and Sinerton, E.N (1975), *Ugandan Asians in Great Britain*, Croom Helm, London.

Kumar, Arun, 'New Economic Policies: An Assessment', *Economic and Political Weekly*, Bombay, 11 December 1993.

Kumar, M. R. (1991), 'Les Investissements Indiens en Afrique a la Recheche d'un Second Souflle', *Marches Tropicaux*, France, 26 July 1991.

Kumar, Nagesh (1990), *Multinational Enterprises in India: Industrial Distribution Characteristic and Performances*, Routledge, London.

Kumar, Nagesh, 'Industrialisation, Liberalisation and Two Way Flows of FDI Case of India' *Economic and Political Weekly*, Bombay, 16 December 1995.

Kumar, R., 'L'Inde: Etat-Nation ou Etat-Civilisation', *Herodote* 71, Paris 1993

Kumar, Sanjeev, 'The Multinational's Dilemma: which Sector to invest in India?', *Third Concept* 10 (119), New Delhi, January 1997.

Kuper, Hilda (1961), *Indian people in Natal*, Natal University Press, Durban.

Lal, B.V., 'Fiji Indians and the Politics of Exclusion', *Foreign Affairs Report*, 38(7,8), Indian Council of World Affairs, New Delhi, July-August 1989.

Lal, Jagdish (1978), *The Foreign Exchange Regulation Act 1973*, Act No. 45 of 1973, Delhi Law House, Allahabad.

Lawrence, Michael and Kumar, Girish, 'A Communal Coup', *India Today*, New Delhi, 15 June 1987.

Lawson, Stephanie, 'Constitutional Change in Fiji: the Apparatus of Justification', *Ethnic and Racial Studies* 15(1), Routledge, London, January 1992.

Lawson, Stephanie, 'The Myth of cultural Homogeneity and its Implications for Chiefly Power and Politics in Fiji', *Comparative Studies in Society & History*, 32(4), Cambridge University Press, Cambridge, 1990.

Lawson, Stephanie (1991), *The Failure of Democratic Politics in Fiji*, Clarendon Press, Oxford.

Lewis, W.A. (1956), *The Theory of Economic Growth*, London.

Lipton, Michael and Fern, John (1975), *The Erosion of a Relationship: India & Britain since 1960*, for RIIA by Oxford University Press, London, Delhi.

Little, I.M.D. (1982), *Economic Development Theory*, Basic Books Inc. Publishers, New York.

Live, Yu Sion, 'Chine-Diaspora: Vers l'integration a l'economie Mondiale'.

Lok Sabha Debates, Parliament Library, New Delhi, India, 1970-1994 as available.

MRTP Act, 1969 and 1991 (1991), Delhi Law House, New Delhi.

Malik, G.K. and Vajpayi, D.K. (eds) (1988), *India: The years of Indira Gandhi*, E.J.Brill, Leiden, New York.

Mamdani, Mahmood, 'Class Struggles in Uganda', *Economic & Political Weekly* 10(33-35), Bombay, August 1975.

Mansergh, Nicholas (ed.) (1963), *Documents and Speeches on Commonwealth Affairs 1952-62*, Oxford University Press, London.

Mansergh, Nicholas (1958), *Survey of British Commonwealth Affairs Problems of Wartime Cooperation & Post-war Change 1939-52*, Oxford University Press, London.

Mansingh, Surjit (1994), *India's Search for Power - Indira Gandhi's Foreign Policy 1966-82*, Sage Publications, New Delhi.

Manual on Industrial Policy and Procedures in India, SIA, New Delhi, September 1998.

McDonald, H., 'Minority Blues', *Far Eastern Economic Review*, Hong Kong, February 1992.

Melady, T.A. and Melady, M.B. (1976), *Uganda: the Asian Exiles*, Orbis Books, New York.

Menon, R., 'Gulf Crisis: An Indian Nightmare', *India Today*, New Delhi, 15 September 1990.

Millar, T.B. (1967), *The Commonwealth & the UN*, Sydney University Press, Sydney.

Miller, J.D.B. (1974), *Survey of British Commonwealth Affairs, Problems of Expansion & Attrition 1953-1969*, Oxford University Press, London.

Ministry of External Affairs - Annual Reports, Parliament Library, New Delhi, India, 1983-1995.

Misra, K.P. (1987), 'Non-Alignment: Indira Gandhi's Contribution', SEMINAR: Indian Foreign Policy under Indira Gandhi (2-5 April 1987), *Nehru Memorial Museum & Library*, (N/P), New Delhi.

Misra, K.P. (ed.) (1977), *Foreign Policy of India*, Thompson Publishers (India), New Delhi.

Mohamed, H. E. (1979), *Asian Legacy in Africa and the White Man's Colour Culture*, Teen Murti Library, New Delhi.

Monthly Newsletter, Indian Investment Centre, New Delhi, 1991-1996.

Morris, S. (1956), 'Indians in East Africa: a Study in a Plural Society', *British Journal of Sociology*, No. 7, London.

Morris, S. (1968), *The Indians in Uganda*, Weidenfeld & Nicholson, London.

Motwani, J. K., Gosine, M. and Barot-Motwani, J. (eds) (1983), *Global Indian Diaspora: Yesterday, Today and Tomorrow*, DPS Enterprises (P) Ltd., New Delhi.

Myrdal, G. (1968), *Asian Drama*, Ian Allan, The Penguin Press, London.

Nabhi's Handbook for NRI (2000), Nabhi Publications, New Delhi.

Naidu and Reddy, 'Stock of Indian Emigrants in the Gulf Countries', *Monthly Commentary*, 32(5), December 1990.

Naidu, G.V.C., 'Crisis in Fiji', *Strategic Analysis*, 11(9), Institute for Defence Studies and Analysis, New Delhi, December 1987.

Nanda, B.R. (ed.) (1976), *Indian Foreign Policy - the Nehru Years*, Vikas Publishing House, New Delhi.

Narula, Rajesh (1996), *Multinational Investment and Economic Structure: Globalisation and Competitiveness*, Routledge Studies in International Business and the World Economy, London and New York.

Naughton, Barry, 'Why has Economic Reform Led to Inflation?', *The American Economic Review* 81(2), Nashville, May 1991.

O'Brian, Justin, 'General Amin and the Uganda Asians', *Round Table* 249, Commonwealth Journal of International Affairs, London, January 1973.

Ollivier, Maurice (ed.) (1954), *The Colonial & Imperial Conferences 1887-37*, Part I, II & III, Ottawa.

Oommen, M. A., 'Bhagwati-Srinivasan Report on Economic Reforms', *Economic and Political Weekly*, Bombay, 2 October 1993.

Pande, D.C. (1988), *India's Foreign Policy as an Exercise in Non-Alignment (1996-1976)*, Gyanodaya Prakashan, Uttar Pradesh.

Parson, Jack D., 'Africanizing Trade in Uganda: the Final Solution', *Africa Today*, 20(1), Denver, Winter 1973.

Patel H.A. (1979), *Power, Race, Class & Citizenship Towards a Conceptual Integration for the Study of Indian Political Activity in Uganda*, University of Rhodesia, Salisburg.

Patnaik, Prabhat, 'Macro-Economic Policy in Times of 'Globalisation'', *Economic & Political Weekly*, 29(16 & 17), Bombay, 16-23 April 1994.

Perkins, D.H., 'Reforming China's Economic System', *Journal of Economic Literature* 26, Nashville, June 1988.

Perkins, Dwight, 'Completing China's Move to the Market', *Journal of Economic Perspectives* 8, Nashville, Spring 1994.

Prasad, Bimal (ed.) (1979), *India's Foreign Policy - Studies in Continuity & Change*, Vikas Publishing House, New Delhi.

Premdas, Ralph R., 'Military Intervention in Fiji: Fear of Ethnic Domination', *Social and Economic Studies*, Institute of Social and Economic Research, Kingston, Jamaica, March 1992.

Press Notes (Series 1991-1996), Government of India, Ministry of Industry, Department of Industrial Development, New Delhi, 1991-96.

Prunier, G. (1990), *L'Ouganda et la Question Indienne (1896-1972)*, Editions Recherche sur les Civilisations, Paris.

Purcell, Victor (1965), 'Overseas Chinese in South East Asia', London.

Purshotamdas Thakurday Research Center (ed.) (1971), *Indians in East Africa*, Teen Murti Library, Bombay.

Racism in South Africa - the Commonwealth Stand, The Commonwealth Secretariat, London.

Rai, Kanleshwar (1979), *Indian & British Colonialism in East Africa 1883-1939*, Associated Book Agency, Patna.

Raj, G.B.V. (1959), *India and the Disputes with the UN*, Bombay.

Rajan, M.S. (ed.) (1976), *India's Foreign Relations during the Nehru Era*, Asia Publishing House, Bombay.

Rajan, M.S. (1990), *India & the Commonwealth*, Konark Publishers, New Delhi.

Rajan, M.S. (1993), *Studies on India's Foreign Policy*, ABC Publishing House, New Delhi.

Rajya Sabha Debates, Parliament Library, New Delhi, India, 1991-94 as available.

Rakshit, Mihir, 'Money and Public Finance Under Structural Adjustment', *Economic and Political Weekly*, 29(16 & 17), Bombay, 16-23 April 1994.

Ramchandani, R.R., 'The Economic Roots of Racial Friction in Uganda', *Economic & Political Weekly*, 8(52), Bombay, December 1973.

Ramchandani, R.R. (1976), *Uganda Asians The End of an Enterprise*, United Asia Publications, Bombay.

Raniner, H.P., 'A Foothold in Two Countries', *Business World*, Bombay, September 1990.

Rao, V.V. B. (1993), *India's Economic Future: Government, People & Attitudes*, Tata McGraw Hill, New Delhi.

Ready Reckoner for NRI Investment, Secretariat for Industrial Assistance (SIA), Department of Industrial Policy and Promotion, Government of India, May 1999.

Reddy, S. Balarami, 'Non Resident Investment - Its Pros & Cons', *Southern Economist*, Bangalore, September 1983.

Regional Security Developments in the South Pacific, Report to the Committee on Foreign Affairs, US House of Representatives - US Government, Washington, March 1989.

Report of the Committee on Capital Account Convertibility, RBI, 1997.

Reserve Bank of India Annual Report (1991-1996), Bombay.

Reserve Bank of India Annual Report, Bombay, 1995-96, 1996-97, 1997-98 and 1998-99.

Reserve Bank of India Bulletin, Bombay, October 1999.

Reserve Bank of India Report on Currency and Finance, Bombay, 1998-99.

Roy, W.T., 'Fiji Today, the Politics of Frustration', *The Round Table* 305, Commonwealth Journal of International Affairs, London, January 1988.

Rutz, H. J., 'Capitalising on Culture: Moral Ironies in Urban Fiji', *Comparative Studies in Society & History* 29(3), July 1987.

Sachdeva, Nirmal, 'Towards Economic Growth', *Third Concept* 10(119), New Delhi, January 1997.

Sagar, Vidya and Puri, Manohar (eds) (1987), *Mother India, Children Abroad*, International Publishers, New Delhi.

Sajjananand, S., '100 years of Indian Presence in Fiji', *The Indian*, Hong Kong, May-June 1979.

Satyanarayana, B. (ed.) (1996), *A Comparative Study of FDI China and India: Problems and Prospective*, Himalaya Publishing House, Bombay.

Sau, Ranjit, 'Foreign Direct Investment, Portfolio Investment and Macro-Economic Stability' *Economic and Political Weekly*, 29(7), Bombay, 12 February 1994.

Secretariat for Industrial Assistance (SIA) Newsletter, Ministry of Industry, Government of India, New Delhi, 6(1), New Delhi, May 1997.

Serpa, Eduardo, 'Indian & Africa', *Africa Insight* 24(3) 1994.

Shridath, Ramphal, 'Our Influence in Fiji is limited', *India Today*, New Delhi, 31 October 1987.

SIA Newsletter, New Delhi, February 1999.

SIA Newsletter, New Delhi, May 1999.

SIA Statistics 5(7), New Delhi, November 1999.

Singh, Ajay, 'The Ugly Indian', *The Indian*, Hong Kong, July 1977.

Singh, L.P. (1993), *India and Afro-Asian Independence*, National Book Organisation, New Delhi.

Singh Joshi, Marcharan (1989), *India's Foreign Policy*, Surjeet Publications, New Delhi.

Sinha, Arun, 'Economic Reforms and Macro-Economic Policy', *Economic and Political Weekly* 29(16 &17), Bombay, 16-23 April 1994.

Sinha, S.L.N., 'Appraising NRI Investment', *Southern Economist*, Bangalore, March 1990.

Sisodia, S.S. (1985), *Foreign Policy of India, Indira Gandhi Era*, Inter-India Publications, New Delhi.

Srivastava, Satya, 'Crisis in Fiji and options available', *Mainstream*, New Delhi, June 1990.

Streeten, P. and Lipton, M. (eds) (1968), *The Crisis of Indian Planning*, Oxford University Press, London.

Subramani (ed.) (1979), *Indo Fijian experience*, New Delhi.

Sunderam, C. (1944), *India in World Politics*, Sultan Chand & Co, New Delhi.

Survey of Important Developments During 1998-99; Achievements and Future Prospects, Annual Report, Ministry of Industry, 1998-99.

Swami, Parthasarthi, 'Banks - Wooing the Non Resident', *India Today*, New Delhi, 15 August 1986.

Tandon, Yash and Raphael, Arnold (1973), 'The New Position of East African Asians: Problems of a Displaced Minority', Report no.16, *Minority Rights Group*, London, 1973 (Rev Ed 6/78 and 11/84).

Tandon, Yash, 'The Future of the Asians in East Africa', *Africa Contemporary Record*, Current Affairs Series, Rex Collins, London, 1973.

Thakur, R., 'India and Overseas Indians - The Case of Fiji', *Asian Survey* 25(3), 1985.

Thakur, Ramesh (1994), *The Politics and Economics of India's Foreign Policy*, Oxford University Press, New Delhi.

Tharoor, S. (1997), *India from Midnight to the Millennium*, Viking Penguin India, New Delhi.

Tharoor, S. (1982), *Reasons of State - Political Development and India's Foreign Policy under Indira Gandhi 1966-77*, Vikas Publishing House, Ghaziabad.

The Image of Contemporary India Abroad, Series of five lectures by Dr V.Singh, Dr G.K. Mukherjee, Dr V.P.Dutt, Dr M.S.Agwani and Shri S.H.Chhabra, India International Centre, New Delhi 1973.

Thompson, L., 'The South African Indians Trapped in the Middle', *Africa Quarterly* 32(1-4), ICCR, New Delhi 1993.

Tinker, H. (1976), *Separate & Unequal: India and the Indians in the British Commonwealth 1920-1950*, C. Hurst & Co., London.

Tinker, H. (1977), *The Banyan Tree: Overseas Immigrants from India, Pakistan & Bangladesh*, Oxford University Press, Oxford.

Trivedi, A., 'Fate of Fijian Indians', *Mainstream*, 28(52), New Delhi, October 1990.

Twaddle, M. (ed.) (1975), *Expulsion of a Minority - Essays on Ugandan Asians*, University of London, Athlone Press, London.

UN Yearbook 1972, UN, New York 1972.

VanFossen, Anthony B., 'Two Military Coups in Fiji', *Bulletin of Concerned Asian Scholars* 19(4), Boulder, October -December 1987.

Venkatasubramani, K. (1993), *Policy and Performance of Indian Economy*, Manoj Prakashan, Madras.

Venkateswaran, A.P., 'Indian Response in betrayal of Gandhian values', *Mainstream*, 28(34), New Delhi, June 1990.

Vivekanandan, B. (1987), 'India & the changing profile of the Commonwealth', SEMINAR: Indian Foreign Policy under Indira Gandhi (2-5 April 1987), *Nehru Memorial Museum & Library*, New Delhi.

Vivekanandan, B. (1983), *The Shrinking Circle - The Commonwealth in British Foreign Policy 1945-74*, Somaya Publications, Bombay.

Vohra, Bikram, 'The Unloved Indian', *The Indian*, Hong Kong, October - November 1978.

Weiner, M., *International Migration and Development - Indians in the Persian Gulf,* Population and Development Review 8(1), 1982.

Willber, C.K. (1984), *The Political Economy of Development and Under Development*, Random House, New York.

World Development Report-1996, Oxford University Press, Oxford 1996.

Yusuf Shahid (1994), 'China's Macroeconomic Performance and Management During Transition', *Journal of Economic Perspectives*, 8(2), Nashville, Spring 1994.

Index

Appendices

Appendix - 1: Government announcements - NRI response

- 27.6.96 India seeks to reverse its brain drain: The push is on to attract wealth and skills of 15m overseas Indians to help in modernising India. The total net worth of the NRIs is estimated between $150 and 300 billion. The previous week there was a gathering of entrepreneurs from the world wide Indian Diaspora in Singapore. (FT)
- 10.7.96 Indus Ind Int. (group of NRIs) give the government a commitment of investing nearly $3billion in the country's industry. (RTN)
- 27.6.96 Foreign companies with an NRI share of more than 60 per cent are allowed to engage in real estate development. (FT)
- 26.6.96 The finance ministry has allowed authorised dealers, mostly banks to sanction rupee loans to NRIs against securities of shares. Also permitted to remit sale proceeds of shares without obtaining prior permission of the RBI. (RTN)
- 16.4.96 Lazard Credit Capital estimated the total outflow in 1996-7 at $13.93 billion and inflows at $16.55 billion. (RTN)
- 21.3.96 The SBI raises interest rates on deposits under its NRNR scheme. Revised rates are 18.5 per cent for 6 months and 18 per cent for 1-3 years. (RTN)
- 8.2.96 The SBI raises interest rates. (RTN)
- 16.1.96 Indian government tries to attract investments from HK Indians. New office: Commissioner for NRIs has been established. (RTN)
- 8.11.95 Banks instructed to increase interest rates on NRI long term deposits from 10 per cent to 12 per cent pa. (SWB)
- 8.11.95 RBI on 1 November granted general permission to NRIs to subscribe to memorandum and articles of association and to take up shares of Indian Companies for incorporation up to the amount of 10.000Rs. (SWB)

- RBI official has urged NRIs to invest more in the services and infrastructure sector, taking advantage of ongoing easing of restrictions which have brought in one billion $ of FDI by NRIs in just 4 years. (SWB)
- 29.9.95 RBI raises interest rates on rupee term deposits held by NRIs from 8 per cent to 10 per cent. (RTN)
- 29.9.95 RBI relaxes investment norms for NRIs to enable them easier market access to the stock exchanges. (RTN)
- 7.8.95 Preparation for Capital Account convertibility, following Government's decision to ease restrictions on foreign institutional investors, NRIs and OCBs to subscribe to the equities of Indian companies engaged in any activity except agriculture and plantation. (RTN)
- 19.7.95 India could expect potential investment of 15 million NRIs who have combined assets of between $40bn-60bn. (SWB)
- 17.7.95 A committee set up by the RBI has recommended that banks should accept deposits from NRIs in all convertible currencies. (RTN)
- 17.7.95 RBI committee has suggested that NRIs be permitted to fully repatriate their profits from investment in housing. Currently this is only possible after a lock in period of 3 years and subject to a ceiling of 16 per cent. (RTN)
- 15.6.95 Increase in deposits by overseas Indians to RS9.15 from 6.79bn during period April 94-March 95. (RTN)
- 26.5.95 Financial services opened to foreign investors and NRIs. They can now invest in the areas of hire-purchase, finance, leasing, trading and other services to a maximum of 24 per cent of a company's equity.
- 16.2.95 The NRIs have complained that the rules under which they can invest are less favourable than those for foreign financial institutions, say the findings of a committee looking into NRI interests. (RTN)
- 3.2.95 Gov. decides to allow foreign companies, corporate houses and NRIs to hold up to 49 per cent equity in small scale units. (Observer)
- 17.11.94 RBI raised interest rates on $ and £ deposits of expatriate Indians. (RTN)
- 20.10.94 India phases out costly expatriate inflow, since forex reserves are comfortable. Deposits of overseas Indians total more than $10 billion. (RTN)
- 17.10.94 RBI cuts interest rate on rupee term deposits by expatriate Indians by 2 per cent to 8 per cent. (RTN)

- 12.10.94 India public sector bodies to float some equity. Seven leading Public Sector Undertakings entered the Capital Market on 5 October, dis-investing equity ranging between 2 per cent - 20 per cent and offering as many as 350m shares for subscription. (Oil & Natural Gas Commission; Indian Oil Ltd; Steel Authority of India; MTNL; National Fertilisers; Shipping Corporation; and Container Corporation) (SWB)
- 5.10 94 RBI permits NRIs and companies owned to 51 per cent by NRIs to buy up to 1 per cent in seven state run companies. (RTN)
- 16.9.94 RBI has removed the lock in period on investments made by NRIs and OCBs under the portfolio investment scheme for repatriation of sales proceeds on the sale and transfer of shares and convertible debentures. (Economic Times, Bombay)
- 11.9.94 Rupee liberalisation in stages; should be made fully convertible by lifting remaining controls on capital outflow after country's forex reserves touch $25bn. Current account convertibility happened on 20 August. (RTN)
- 25.8.94 RBI would allow companies owned by NRIs to acquire up to 100 per cent stake in local firms involved in development of housing, real estate, townships, urban infrastructure, manufacturing of building materials and financing of housing development. (RTN)
- 20.8.94 Rupee convertible in all Current Account transactions. The move will give India article 8 status in the IMF, which is a fundamental indicator of good standing in the fund. (Trade Account convertibility in March 1993) (FT)
- 18.5.94 PM N.Rao opposes dual citizenship for NRIs. (Statesman)
- 14.5.94 RBI cut rupee deposit interest rate from 11 per cent to 10 per cent. (RTN)
- 27.4.94 Indus Ind Bank set up with a capital of Rs1bn in Bombay on 11.4. (SWB)
- 28.2.94 India announced that it was rationalising the tax structure for foreigners and NRIs and would tax them at a uniform rate of 20 per cent. Period of stay for NRIs raised from 149 to 181 days. (RTN)
- 11.1.94 Demand of dual citizenship by the 13th India-NRI World Convention. A memorandum was submitted to the PM Narasimha Rao. (HT)
- 31.12.93 Indian Government has approved investment worth 79.9bn for the first 11 months this year, doubling last years figure of Rs 38.9bn and outstripping the Rs 5.3bn approved in 1991. NRIs worldwide contributed Rs 6.82bn to the total. (FT)

- 20.11.93 India is allowing foreign financial institutions to own shares in new private banks in order to inject greater efficiency into its state dominated banking sector. They will be able to hold up to 20 per cent while expatriate Indians will be allowed up to 40 per cent. (IND)
- 23.9.93 NRIs are now permitted to acquire, hold, transfer or dispose of by sale or inheritance immovable property situated in India provided they are for the bonafide residential use of the purchasers and the sale consideration is met out of foreign exchange remitted to India through normal banking channels or NRI/FCNR accounts. They are allowed to acquire up to two houses. (Hindu)
- 16.9.93 RBI allowed NRIs to rent out immovable property, but income from the rents could not be repatriated. (RTN)
- 10.3.93 There has been a net outflow of $203 million NRI deposits. (SWB)
- 1.3.93 The Finance Minister has proposed substantial reductions in customs, excise and import duties, particularly in items of mass consumption. (SWB)
- 21.9.92 A NRI group headed by BR Parmar will be investing $1 billion in the next 2,5 years. The group is planning to set up an export-oriented oil refinery in coastal Gujerat. (Pioneer)
- 12.8.92 Outflow of NRI funds continues. The net outflow from NRI accounts during June 92 amounted to $67 million. This included $45 million from the more volatile Foreign Currency Non Resident (FCNR) accounts and the rest of $22 million from the Non Resident (External) Rupee account. (FE)
- 19.7.92 Further concession to NRIs: they are no longer required to surrender their foreign currency assets held abroad when they return to India, nor will they be have to surrender legally acquired foreign currency holdings, provided they have been NR for the continuous period of at least one year. (ET)
- 18.7.92 Indian Government exempted NRIs from the obligation to surrender foreign currency assets held abroad when they return to India. (FT)
- 21.6.92 There is room for much more on the reforms front. The present reforms will take some time to bear fruits as they clash with the stabilisation exercise. (FE)
- 20.6.92 Green card for NRIs under consideration. (BP)
- 18.6.92 The second world conference of the Overseas Indians will be held in Paris from 10-14 July. First one held in the USA in 1989. One

of the issues to be discussed will be the setting up of a special ministry in New Delhi to deal with NRI issues. (BS)

- 11.6.92 RBI has formulated a new deposit scheme for NRIs under which accounts in Indian rupees can be opened with authorised forex dealers. The funds are non-repatriable. (FT)
- 8.6.92 Government has set up a bureau to bring NRI scientists and technologists in contact with Indian industries. (Interface for NRI scientists- INRIST) An estimated 375000 highly qualified scientists of Indian Origin are working overseas. (ET)
- 26.5.92 Government is soon expected to initiate steps to reduce its dependence on the NRI deposits and to convert some of the country's debt into equity. (FE)
- 23.5.92 A free trade zone should be set up in the country to attract Indian Capital and labour from Hong Kong which would become a part of China in 1997. (SN)
- 13.5.92 RBI announced that Indian companies will now not be required to seek the RBI's permission for accepting capital contributions from NRIs. Nor will the RBI's permission be required to issue shares and debentures to NRIs and to OCBs on a non-repatriation basis. (SWB)
- 12.5.92 Hindujas offer to invest $2.8 billion by setting up 4 mega projects in the energy, oil, wireless and vehicles sectors. (ET)
- 4.5.92 A delegation of the US based federation of Indian Associations (FIA) has called on PM Narasimha Rao and urged him to grant dual citizenship to NRIs settled abroad. (HT)
- 29.4.92 RBI announces simplifications in the procedures relating to NRI investment, regulations governing direct investment by NRIs on non repatriation basis and shares or debentures in Indian companies. (FE)
- 14.4.92 The Union Commerce Minister P.Chidambaram hoped India would be able to attract at least $2billion in direct foreign investment a year to finance new and for updating existing ventures in the country. (HU)
- 13.4.92 The Law ministry has held up the scheme seeking to introduce large scale investment by NRIs in housing and real estate. (ET)
- 4.4.92 Ram Buxani, Chairman of the overseas Indian economic forum, UAE favoured dual citizenship in an interview. (FE)
- 30.3.92 GD Tandon, president of the Hindu international and Chairman of the Virat Hindu Sammelan, welcomed the new budget, but is

pleading for more steps to streamline the procedures. He is also an advocate of dual citizenship. (HT)

- 24.3.92 NRI remittance to Kerala go up; NRIs have also subscribed heavily to the India Development Bonds. (ET)
- 21.3.92 The Government has in the first 7 months since it deregulated industrial licensing and liberalised foreign investment rules, approved proposals envisaging an investment of Rs 1.141.84 crores. This was 13 times more than the investment approved in the corresponding period of 1990-91. (HU)
- 21.3.92 Migrant workers and other NRIs will soon be able to exchange their entire remittances at market rate as against the 60-40 formula wherein 60 per cent of the remittance is exchanged at market rate and 40 per cent at RBI rates. (IE)
- 15.3.92 Union Minister SB Chavan urged the NRIs to contribute towards the economic development of the country. He said the prosperity of the country was linked to the prosperity of the NRIs. (FE)
- 10.3.92 Dual citizenship for NRIs likely soon. The Government may leave out the pre 1947 Indian emigrants from the scheme. (TG)
- 2.3.92 Leading NRIs have applauded the Manmohan Singh Budget, although some say the Government should do a little more to curb inflation at home.
- 28.2.92 Unable to obtain fresh commercial borrowings abroad, India suffered a net outflow of $952m between April and June 91 from expatriate Indians taking out their non resident deposits. The survey says that the net outflow of NR deposits only came to a stop in January. (FT)
- 27.2.92 Lured by the idea of drawing in the massive NRI funds abroad, the Government is at last seriously thinking of amending the Indian Citizenship Act to introduce dual citizenship for NRIs. (PR)
- 17.2.92 The Union Government's policy to attract direct investment to projects from NRIs has so far got a poor response. The expectation was that NRI investment in projects would increase after the government allowed 100 per cent investment by NRIs or OCBs in projects. However not a single NRI application for a 100 per cent foreign equity participation in any project has yet come. (ET)
- 30.1.92 India announced that foreign companies would be permitted up to a 51 per cent stake in joint ventures. Previously they were only allowed 40 per cent. (RTN)

- 12.1.92 Last week the Bombay stock exchange opened an NRI cell. (ET)
- 8.1.92 Permission for NRIs to buy, hold and sell property. (TI)
- 5.1.92 An NRI delegation was told that the Government was actively considering granting them the right of dual citizenship. (PT)
- 30.12.91 The Union Commerce Minister P.Chidambaram said that all licenses and controls of trade would go by next March end. (TI)
- 29.10.91 Automatic approval for investment up to 100 per cent in high priority industries with full repatriation benefits. (TI)
- 22.9.91 The PM Narasimha Rao has assured the NRIs that the government would do its utmost to solve the problems being faced by them. (FE)
- 12.9.91 The Lok Sabha approved a Bill seeking to provide certain direct tax exemptions to persons receiving remittances in forex and owning foreign exchange bonds. (TB)
- 5.9.91 If the terms finalised for the issue of the proposed India development Bonds by the SBI are any guide, these bonds will prove to be an attractive conduit for Indians having funds abroad or black money at home, to white wash their unaccounted wealth. The terms may even tempt NRIs to divert a part of their funds lying in the vaults of foreign banks abroad. (FE)
- 1.9.91 Devaluation fails to stem NRI deposit outflow. (ET)
- 30.8.91 Dual citizenship issue raised at a high level meeting by Dr Manmohan Singh earlier in the month, as a measure to bring in greater NRI involvement. (BS)
- 18.8.91 The new government has made no bones about wooing the NRIs in a big way: 'we are ready to give them all concessions to put their money and revive their age-old links with their motherland.' (Narasimha Rao) (ET)
- 24.6.91 PM's policy address: 'I see a very special role for NRIs to play in this process. We shall make investment in India a rewarding experience.' (SWB)

PRE-1991 REFORMS

- 24.12.90 Among measures under review to increase forex earnings are potentially controversial schemes to allow Resident Indians to repatriate forex illegally held abroad and to offer dual nationality to NRIs. (FT)

- 10.12.90 The Finance Minister has formulated a blueprint to woo NRIs to tide over the present forex crisis by letting them invest freely in real estate, reduce investigations and probes in case of gifts, order Indian Banks with NRI deposits to become more aggressive in this area and remove RBI restrictions on inflow of foreign exchange deposited in foreign branches of Indian Banks. (FE)
- 15.9.90 RBI scheme to attract emergency money from the Gulf by creating a special deposit facility has flopped, and the inflow into this facility has been virtually zero. (TI)
- 5.7.90 The External Affairs Minister, I.K.Gujral said that the Government had set up a separate division in his ministry to co-ordinate the activities and find solutions to the problems facing overseas Indians.
- 22.9.89 The Union Government cleared 806 proposals for investment by NRIs in the country during the last 5 years (January 84-March 89). Total number of applications was placed at 974. So far 103 projects have been set up with another 351 under implementation. (ET)
- 14.12.88 It is important to note that the visible NRI projects, implemented in the country so far were not launched with any government contact or inducement (such as Orson, Indo-Gulf Fertilisers, Apollo Hospitals, Double Cola, etc.).
- 15.10.88 The Indian government sought to bolster the country's forex reserves with an issue of bonds designed to attract funds from Indians living abroad. The move comes at a time when the balance of payments has been under pressure from a widening trade deficit and the forex reserves were down 19 per cent at the end of August, compared to the previous year. Bonds will be issued in $ over a 7 year maturity, redeemable only in Rs. Aimed at Indians planning to return home. It will be exempt from wealth and gift tax. (FT)
- 21.7.88 The PM recently indicated that a new plan for encouraging NRIs to invest in India without their having to return to the country was under consideration. (Patriot)
- 8.4.88 NRIs and Persons of Indian Origin are allowed to invest in Bonds issued by the Public Sector Undertakings on a non-repatriation basis. (LSD, Q6362)
- 18.3.88 Government has decided to introduce a new scheme of foreign currency denominated Bonds/ Deposit certificates for NRIs on non-repatriation basis; maturity period is 7 years; free from income, wealth and gift tax. (LSD, Q3839)

- 27.10.87 Indo-NRI chamber of commerce and culture set up to promote the overseas' Indian case. The NRI is not welcome for the reason that he might upset too many apple carts. The smug family oligarchies fed on the 'license permit' system would feel threatened. (Deccan Herald)
- 11.11.87 The Indo-NRI Chamber of Commerce and Culture called for the creation of and NRI lobby in the Indian Parliament. NRIs have demanded the right to vote and be elected to India's legislative bodies and to hold double citizenship. (News Time)
- 17.11.87 Expatriate Indians are permitted, acting through Indian stock exchanges, to buy up to 1 per cent of an Indian company's paid-up capital, subject to an overall ceiling of 5 per cent for the expatriate Indian Community as a whole.'(FT)
- 27.3.87 Grindlays Bank and Investors in Industry of the UK have launched an investment fund from Guernsey for expatriate Indians and other overseas investors. The principal objective of the India Investment Fund is long term appreciation through investment in both young and mature Indian companies and by providing venture capital to make the fund India's first overseas venture capital financing unit. (FT)
- 25.2.87 The Indian Investment Centre, an autonomous agency under the administrative control of the Ministry of Finance has been designated as nodal agency for NRI and foreign investment. HQ are in New Delhi, overseas offices are in NY, London, Frankfurt, Abu Dhabi, Tokyo & Singapore. (LSD, Q359)
- 5.12.86 The Finance Minister is considering the formulation of a new scheme to permit portfolio investment by NRIs up to 40 per cent of the equity on the basis of non-repatriation of profits and capital. This is subject to the condition that the Indian company concerned has no objection to allotment of shares beyond the 5 per cent limit. (FE)
- 12.5.86 State Bank of India (SBI) plans to improve the quality of its loan portfolio and increase the range of income by floating a subsidiary to provide services ranging from issuing shares to portfolio management's for Expatriate Indians. (FT)
- 17.3.86 Government has entered into a labour agreement with the State of Qatar for regulating the recruitment and treatment of Indian Workers. (LSD, Q3097)
- 14.3.86 The 1986 Finance Bill proposes that money and assets brought by NRIs within 1 year immediately proceeding the date of return be exempted under the wealth tax act for 7 years. (LSD,Q2805)

- 7.3.86 A Special Approval Committee (SAC) has been constituted in the department of Industrial Development for the expeditious clearance of industrial investment proposals of NRIs. Proposals involving industrial license are cleared within 45 days, proposals involving the import of capital goods 60 days and composite 90 days. (LSD, Q1910)
- 8.1.86 Swaraj Paul withdraws from share battle over Escorts and DCM. (FT)
- 22.11.85 The Government have received a memorandum from a delegation of NRIs which contains the following suggestions: removal of the 5 per cent ceiling on portfolio investment, reduction/removal of 1 year lock in period for resale of shares, extension of tax concessions available to individual NRIs to OCB owned predominantly by NRIs, issue of debentures/deposits by public limited companies and security by central Government in designated foreign currency for subscription of NRI investors. It was examined by the Ministry and found not feasible. (LSD, Q81)
- 3.6.85 India's trade gap soared to a record Rs 59.95bn in 1983/84. There is no short term crisis because a strong inflow of capital from NRIs has boosted foreign exchange reserves. (FT)
- 3.6.85 Last year's foreign investment approval granted by the government to the NRIs amounted to Rs146m. Comparable figures for the US were Rs 89m, UAE Rs 75m, W Germany Rs 28m and the UK Rs 18m. (FT)
- 6.4.84 Private transfers/ receipts including remittances received from NRIs of Indian nationality: (in crores) 1977/78 - Rs 917.3; 78/79 - Rs 943.8; 79/80 - Rs 1472.1; 80/81 - Rs 2129.7; 81/82 - Rs 2082.9. (LSD, Q6771)
- 12.8.83 Between 1 and 2 March 1983 80,000 shares of Delhi Cloth and General Mills company ltd. were purchased on behalf of 13 overseas companies of the Caparo Group UK. These shares constituted 12.95 per cent of the total paid up equity of Rs 20.06 crores of DCM. The Board meeting of 15 July 1983 rejected the transfer of 10.33.192 shares. (LSD, Q3325)
- 7.5.83 As from this week NRIs may acquire no more than 5 per cent of the equity of companies registered in the subcontinent. This limit has been introduced to curb the activities of expatriates like Mr. Swaraj Paul, chairman of the British group Caparo.(...) This surge in foreign purchases left all quoted Indian companies terrified of being taken

over, is due to the introduction of generous tax concessions originally designed to attract investments from Indians resident abroad. (ECN)

- 22.4.83 Indian businessmen have asked the Government to prevent the take-over of established and profitable companies by expatriate Indians for whose benefit various investment incentives were announced last February. They have suggested a ceiling of 2 per cent of the total equity of any company. (FT)
- 24.5.82 Serious bid to attract the NRIs: though remittances from Indians overseas are already a major factor in India's economy (estimated $5bn in 1981) the budget speech announced that NRIs would now be treated on the same footing as Indian nationals in a number of investment areas and would for the first time be allowed to purchase shares on the Indian stock exchange. (FT)
- 28.4.82 Budget measures: NRIs were for the first time permitted to invest in new company shares up to 40 per cent of equity capital on a repatriable basis. (FT)
- 24.3.82 Details on distinguished scientists and technologists of Indian Origin settled abroad are being collected to maintain a register. (LSD, Q439)
- 26.3.81 Steps taken by the Indian Government to protect interests of Indian workers abroad are arrangements made to register with the proctor of emigrants the employment contract in order to avail of legal and administrative help if necessary; and arrangements including warnings through the media to caution Indian job seekers, and instructing missions to be in constant touch with Indian workers. (LSD, Q5129)
- Very few proposals that are being screened for investments are in the high technology sector, most are in the service sector or other low priority areas. This causes problems to the Indian economy as the capital and the profits which might be repatriated would be much higher than what they bring into India. Nothing came out of Mrs. Gandhi's plan to set up a 'NR scientists city' with Indian investment of Rs125 crores. (Statesman)
- 21.10.78 Indian polity with regard to NRI investment has grown more confident since 1972; India has liberalised the import of capital goods, withdrawn the restriction of substantial ownership of not less than 51 per cent, done away with the insistence on taking up Indian citizenship, and discontinued provision of blocked accounts. (FE)

- 14.4.78 Incentives to NRIs returning permanently to India include 25 per cent of the total amount of foreign currency repatriated to India or held in bank accounts abroad at the time of transfer can be used for certain specified personal purposes such as visits abroad, medical treatment, education of dependants and gifts to relatives for three years after applying to the RBI. (LSD, Q6854)
- 10.7.77 Emigrants shy of investing in India, absence of a central co-ordinating agency to help Indians abroad set up Industry major stumbling block. NRIs who wish to invest feel that they are looked upon with some degree of suspicion if not hostility. This is especially so if the potential investor has no potential patronage or 'contacts' in the bureaucracy. (TOI)
- 30.6.76 Response to foreign currency deposits has been good, but scheme for attracting foreign capital of NRIs has been less successful - only one project so far has taken concrete shape. (Tribune)
- 6.4.76 More incentives announced by the Government: NRIs permitted equity participation up to 74 per cent in 19 selected industries, (metallurgy, boilers & steam-generating equipment, electrical generators, electrical equipment, transportation, machine tools, earth moving machinery, fertilisers, other chemicals, drugs, paper & pulp, car tires & tubes, plate glass, ceramics and cement products; Investment also permitted in other industries up to 74 per cent provided they export 60 per cent of the output. (Hindu)
- 28.8.75 variety of inducements for NRIs to invest their savings into India: concessions include allotment of housing sites by urban development authorities against payment in foreign currency and special tax treatment to capital repatriated from abroad to deposit in NR accounts. (HT)
- 26.8.75 Government announces further concessions for NRIs to remit money home; decides to persuade Indian passport holders who may be earning more than $12000 pa to remit 10 per cent of their earnings through legal channels. NRIs will be allowed to acquire more than 20 per cent of share capital in any venture, and entire dividend income is tax free (tax exemption limit abolished). (FE)
- 5.3.75 CSIR study conducted in 1971 estimates the number of Indian scientists and technologists abroad at around 30,000. Steps taken by the government to bring them back include the maintenance of a register, payment of travel grant for appointment in research institutions,

package schemes to start own industries, and creation of a scientists pool to provide temporary placements. (LSD, Q2381)

- 15.11.74 Question to the Minister of Finance whether the Central Government had framed a scheme for giving incentives including benefits over official rates to Indians abroad remitting money to India through Banking channels was answered with 'No'. (LSD, Q701)

Appendix - 2

Table A: Foreign exchange resources: Historical perspective (US$ million)

Years	Foreign Exchange Reserves [a, b]	Import cover (No. of months)[c]	Current Payment Cover[d] (No. of months)[c]
1950-51	1914	16.8	14.6
1955-56	1648	12.2	10.6
1960-61	390	2.0	1.7
1965-66	383	1.6	1.3
1970-71	584	2.9	2.2
1975-76	1657	3.2	2.8
1980-81	5850	4.3	3.8
1985-86	5972	4.1	3.5
1990-91	2236	1.0	0.8
1991-92	5631	3.2	2.3
1992-93	6434	3.3	2.5
1993-94	15068	7.2	5.4
1994-95	20809	7.8	5.8
1995-96	17044	4.9	3.8
1996-97[e]	19847	5.5	4.0

Source: Economic Survey, 1996-97, Government of India.

a) Excluding gold and SDRs.
b) Years-end level.
c) Based on Foreign Exchange resources of respective Year-end level.
d) Current payments represent sum of merchandise imports and invisible payments.
e) Reserve level at end-January, 1997.